"Informed by the maxim that you can't study what you can't see, Baer's book provides the necessary psychometric underpinning to further our understanding of core change processes in mindfulness-based interventions."

—Zindel V. Segal, Ph.D., Cameron Wilson Chair in Depression Studies at the Centre for Addiction and Mental Health and author of *The Mindful Way Through Depression*

"Mindfulness meditation has become a leading clinical intervention for clients with multiple problems, ranging from pain and physical discomfort (mindfulness-based stress reduction) to mental health problems such as depression (mindfulness-based cognitive therapy). Although mindfulness training has been shown to be effective in various clinical outcome studies, questions have been raised about the mechanisms of change that help explain these successful results. This new book, edited by Ruth Baer, provides a variety of perspectives on potential mechanisms of change, including decentering, psychological flexibility, values processes, emotion regulation, self-compassion, and spiritual engagement. I highly recommend this book as a cutting-edge approach to understanding mindfulness and acceptance processes in clients."

—G. Alan Marlatt, Ph.D., professor of psychology at the University of Washington and director of the Addictive Behaviors Research Center

"Ruth Baer has consistently been at the forefront of careful study of the efficacy of mindfulness-based treatments. In this edited volume, she provides readers with a thoughtful review of a crucial area of study: potential mechanisms that may underlie the efficacy of mindfulness and acceptance-based psychotherapies. Each chapter provides a conceptual and empirical review of a relevant process (e.g., decentering, emotion regulation), as well as relevant assessment methods. This kind of attention to the reasons why mindfulness-based intervention may be beneficial will help stimulate informative research in the area and also help clinicians provide therapy that enhances these important skills."

—Lizabeth Roemer, Ph.D., professor of psychology at the University of Massachusetts and coauthor of *Mindfulness- and Acceptance-Based Behavioral Therapies in Practice*

"In this comprehensive and much-needed book, Ruth Baer and colleagues present the most up-to-date findings on exactly *how* mindfulness and acceptance might work to increase psychological well-being. An excellent resource not only for mindfulness researchers and practitioners, but for anyone interested in what leads to mental health and emotional balance."

—Cassandra Vieten, Ph.D., director of research at the Institute of Noetic Sciences and author of *Mindful Motherhood*

"A fascinating journey to the heart of what actually changes in mindfulness and acceptance-based treatment. Ruth Baer and her colleagues offer a brilliant and careful review of one of the most exciting areas of behavioral research in decades. This book is highly recommended for psychotherapists, health care professionals, and anyone seeking the very latest scientific understanding of psychological change."

—Christopher K. Germer, Ph.D., clinical instructor in psychology at Harvard Medical School and author of *The Mindful Path to Self-Compassion*

"A cutting edge text which responds with rigor and clarity to the salient questions in the field of mindfulness-based interventions, namely, what are the mechanisms and processes of change? And how can these processes be assessed? Baer does an excellent job weaving different perspectives and theories from a wide range of experts to provide a pioneering response to these compelling questions."

—Shauna L. Shapiro, Ph.D., coauthor of *The Art and Science of Mindfulness*

"This is an important and timely book. Ruth Baer has brought together international experts in the clinical and research fields to build a critically important bridge between ancient wisdom and modern psychological science. This book will be essential reading for students, researchers, and practitioners of mindfulness and acceptance-based approaches."

—Mark Williams, professor of clinical psychology at the University of Oxford and coauthor of *The Mindful Way Through Depression*

ASSESSING MINDFULNESS & ACCEPTANCE PROCESSES IN CLIENTS

Illuminating the Theory & Practice of Change

Edited by
RUTH A. BAER, PH.D.

CONTEXT PRESS
An Imprint of New Harbinger Publications, Inc.

Distributed in Canada by Raincoast Books

New Harbinger Publications, Inc.
5674 Shattuck Avenue
Oakland, CA 94609
www.newharbinger.com

Printed in the United States of America

Acquired by Catharine Sutker; Cover design by Amy Shoup;
Edited by Jasmine Star; Text design by Tracy Carlson

Library of Congress Cataloging-in-Publication Data

Assessing mindfulness and acceptance processes in clients : illuminating the theory and practice of change / Ruth A. Baer, editor ; Including contributions from Kelly Wilson ... [et al.].

p. cm.

Includes bibliographical references and index.

ISBN 978-1-57224-694-2

1. Mindfulness-based cognitive therapy. 2. Meditation--Therapeutic use. I. Baer, Ruth A. II. Wilson, Kelly G.

RC489.M55A87 2010

616.89'1425--dc22

2010002416

12 11 10

10 9 8 7 6 5 4 3 2 1 First printing

Contents

Introduction

Mindfulness- and Acceptance-Based Interventions and Processes of Change

Ruth A. Baer, University of Kentucky

Psychological interventions based on mindfulness and acceptance have attracted extraordinary interest in a very short time. The *New York Times* recently described mindfulness meditation as "perhaps the most popular new psychotherapy technique of the past decade" (Carey, 2008). Although mindfulness meditation originates in ancient Buddhist traditions that have evolved over many centuries, the incorporation of secular forms of mindfulness practice into contemporary Western settings is quite recent.

Mindfulness-based principles and practices are applied to psychological treatment in many ways. Some therapists maintain a personal practice of mindfulness meditation to improve their own well-being and peace of mind and develop a more attentive, balanced, and compassionate presence during therapy sessions, but don't teach mindfulness to their clients (Germer, Siegel, & Fulton, 2005). Others incorporate wisdom and insight from Buddhist teachings on concepts such as impermanence and acceptance into their discussions with clients without explicitly teaching their clients to engage in mindfulness practices (Shapiro & Carlson, 2009). Most of the empirical literature, however, describes structured treatments in which formal or informal mindfulness practices are explicitly taught as a central therapeutic ingredient. The best known of these, which have accrued substantial support for their efficacy, are acceptance and commitment therapy

(ACT; Hayes, Strosahl, & Wilson, 1999), dialectical behavior therapy (DBT; Linehan, 1993), mindfulness-based cognitive therapy (MBCT; Segal, Williams, & Teasdale, 2002) and mindfulness-based stress reduction (MBSR; Kabat-Zinn, 1982, 1990). Research on these approaches, including variations and adaptations for specific disorders and populations, appears regularly in the empirical literature, as do new books for professional and lay audiences. Professional training in the implementation of these interventions is increasingly available.

Much of the literature supporting these treatments emphasizes the reduction of symptoms or distress as the primary outcome of interest. Fewer studies have examined the processes and mechanisms by which beneficial outcomes are obtained. For people seeking treatment, reduction of symptoms is often the primary goal. However, the advancement of science and practice is better served when studies investigate not just whether treatments work, but how they work. If we understand how treatments work, we can increase their effectiveness by refining components that are responsible for therapeutic change and de-emphasizing or eliminating components that aren't active ingredients.

For example, it is generally assumed, both in Buddhist meditation traditions and in contemporary interventions, that mindfulness training should enable participants to be more mindful of the experiences of daily life. In turn, being more mindful should lead to reductions in suffering and increases in well-being. But do mindfulness-based treatments actually work this way? Do participants learn to be more mindful in daily life? Is that why their psychological health improves? Is it possible that improvements are due to other factors, such as social support, attention from a caring therapist or teacher, increased ability to relax, or the general psychological education and discussion that occurs while participating in a structured treatment? Answering these questions requires understanding the processes of change, and this requires methods for assessing the relevant processes. Without such methods, we cannot say whether participants in mindfulness training learn to be more mindful in daily life, or whether this is important in accounting for the benefits of mindfulness training.

The purpose of this book is to examine important questions about how mindfulness- and acceptance-based treatments work. What is changing when people participate in these interventions? Are they becoming more mindful or more accepting? If so, are these changes important in accounting for the improvements in psychological functioning, well-being, and quality of life that typically result from these interventions? The following

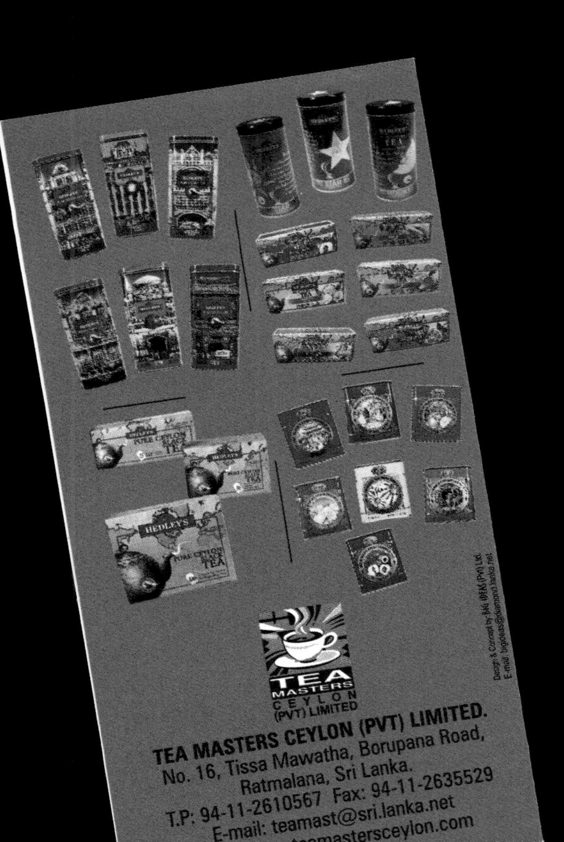
TEA
MASTERS
CEYLON
(PVT) LIMITED
TEA MASTERS CEYLON (PVT) LIMITED.
No. 16, Tissa Mawatha, Borupana Road,
Ratmalana, Sri Lanka.
T.P: 94-11-2610567 Fax: 94-11-2635529
teamast@sri.lanka.net
E-mail:

H

HEDLEY'S®

chapters address these questions for several important processes in a variety of populations. In this introduction, I provide historical background about the origins of mindfulness-based interventions, a brief review of the populations and disorders to which they are often applied, and an overview of the processes believed to be central to their mechanisms of action.

ORIGINS AND APPLICATIONS OF MINDFULNESS TRAINING

Mindfulness meditation originated in ancient Buddhist traditions that are approximately 2,500 years old. As Buddhism spread across Asia, it evolved into several subtraditions and schools of thought that vary in their specific practices. The three primary branches are described by Kabat-Zinn (2003) as the Theravada tradition, the Mahayana or Zen tradition, and the Vajrayana or Tibetan tradition. The ancient texts that elucidate the nature of mindfulness are core teachings for all of these branches and their subdivisions. These texts describe mindfulness as an attentional stance that is embedded within an ethical framework centered on nonharming of self and others. The practice of mindfulness within this ethical context is believed to cultivate insight into the nature of human suffering and how to relieve it (see also Gunaratana, 2002; Nhat Hanh, 1976).

In recent decades, several forms of Buddhist meditation have been introduced into Western culture (Goldstein, 2002). Westerners who have studied extensively with Buddhist masters in Asian countries have founded meditation centers in North American and Europe, where they offer mindfulness retreats of varying lengths. Guidance and instruction in mindfulness meditation is also available at many wellness centers and mental health facilities. Numerous books for the lay audience describe mindfulness meditation practices (e.g., Goldstein & Kornfield, 1987; Gunaratana, 2002). In addition, as noted earlier, several recently developed structured interventions incorporate mindfulness training and now have considerable empirical support for their efficacy. These interventions are briefly reviewed here.

MBSR

MBSR was developed by Jon Kabat-Zinn (1982, 1990) and first offered in 1979 at the University of Massachusetts Medical School. The goal of the program was to make mindfulness meditation available and accessible in a Western medical setting while remaining true to the essence of Buddhist teachings. Kabat-Zinn had practiced and studied mindfulness meditation for years and began offering a ten-week group program for patients with a wide variety of stress-related and chronic pain conditions who were referred by their physicians because their medical treatment had been unsatisfactory. The program is described as educational rather than a form of psychotherapy and is based on intensive practice of several forms of mindfulness meditation. It also includes didactic instruction on the nature of stress and discussion of how to apply mindfulness to the difficulties of daily life. The program was originally called stress reduction and relaxation because of concerns that meditation wouldn't be viewed as an acceptable activity for patients in an academic medical center. Now known as MBSR, in its standard form it is an eight-week group program for up to thirty participants with a wide range of stress-related conditions. Groups meet weekly for 2.5-hour sessions, and week six often includes an all-day session.

MBSR has been used with many populations in a variety of settings. Medical populations that have shown reduced distress or increased well-being include patients with cancer (Carlson, Speca, Patel, & Goodey, 2003), heart disease (Tacon, McComb, Caldera, & Randolph, 2003), fibromyalgia (Weissbecker et al., 2002), other forms of chronic pain (Kabat-Zinn, 1982), and chronic fatigue syndrome (Surawy, Roberts, & Silver, 2005), as well as mixed medical populations (Reibel, Greeson, Brainard, & Rosenzweig, 2001). Significant benefits for nonclinical populations also have been reported, including mental health and medical professionals and students (Shapiro, Astin, Bishop, & Cordova, 2005; Shapiro, Brown, & Biegel, 2007) and healthy adults with work-related stress (Davidson et al., 2003; Williams, K., 2006).

Variants of MBSR for other populations also have been developed. For example, mindfulness-based relationship enhancement (MBRE; Carson, Carson, Gil, & Baucom, 2004), which is designed for couples, has been shown to provide significant improvements in relationship quality and personal adjustment. Mindfulness-Based Eating Awareness Treatment (MB-EAT; Kristeller, 2003; Kristeller & Hallett, 1999) is a treatment for binge eating that incorporates elements of MBSR with mindful eating of several types of food, as well as guided meditations related to body shape and weight, hunger and satiety cues, and binge-eating triggers. Other adaptations with at least preliminary support include mindfulness-based art therapy (MBAT; Monti et al., 2005), which combines elements of MBSR with art-making activities and was developed for medical populations, and mindfulness-based relapse prevention for substance abuse (MBRP; Witkiewitz, Marlatt, & Walker, 2005). In most published studies, the eight-week format is maintained. However, several authors have reported on shorter versions of MBSR for a variety of populations and outcome data suggest that these can be as effective as the standard eight-week version (Carmody & Baer, 2009). Other reviews of the MBSR literature are provided by Baer (2003); Grossman, Neimann, Schmidt, and Walach (2004); and Salmon and colleagues (2004).

MBCT

MBCT is an adaptation of MBSR designed to prevent relapse in participants with a history of depressive episodes (Segal et al., 2002). It was developed in consultation with Kabat-Zinn and his colleagues and includes many of the same mindfulness practices used in MBSR. It also incorporates cognitive therapy exercises that cultivate the understanding that thoughts are not facts and do not have to control behavior. Like MBSR, MBCT is an eight-session group program with 2 or 2.5-hour weekly sessions and an all-day session in week six. Groups are usually limited to twelve participants. Although MBCT was originally developed for people whose depression has remitted, recent research suggests it is probably effective for those with ongoing depressive episodes (Barnhofer et al., 2009; Kenny & Williams, 2007). In addition, preliminary support for adaptations with other populations is beginning to appear. Examples include MBCT for bipolar disorder (Williams, J. M. G., et al., 2008), generalized anxiety disorder (Craigee, Rees, Marsh, & Nathan, 2008; Evans et al., 2008), binge eating (Baer, Fischer, & Huss, 2005a, 2005b), anxious children (Semple, Lee, & Miller, 2006), and older adults with depression and anxiety (Smith, 2006; Smith, Graham, & Senthinathan, 2006).

DBT

DBT was developed at the University of Washington, beginning in the late 1970s, by Marsha Linehan, who was working with suicidal and self-injurious women, many of whom met criteria for borderline personality disorder (BPD). Her clients typically had severe and chronic negative affect and multiple problematic behaviors. Although their level of suffering was very high, they often found suggestions about behavior change to be invalidating and reacted with anger, which led to high rates of attrition (Linehan, 1997). However, if they didn't work on behavior change, their lives remained chaotic and miserable. Linehan studied historical and biographical accounts of torture victims, holocaust survivors, and others who had endured great suffering and found that the concept of acceptance was often central to descriptions of their experiences. It appeared that those who were able to accept the reality of their circumstances without avoidance, suppression, or denial were more likely to experience personal growth (Linehan, 2002). To learn more about acceptance, which was not widely discussed in psychology at that time, Linehan studied Zen Buddhism (Butler, 2001). She began incorporating acceptance-based methods, including validation and mindfulness skills, with traditional cognitive behavioral strategies. Because her clients were unwilling or unable to engage in lengthy meditation practices, she developed behavioral exercises for teaching mindfulness and acceptance skills without engaging in formal meditation. These skills appear to enable clients to tolerate the emotional pain associated with changing their behaviors to build better lives and to accept undesirable aspects of their histories and current circumstances that cannot be changed.

DBT has been very favorably received by clinicians looking for effective treatment for clients with BPD (Scheel, 2000; Swenson, 2000). DBT programs are now widely available (although more are needed). Standard outpatient DBT typically includes weekly individual therapy and group skills training, telephone consultation as needed, and a therapists' consultation group. Duration is usually one year, although shorter versions have been developed. Applications for substance abuse problems, eating disorders, intimate partner violence and other family problems, self-harm in adolescents, and depression with comorbid personality disorders in older adults have been developed and studied, along with adaptations for inpatient psychiatric and forensic settings and outpatient private practices (Dimeff & Koerner, 2007; Marra, 2005; Safer, Telch, & Chen, 2009; Rathus, Cavuoto, & Passarelli, 2006). Recent reviews of the DBT literature are provided by Lynch, Trost, Salsman, and Linehan (2007) and Robins and Chapman (2004).

ACT

ACT, developed by Steven Hayes and colleagues beginning in the late 1970s, is based on a philosophy known as functional contextualism and a theory of human language and cognition known as relational frame theory (RTF), both of which are beyond the scope this introduction (see Hayes et al., 1999, and Hayes, Barnes-Holmes, & Roche, 2001, for more detail). In its original form, the therapy was called comprehensive distancing because it emphasized the development of a particular perspective on thoughts. From this perspective, which is very similar to the concept of decentering in cognitive therapy, thoughts are seen as just thoughts—mental events that come and go and don't necessarily reflect truth, reality, or personal worth and need not influence behavior. Comprehensive distancing encouraged participants to notice and identify their troubling thoughts as just thoughts, and to engage in adaptive behavior while having these thoughts, regardless of the content of the thoughts. The name of the treatment was changed to acceptance and commitment therapy to signify acceptance of a wide range of internal experiences (thoughts, emotions, sensations) while choosing and committing to potentially effective behavior consistent with goals and values. ACT incorporates many mindfulness exercises to facilitate awareness and acceptance of thoughts and feelings.

ACT was designed to be applicable to numerous populations and settings. The current literature describes adaptations for depression (Zettle, 2007), anxiety (Eifert & Forsyth, 2005), anger (Eifert, McKay, & Forsyth, 2006), smoking and substance abuse, chronic pain and other medical conditions, living with psychosis, self-harm in BPD, worksite stress, and stigma and burnout in mental health professionals, among others (Hayes & Strosahl, 2004). Adaptations for children and adolescents (Greco & Hayes, 2008) and for group interventions (Walser & Pistorello, 2004) have also been described. A recent review of the ACT literature is provided by Hayes, Luoma, Bond, Masuda, and Lillis (2006).

WHAT IS CHANGING WHEN PEOPLE PARTICIPATE IN MINDFULNESS- AND ACCEPTANCE-BASED TREATMENTS?

Researchers and clinicians are studying several interesting psychological processes that may help to explain why mindfulness- and acceptance-based treatments lead to reduced distress and improved well-being. Each of these is discussed in more detail in one of the chapters in this volume. Here we present a brief overview.

Mindfulness. Participants in the treatments just described devote substantial time and effort to the practice of mindfulness skills. In MBSR and MBCT, participants are asked to engage in formal mindfulness meditation for forty-five minutes per day, six day per week, and to practice mindfulness informally while doing routine daily activities. It seems reasonable to assume that engaging in these practices will cultivate greater mindfulness of the experiences of daily life, and that this will lead to reductions in suffering and increases in psychological health. Until recently, this assumption could not be tested because no methods were available for assessing the tendency to be mindful in general daily life. However, assessment tools designed to measure mindfulness have become available within the last few years. Developing these measures has required discussion of what it means, in concrete behavioral terms, to be mindful and why it should be helpful to adopt a mindful stance toward ongoing experience. Although many questions remain, the recent literature on this topic has grappled productively with these issues and is contributing to a clearer understanding of the nature of mindfulness, the changes that occur in people who practice mindfulness, and how these changes contribute to symptom reduction and increased well-being (Baer, Smith, Krietemeyer, Hopkins, & Toney, 2006; Baer et al., 2008).

Decentering. In the early days of cognitive therapy, decentering was described as a particular way of relating to thoughts in which they are observed as transitory mental phenomena that are not necessarily true or important and do not reflect on personal worth or require particular behaviors in response (Hollon & Beck, 1979). A decentered relationship to a specific thought (e.g., "I'm an idiot") includes noticing the thought when it arises and recognizing that it is a thought, rather than a fact, and that it is separate from the person having the thought. Decentering is closely related to mindfulness and is believed to play a central role in accounting for the benefits of mindfulness training. Recent advances in the assessment of decentering have made it possible to study this process and its relationship to psychological distress in people who participate in mindfulness-based interventions (Fresco et al., 2007).

Psychological flexibility. In ACT, the central therapeutic goal is helping the client develop psychological flexibility, a term that encompasses the acceptance and the commitment processes reflected in this therapy's name. Psychological flexibility includes mindful awareness of the present moment and willingness to experience unpleasant or unwanted internal stimuli (thoughts, sensations, emotions) while either changing or maintaining overt behavior in the service of important goals and values. Recent work on the assessment of psychological flexibility has greatly advanced our understanding of the changes that occur in ACT and how these lead to improvements in the problems for which people seek treatment. The literature suggests that increases in psychological flexibility are important mediators of therapeutic change (Hayes et al., 2006).

Values. An important element of psychological flexibility is the clarification of personal values. In ACT, participants are encouraged to think deeply about what is most important to them in life (such as being a loving spouse or parent or doing work that feels meaningful and worthwhile) and to identify specific behaviors that are necessary to move their lives in these directions. Although identifying values is an element of psychological flexibility, it has received less attention in the literature than it deserves, and for this reason it has its own chapter in this book. Recent work on the assessment of values provides interesting insights about how changes in the extent to which people are acting in accordance with their values are related to changes in other aspects of their psychological functioning (Wilson & DuFrene, 2008).

Emotion regulation. The current literature includes several definitions of emotion regulation. Some of these emphasize control and reduction of negative emotions. These definitions are not consistent with mindfulness- and acceptance-based treatments, which emphasize awareness and acceptance of all emotions as they arise and controlling behavior while experiencing negative emotions by inhibiting maladaptive impulsive behavior and engaging in goal-directed behavior. Recent work on the assessment of emotion regulation as defined in this way suggests that acceptance-based treatment encourages improvement in these adaptive ways of responding to emotions, and that these changes are related to other improvements in psychological functioning (Gratz & Roemer, 2004; Gratz & Gunderson, 2006).

Self-compassion. Ancient Buddhist writings have much to say about compassion for oneself and others. Development of compassion is described as one of the central effects of the regular practice of mindfulness meditation. Self-compassion, a relatively unfamiliar concept in the Western psychological literature, includes treating oneself kindly rather than judgmentally, recognizing that painful emotions and hardships are part of the human experience, and maintaining mindful awareness of difficult experiences rather than trying to avoid them or becoming excessively immersed in them. A recently developed measure of self-compassion has allowed for interesting studies and growing evidence that treating oneself kindly is associated with numerous aspects of healthy psychological functioning (Neff, 2009). It also appears that participants in mindfulness-based interventions are likely to show increases in self-compassion.

Spirituality. Although mindfulness meditation originates in a spiritual tradition, mindfulness- and acceptance-based treatments are intentionally secular. However, several authors have argued that spirituality is an important dimension of human functioning and that understanding the psychology of spiritual experience may contribute to knowledge of how mindfulness-based therapies achieve their beneficial outcomes. Spirituality is difficult to define and measure. Nevertheless, recent work suggests that the practice of mindfulness can lead to increases in spirituality and that these are associated with improvements in many domains of psychological functioning (Carmody, Reed, Kristeller, & Merriam, 2008).

Changes in the brain. Recent advances in imaging technologies have provided ways of studying the effects of mindfulness meditation on the brain. Evidence is growing that the practice of mindfulness leads to changes in the structure and function of the brain and that these changes are associated with cognitive and emotional benefits. The initial studies compared long-term meditation practitioners to nonmeditators, making it impossible to determine whether observed differences were due to meditation in particular or to other factors associated with meditation, such as openness to experience or dietary differences. However, recent studies have shown meaningful changes in the brain in people with no previous meditation experience who completed an MBSR program. These changes appear to be related to healthy psychological functioning (Davidson et al., 2003).

Changes in attention and working memory. Recent findings also suggest that the practice of mindfulness is associated with changes in attention skills and working memory. In some ways, this isn't surprising. Directing one's attention in particular ways is central to the practice of mindfulness. It therefore seems plausible that repeated practice might lead to generalized changes in attention skills, which are closely related to working memory capacity. Advances in the ability to measure such changes, using objective computer-based tests of attention and working memory, have begun to shed light on the nature of these changes and how they may be related to the beneficial outcomes of engaging in mindfulness practices (Jha, Krompinger, & Baime, 2007).

HOW DO WE KNOW IF CHANGE IN A PARTICULAR PROCESS IS RESPONSIBLE FOR IMPROVED WELL-BEING?

In psychological research, we study mediation to determine whether change in a particular process is responsible for improved well-being. A mediator is a variable that is responsible for the effect that an independent variable (such as a psychological treatment) exerts on a dependent variable (such as the level of psychological symptoms or well-being). A large body of research literature on the outcomes of mindfulness- and acceptance-based treatments provides substantial evidence that these interventions have a significant therapeutic impact on participants' levels of symptoms and well-being. Thus, the relationship between the independent variable (mindfulness-based treatment) and the dependent variable (improved psychological health) is well established. Examining the mechanisms through which these beneficial effects occur is the central purpose of this book. The general hypothesis in most of the following chapters is that changes in a particular process (mindfulness, decentering, emotion regulation, self-compassion, and so on) mediate the improvements in well-being that occur with treatment.

How do we test this hypothesis? Several steps are required. As already noted, first we must show that mindfulness training leads to beneficial outcomes. The evidence for this is clear. We must also investigate whether mindfulness training leads to increases in the potential mediators. As the following chapters will explain in detail, the evidence is strong, or at least suggestive, for the processes considered in this volume. Studies show that participants in mindfulness-based treatments, or people with a long-term practice of mindfulness meditation, have higher scores on measures of decentering, psychological flexibility, self-compassion, and other potential mechanisms of change. Thus, the practice of mindfulness appears to cultivate these processes. Another important step is to examine whether the potential mediating variables are correlated with measures of symptoms and well-being. Again, the evidence is clear that the processes examined in this book show the expected relationships. People with higher scores on self-reported mindfulness, decentering, self-compassion, and other processes consistently show lower levels of psychological symptoms and a higher degree of well-being. Finally, the potential mediator must predict psychological outcomes after controlling statistically for having participated in the treatment. This means that other aspects of treatment, such as social support or psycho-education, are not responsible for the observed improvements. Studies have shown this for several of the processes of change described in this volume.

Although recent research is encouraging, conclusive tests of mediation are difficult to conduct. The primary difficulty lies in establishing that the mediator leads to the outcome, rather than the reverse. For example, we would like to be certain that increases in mindfulness skills lead to improved psychological health, but we must acknowledge that the reverse may be true. A useful example of a mediational study that illustrates this problem was conducted by Carmody and Baer (2008). Participants in an MBSR program recorded their home practice time (in minutes) for mindfulness meditation exercises throughout the eight-week course. They also completed self-report measures of mindfulness, psychological symptoms, and well-being at the beginning and end of the intervention. Results showed that the more time they spent practicing, the more improvement they showed in their ability to be mindful in daily life and in their psychological symptoms and well-being. Statistical analyses showed that improved mindfulness in daily life predicted changes in psychological health after controlling for practice time. The results were interpreted to mean that the practice of mindfulness meditation leads to increases in the ability to be mindful in daily life, and that this in turn leads to improved psychological health. That is, increased mindfulness in daily life was described as the mediator, or the mechanism through which improvement in psychological health occurred. This makes theoretical sense and is consistent with the Buddhist traditions, which describe the potential outcomes of mindfulness practice in a similar way.

However, because mindfulness and psychological health were measured at the same two time points (before and after MBSR), we can't be certain of the direction of causality. It's possible that practicing mindfulness led directly to improved psychological health, and that this in turn led to an improved ability to be mindful in daily life. That is, perhaps people can more easily be mindful after they feel better. According to statistical analyses that are beyond the scope of this introduction, the findings of Carmody and Baer (2008) were less consistent with this possibility. However, conclusively ruling it out requires measuring all relevant variables at three points in time. If it can be shown that, over time, mindfulness training leads to a change in the proposed mediator (such as mindfulness or decentering), which then leads at a later time to a change in psychological health (symptoms or well-being), we could be more certain that the proposed mediator is truly a mechanism of change and not an outcome of improved psychological health. So far, very few studies have used this methodology. Most of them can be found in the ACT literature and are described in chapter 2 of this book.

The statistical methods used to test mediation are beyond the scope of this volume. Interested readers are referred to Baron and Kenny (1986), whose methods, based on regression analysis, have been widely used. Further refinements of these methods and alternative methods have been proposed. Additional helpful resources include MacKinnon, Lockwood, Hoffman, West, and Sheets (2002) and Kraemer, Wilson, Fairburn, and Agras (2002).

HOW DISTINCT ARE THESE PROCESSES OF CHANGE?

Close examination of the processes of change discussed in this volume suggests that many of them are highly overlapping. As noted in chapter 1, mindfulness and decentering have very similar definitions. In the context of mindfulness-based treatments, both include nonjudgmental observation and acceptance of thoughts and feelings. Psychological flexibility, the focus of chapter 2, includes six processes, four of which are identified as mindfulness and acceptance processes. These include contact with the present moment, acceptance, defusion (which is similar to decentering), and recognition of the self as the context in which thoughts and feelings occur (rather than equating the self with the thoughts and feelings that come and go). Psychological flexibility also includes clarity about personal values (the topic of chapter 3) and engaging in values-consistent behavior even when unpleasant internal experiences are present. Similarly, emotion regulation, as defined in this volume and discussed in chapter 4, includes awareness and acceptance of emotions, along with willingness to engage in goal-directed behavior while experiencing negative emotions. A prominent definition of self-compassion, the focus of chapter 5, includes mindfulness as a central component. Spirituality, the topic of chapter 6, is defined in a variety of ways but can include compassion and a sense of higher meaning. The latter might be consistent with values as conceptualized in ACT. Spirituality defined as the transcendence of self might also be consistent with the self-as-context element of psychological flexibility (see Hayes, 1984). Additional research is required to clarify the commonalities and distinctions among these processes.

WHAT ABOUT OTHER PROCESSES?

The recent literature addresses many other psychological processes that may be important in various forms of psychopathology. An excellent discussion can be found in Harvey, Watkins, Mansell, and Shafran (2004), a book that identifies several processes that appear to be transdiagnostic; that is, they are common to several disorders and may be causal or maintaining factors. Examples include selective attention, overgeneral memory, thought suppression, and rumination. These processes are not the focus of chapters in this volume because they are conceptualized as intermediate outcomes between the processes described here and improved psychological functioning. That is, the development of mindfulness, decentering, psychological flexibility, acceptance-based emotion regulation, and so on, should cultivate flexibility of attention, observational noting of thoughts as thoughts rather than rumination, and willingness to experience unpleasant thoughts, memories, and emotions as they arise rather than attempting to avoid or suppress them.

CONCLUSIONS

The processes of change addressed in this volume are exciting because they are relatively new to the literature and have previously received little or no attention in empirically supported treatment approaches (Hayes, Follette, & Linehan, 2004). The study of mediation is also relatively new. Until recently, the treatment outcome literature rarely included analyses of mediation. Now mediational studies of mindfulness- and acceptance-based treatments are making substantial contributions to our understanding of how these treatments work. The evidence suggests that they work according to the theorized processes and that they work differently from traditional cognitive behavioral treatments (Zettle, Rains, & Hayes, in press). Chapters in part 1 of this book will discuss each of the processes introduced here. Although they are addressed separately, it is important to remember that several of them are highly overlapping and that future work will elucidate their similarities and differences. Chapters in part 2 of this book discuss processes of change in specific populations, including children and adolescents, medical populations, and adults in the workplace.

REFERENCES

Baer, R. A. (2003). Mindfulness training as a clinical intervention: A conceptual and empirical review. *Clinical Psychology: Science and Practice, 10*, 125-143.

Baer, R. A., Fischer, S., & Huss, D. B. (2005a). Mindfulness-based cognitive therapy applied to binge eating: A case study. *Cognitive and Behavioral Practice, 12*, 351-358.

Baer, R. A., Fischer, S., & Huss, D. B. (2005b). Mindfulness and acceptance in the treatment of disordered eating. *Journal of Rational Emotive and Cognitive Behavioral Therapy, 23*, 281-300.

Baer, R. A., Smith, G. T., Krietemeyer, J., Hopkins, J., & Toney, L. (2006). Using self-report assessment methods to explore facets of mindfulness. *Assessment, 13*, 27-45.

Baer, R. A., Smith, G. T., Lykins, E., Button, D., Krietemeyer, J., Sauer, S., et al. (2008). Construct validity of the Five Facet Mindfulness Questionnaire in meditating and nonmeditating samples. *Assessment, 15*, 329-342.

Barnhofer, T., Crane, C., Hargus, E., Myanthi, A., Winder, R. Williams, J. M. G., et al. (2009). Mindfulness-based cognitive therapy as a treatment for chronic depression: A preliminary study. *Behaviour Research and Therapy, 47*, 366-373.

Baron, R., & Kenny, D. A. (1986). The moderator-mediator variable distinction in social psychological research: Conceptual, strategic, and statistical considerations. *Journal of Personality and Social Psychology, 51*, 194-198.

Butler, K. (2001). Revolution on the horizon: DBT challenges the borderline diagnosis. *Psychotherapy Networker, 25*, 26-39.

Carey, B. (2008, May 27). Lotus therapy. *New York Times.*

Carmody, J., & Baer, R. A. (2008). Relationships between mindfulness practice and levels of mindfulness, medical and psychological symptoms and well-being in a mindfulness- based stress reduction program. *Journal of Behavioral Medicine, 31*, 23-33.

Carmody, J., & Baer, R. A. (2009). How long does a mindfulness-based stress reduction program need to be? A review of class contact hours and effect sizes for psychological distress. *Journal of Clinical Psychology, 65*, 627-638.

Carmody, J., Reed, G., Kristeller, J., & Merriam, P. (2008). Mindfulness, spirituality, and health-related symptoms. *Journal of Psychosomatic Research, 64*, 939-403.

Carlson, L. E., Speca, M., Patel, K. D., & Goodey, E. (2003). Mindfulness-based stress reduction in relation to quality of life, mood, symptoms of stress, and immune parameters in breast and prostate cancer outpatients. *Psychosomatic Medicine, 65*, 571-581.

Carson, J. W., Carson, K. M., Gil, K. J., & Baucom, D. H. (2004). Mindfulness-based relationship enhancement. *Behavior Therapy, 35*, 471-494.

Craigee, M. A., Rees, C. S., Marsh, A., & Nathan, P. (2008). Mindfulness-based cognitive therapy for generalized anxiety disorder: A preliminary investigation. *Behavioural and Cognitive Psychotherapy, 36*, 553-568.

Davidson, R. J., Kabat-Zinn, J., Schumacher, J., Rosenkranz, M., Muller, D., Santorelli, S. F., et al. (2003). Alterations in brain and immune function produced by mindfulness meditation. *Psychosomatic Medicine, 65*, 564-570.

Dimeff, L., & Koerner, K. (Eds.). (2007). Dialectical behavior therapy in clinical practice: Applications across disorders and settings. New York: Guilford.

Eifert, G. H., & Forsyth, J. P. (2005). *Acceptance and commitment therapy for anxiety disorders*. Oakland, CA: New Harbinger.

Eifert, G. H., McKay, M., & Forsyth, J. (2006). *ACT on life not on anger: The new acceptance and commitment therapy guide to problem anger*. Oakland, CA: New Harbinger.

Evans, S., Ferrando, S., Findler, M., Stowell, C., Smart, C., & Haglin, D. (2008). Mindfulness-based cognitive therapy for generalized anxiety disorder. *Journal of Anxiety Disorders, 22*, 716-721.

Fresco, D. M., Moore, M. T., van Dulmen, M., Segal, Z. V., Ma, S. H., Teasdale, J. D. et al. (2007). Initial psychometric properties of the Experiences Questionnaire: Validation of a self-report measure of decentering. *Behavior Therapy, 38*, 234-246.

Germer, C. K., Siegel. R. D., & Fulton, P. R. (2005). *Mindfulness and psychotherapy.* New York: Guilford.

Goldstein, J. (2002). *One dharma: The emerging Western Buddhism.* New York: Harper Collins.

Goldstein, J., & Kornfield, J. (1987). *Seeking the heart of wisdom: The path of insight meditation.* Boston: Shambhala.

Gratz, K. L., & Gunderson, J. G. (2006). Preliminary data on an acceptance-based emotion regulation group intervention for deliberate self-harm among women with borderline personality disorder. *Behavior Therapy, 37,* 25-35.

Gratz, K. L., & Roemer, L. (2004). Multidimensional assessment of emotion regulation and dysregulation: Development, factor structure, and initial validation of the Difficulties in Emotion Regulation Scale. *Journal of Psychopathology and Behavioral Assessment, 26,* 41-54.

Greco, L. A., & Hayes, S. C. (Eds.). (2008). *Acceptance and mindfulness treatments for children and adolescents: A practitioner's guide.* Oakland, CA: New Harbinger.

Grossman, P., Neimann, L., Schmidt, S., & Walach, H. (2004). Mindfulness-based stress reduction and health benefits: A meta-analysis. *Journal of Psychosomatic Research, 57,* 35-43.

Gunaratana, B. H. (2002). *Mindfulness in plain English.* Boston: Wisdom Publications.

Harvey, A., Watkins, E., Mansell, W., & Shafran, R. (2004). *Cognitive behavioural processes across psychological disorders: A transdiagnostic approach to research and treatment.* Oxford, UK: Oxford University Press.

Hayes, S. C. (1984). Making sense of spirituality. *Behaviorism, 12,* 99-110.

Hayes, S. C., Barnes-Holmes, D., & Roche, B. (2001). *Relational frame theory: A post-Skinnerian account of human language and cognition.* New York: Kluwer.

Hayes, S. C., Follette, V. M., & Linehan, M. M. (Eds.). (2004). *Mindfulness and acceptance: Expanding the cognitive-behavioral tradition.* New York: Guilford.

Hayes, S. C., Luoma, J. B., Bond, F. W., Masuda, A., & Lillis, J. (2006). Acceptance and commitment therapy: Model, processes, and outcomes. *Behaviour Research and Therapy, 44,* 1-25.

Hayes, S. C., & Strosahl, K. D. (Eds.). (2004). *A practical guide to acceptance and commitment therapy.* New York: Springer.

Hayes, S. C., Strosahl, K. D., & Wilson, K. G. (1999). *Acceptance and commitment therapy.* New York: Guilford.

Hollon, S. D., & Beck, A. T. (1979). Cognitive therapy of depression. In P. C. Kendall & S. D. Hollon (Eds.), *Cognitive-behavioral interventions: Theory, research, and procedures.* New York: Academic Press.

Jha, A. P., Krompinger, J., & Baime, M. J. (2007). Mindfulness training modifies subsystems of attention. *Cognitive, Affective, and Behavioral Neuroscience, 7,* 109-119.

Kabat-Zinn, J. (1982). An outpatient program in behavioral medicine for chronic pain patients based on the practice of mindfulness meditation: Theoretical considerations and preliminary results. *General Hospital Psychiatry, 4,* 33-47.

Kabat-Zinn, J. (1990). *Full catastrophe living: Using the wisdom of your body and mind to face stress, pain, and illness.* New York: Delacorte.

Kabat-Zinn, J. (2003). Mindfulness-based interventions in context: Past, present, and future. *Clinical Psychology: Science and Practice, 10,* 144-156.

Kenny, M. A., & Williams, J. M. G. (2007). Treatment-resistant depressed patients show a good response to mindfulness-based cognitive therapy. *Behaviour Research and Therapy, 45,* 617-625.

Kraemer, H. C., Wilson, G., Fairburn, C., & Agras, W. S. (2002). Mediators and moderators of treatment effects in randomized clinical trials. *Archives of General Psychiatry, 59,* 877-884.

Kristeller, J. L. (2003). Mindfulness, wisdom, and eating: Applying a multi-domain model of meditation effects. *Journal of Constructivism in the Human Sciences, 8,* 107-118.

Kristeller, J. L., & Hallett, C. B. (1999). An exploratory study of a meditation-based intervention for binge eating disorder. *Journal of Health Psychology, 4,* 357-363.

Linehan, M. M. (1993). *Cognitive-behavioral treatment of borderline personality disorder.* New York: Guilford.

Linehan, M. M. (1997). Validation and psychotherapy. In A. C. Bohart & L. S. Greenberg (Eds.), *Empathy reconsidered: New directions in psychotherapy*. Washington, DC: American Psychological Association.

Linehan, M. M. (2002). Introduction. On *From suffering to freedom through acceptance* [CD]. Seattle, WA: Behavioral Technology Transfer Group.

Lynch, T. R., Trost, W. T., Salsman, N., & Linehan, M. M. (2007). Dialectical behavior therapy for borderline personality disorder. *Annual Review of Clinical Psychology, 3*, 181-205.

MacKinnon, D. P., Lockwood, C. M., Hoffman, J. M., West, S. G., & Sheets, V. (2002). A comparison of methods to test mediation and other intervening variable effects. *Psychological Methods, 7*, 83-104.

Marra, T. (2005). *Dialectical behavior therapy in private practice.* Oakland, CA: New Harbinger.

Monti, D. A., Peterson, C., Kunkel, E. J., Hauck, W. W., Pequignot, E., Rhodes, L., et al. (2005). A randomized, controlled trial of mindfulness-based art therapy (MBAT) for women with cancer. *Psycho-Oncology, 15*, 363-373.

Neff, K. D. (2009). Self-Compassion. In M. R. Leary & R. H. Hoyle (Eds.), *Handbook of individual differences in social behavior.* New York: Guilford.

Nhat Hanh, T. (1976). *The miracle of mindfulness.* Boston: Beacon Press.

Rathus, J. H., Cavuoto, N., & Passarelli, V. (2006). Dialectical behavior therapy (DBT): A mindfulness-based treatment for intimate partner violence. In R. A. Baer (Ed.), *Mindfulness-based treatment approaches: A clinician's guide to evidence base and applications.* San Diego, CA: Elsevier.

Reibel, D. K., Greeson, J. M., Brainard, G. C., & Rosenzweig, S. (2001). Mindfulness-based stress reduction and health-related quality of life in a heterogeneous patient population. *General Hospital Psychiatry, 23*, 183-192.

Robins, C. J., & Chapman, A. L. (2004). Dialectical behavior therapy: Current status, recent developments, and future directions. *Journal of Personality Disorders, 18*, 73-89.

Safer, D. L., Telch, C. F., & Chen, E. Y. (2009). *Dialectical behavior therapy for binge eating and bulimia.* New York: Guilford.

Salmon, P., Sephton, S., Weissbecker, I., Hoover, K., Ulmer, C., & Studts, J. (2004). Mindfulness meditation in clinical practice. *Cognitive and behavioral practice, 11*, 434-446.

Scheel, K. R. (2000). The empirical basis of dialectical behavior therapy: Summary, critique, and implications. *Clinical Psychology: Science and Practice, 7*, 68-86.

Segal, Z. V., Williams, J. M. G., & Teasdale, J. D. (2002). *Mindfulness-based cognitive therapy for depression: A new approach to preventing relapse.* New York: Guilford.

Semple, R. J., Lee, J., & Miller, L. F. (2006). Mindfulness-based cognitive therapy for children. In R. A. Baer (Ed.), *Mindfulness-based treatment approaches: A clinician's guide to evidence base and applications.* San Diego, CA: Elsevier.

Shapiro, S. L., Astin, J. A., Bishop, S. R., & Cordova, M. (2005). Mindfulness-based stress reduction for health care professionals: Results from a randomized trial. *International Journal of Stress Management, 12*, 164-176.

Shapiro, S. L., Brown, K. W., & Biegel, G. M. (2007). Teaching self-care to caregivers: Effects of mindfulness-based stress reduction on the mental health of therapists in training. *Training and Education in Professional Psychology, 1*, 105-115.

Shapiro, S. L., & Carlson, L. E. (2009). *The art and science of mindfulness: Integrating mindfulness into psychology and the helping professions.* Washington, DC: American Psychological Association.

Smith, A. (2006). "Like waking up from a dream": Mindfulness training for older people with anxiety and depression. In R. A. Baer (Ed.), *Mindfulness-based treatment approaches: A clinician's guide to evidence base and applications.* San Diego, CA: Elsevier.

Smith, A., Graham, L., & Senthinathan, S. (2006). Mindfulness-based cognitive therapy for recurring depression in older people: A qualitative study. *Aging and Mental Health, 11*, 346-357.

Surawy, C., Roberts, J., & Silver, A. (2005). The effect of mindfulness training on mood and measures of fatigue, activity, and quality of life in patients with chronic fatigue syndrome on a hospital waiting list: A series of exploratory studies. *Behavioural and Cognitive Psychotherapy, 33*, 103-109.

Swenson, C. R. (2000). How can we account for DBT's widespread popularity? *Clinical Psychology: Science and Practice, 7*, 87-91.

Tacon, A. M., McComb, J., Caldera, Y., & Randolph, P. (2003). Mindfulness meditation, anxiety reduction, and heart disease: A pilot study. *Family and Community Health, 26*, 25-33.

Walser, R. D., & Pistorello, J. (2004). ACT in group format. In S. C. Hayes & K. D. Strosahl (Eds.), *A practical guide to acceptance and commitment therapy.* New York: Springer.

Weissbecker, I., Salmon, P., Studts, J. L., Floyd, A. R., Dedert, E. A., & Sephton, S. E. (2002). Mindfulness-based stress reduction and sense of coherence among women with fibromyalgia. *Journal of Clinical Psychology in Medical Settings, 9*, 297-307.

Williams, J. M. G., Alatiq, Y., Crane, C., Barnhofer, T., Fennell, M. J. V., Duggan, D. S., et al. (2008). Mindfulness-based cognitive therapy (MBCT) in bipolar disorder: Preliminary evaluation of immediate effects on between-episode functioning. *Journal of Affective Disorders, 107*, 275-279.

Williams, K. (2006). Mindfulness-based stress reduction (MBSR) in a worksite wellness program. In R. A. Baer, (Ed.), *Mindfulness-based treatment approaches: Clinician's guide to evidence base and applications.* San Diego, CA: Elsevier.

Wilson, K. W., & DuFrene, T. (2008). *Mindfulness for two: An acceptance and commitment therapy approach to mindfulness in psychotherapy.* Oakland, CA: New Harbinger.

Witkiewitz, K., Marlatt, G. A., & Walker, D. (2005). Mindfulness-based relapse prevention for alcohol and substance use disorders. *Journal of Cognitive Psychotherapy, 19*, 211-228.

Zettle, R. D. (2007). *ACT for depression: A clinician's guide to using acceptance and commitment therapy in treating depression.* Oakland, CA: New Harbinger.

Zettle, R. D., Rains, J. C., & Hayes, S. C. (in press). Processes of change in acceptance and commitment therapy and cognitive therapy for depression: A mediational reanalysis of Zettle and Rains (1989). *Behavior Modification.*

PART 1

Processes of Change

CHAPTER 1

Mindfulness and Decentering as Mechanisms of Change in Mindfulness- and Acceptance-Based Interventions

Shannon Sauer and Ruth A. Baer,
University of Kentucky

Mindfulness and decentering are closely related processes of critical importance in acceptance- and mindfulness-based treatments. Both are believed to play a key role in accounting for the benefits of mindfulness training, including reduction of symptoms and improvements in well-being. In this chapter, we describe how mindfulness and decentering are defined and measured and how they contribute to healthy psychological functioning. We conclude with a discussion of the relationship between mindfulness and decentering, including their similarities and differences.

MINDFULNESS

Mindfulness has been described as intentionally focusing one's attention on experiences occurring in the present moment in a nonjudgmental or accepting way (Kabat-Zinn, 1990). Mindfulness, and its cultivation through the practice of meditation, has its roots in Eastern spiritual traditions, primarily

Buddhism (Linehan, 1993); these traditions describe mindfulness meditation as a way of reducing suffering and encouraging the development of positive qualities, such as awareness, insight, and compassion (Goldstein, 2002; Kabat-Zinn, 2003). Mindfulness practices have been secularized for empirical study and included in interventions for a variety of mental health concerns, such as depression and anxiety (Segal, Williams, & Teasdale, 2002; Eifert & Forsyth, 2005); borderline personality disorder (Linehan, 1993); chronic pain, illness, and stress (Kabat-Zinn, 1982, 1990); substance abuse (Witkiewitz, Marlatt, & Walker, 2005); and binge eating (Kristeller & Hallett, 1999; Leahey, Crowther, & Irwin, 2008). A growing body of empirical literature supports the efficacy of mindfulness-based interventions for these and other problems (Baer, 2003; Grossman, Neimann, Schmidt, & Walach, 2004; Hayes, Luoma, Bond, Masuda, & Lillis, 2006; Lynch, Trost, Salsman, & Linehan, 2007; Robins & Chapman, 2004).

Although mindfulness-based interventions appear to be effective in the treatment of a wide variety of disorders, the mechanisms leading to these beneficial outcomes are unclear. This may be attributable in part to a lack of consensus regarding a secularized, clinically relevant definition of mindfulness. Thus, it is first important to describe current conceptualizations of mindfulness and to clarify what conceptualization of mindfulness may be most clinically useful.

Conceptualizing Mindfulness

Several authors have noted that the nature of mindfulness is subtle, somewhat elusive, and difficult to define (Block-Lerner, Salters-Pedneault, & Tull, 2005; Brown & Ryan, 2004). The published literature includes many definitions and descriptions of mindfulness. For example, Brown and Ryan (2003) define mindfulness as "the state of being attentive to and aware of what is taking place in the present" (p. 822). Other descriptions place more emphasis on particular qualities of attention that are brought to bear on present-moment experience, such as acceptance and nonjudgment. One of the most commonly cited definitions states that mindfulness is "paying attention in a particular way: on purpose, in the present moment, and nonjudgmentally" (Kabat-Zinn, 1994, p. 4). Bishop and colleagues (2004) describe mindfulness as having two components: self-regulation of attention to focus on current experiences (thoughts, feelings, sensations), and an attitude of curiosity, experiential openness, and acceptance of these experiences, regardless of how pleasant or aversive they may be. Similarly, Segal and colleagues (2002) suggest that mindfulness involves attending to whatever experiences are occurring in the present moment with kindly curiosity and without automatic judgments or reactivity. These authors also note that mindfulness can be contrasted with behaving mechanically and without awareness of one's actions, in a manner often referred to as automatic pilot. Kabat-Zinn (2003) suggests that "mindfulness includes an affectionate, compassionate quality within the attending, a sense of openhearted friendly presence and interest" (p. 145). Similarly, Marlatt and Kristeller (1999) note that mindfulness includes "an attitude of acceptance and loving-kindness" that is applied to observation of present-moment experiences (p. 70).

The instructions typically used to teach mindfulness are broadly consistent with these definitions and descriptions. Participants in mindfulness training are encouraged to focus their attention on particular stimuli that can be observed in the present moment, such as the sensations and movements of breathing or sounds in the environment. If cognitions, emotions, urges, or other experiences arise, participants are encouraged to observe them closely. Brief mental labeling of observed internal or external experiences is often suggested. For example, participants may silently say, "anger," "planning," "aching," "urge," or "hearing," as they observe internal and external phenomena. Some teaching methods suggest the use of complete sentences to describe experiences, such as "A feeling of sadness has arisen" or "I'm having self-critical thoughts" (Hayes, Strosahl, & Wilson, 1999; Linehan, 1993). Participants are asked to bring an attitude of acceptance, allowing, openness, willingness, kindness, compassion, and friendly curiosity to all observed experiences, regardless of how pleasant or unpleasant they may be, and to refrain from efforts to judge, evaluate, change, or terminate them. In dialectical behavior therapy (DBT; Linehan, 1993) mindfulness is taught as a set of interrelated skills in which there is a dual focus on what one does when being mindful (the "what" skills) and how one does it (the "how" skills). The "what" skills include observing (noticing or attending to present-moment experiences), describing (noting or labeling these experiences with words), and participating (focusing complete attention on ongoing activity). The "how" skills include being nonjudgmental (accepting, allowing, or refraining from evaluation of present-moment experience), one-mindful (having undivided attention), and effective (using skillful means).

In combination, these definitions, descriptions, and instructions for teaching mindfulness suggest the utility of conceptualizing mindfulness as a multifaceted construct that includes paying attention to present-moment experiences, labeling them with words, acting with awareness, avoiding automatic pilot, and bringing an attitude of openness, acceptance, willingness, allowing, nonjudging, kindness, friendliness, and curiosity to all observed experiences.

Assessing Mindfulness

Several tools for assessing mindfulness have been developed in recent years, most in the form of self-report questionnaires. Writing an effective questionnaire requires a clear and detailed conception of the construct to be measured (Clark & Watson, 1995). Thus, every questionnaire in the literature represents an attempt to operationalize the nature of mindfulness. So far, at least six independent research teams have attempted this task, and the resulting measures have provided a large and growing body of information about the nature of mindfulness and its relationships with other variables. All of the mindfulness questionnaires described below have shown at least preliminary evidence for their psychometric soundness, including internal consistency, significant correlations with variables that theoretically should be related to mindfulness, and low correlations with variables that should not be related to mindfulness. Some have shown higher scores in meditators than in nonmeditators or increases with participation in a meditation practice or a mindfulness-based intervention. Most are subject to ongoing study, and new articles reporting findings for one or more of these questionnaires appear regularly in the literature. Although all of these questionnaires are designed to measure mindfulness, they differ somewhat in their content and structure, especially in how they define the components of mindfulness and whether they assess them separately.

The Mindful Attention Awareness Scale (MAAS; Brown & Ryan, 2003) measures general tendency to be attentive to and aware of present-moment experiences in daily life and yields a single total score. This is consistent with Brown and Ryan's work (2003, 2004) suggesting that mindfulness consists of a single factor. Items describe being inattentive, preoccupied, and functioning on automatic pilot and are reverse scored, so that higher scores represent higher levels of mindfulness. Example items include "I find myself doing things without paying attention" and "I break or spill things because of carelessness, not paying attention, or thinking of something else."

The Freiburg Mindfulness Inventory (FMI; Buchheld, Grossman, & Walach, 2001) assesses nonjudgmental present-moment observation and openness to negative experience. Items include "I watch my feelings without becoming lost in them" and "I am open to the experience of the present moment." Although the FMI was designed to capture several elements of mindfulness (present-moment attention, nonjudging, openness), it doesn't measure them separately and yields only a total mindfulness score. The original version of the FMI was developed with experienced meditators participating in mindfulness retreats and assumed that respondents would have some knowledge of mindfulness. In a subsequent study, Walach, Buchheld, Buttenmuller, Kleinknecht, and Schmidt (2006) developed a version for people without previous meditation experience.

The Cognitive and Affective Mindfulness Scale–Revised (CAMS-R; Feldman, Hayes, Kumar, Gresson, & Laurenceau, 2007) assesses attention, awareness, present-moment focus, and acceptance of thoughts and feelings in general daily life. These components are not assessed separately but are combined to provide a total mindfulness score. Items include "I am able to accept the thoughts and feelings that I have" and "I try to notice my thoughts without judging them."

The Southampton Mindfulness Questionnaire (SMQ; Chadwick, Hember, Mead, Lilley, & Dagnan, 2005) specifically assesses mindful responding to distressing thoughts and images. It was designed to include four components of mindfulness (mindful observation, nonaversion, nonjudgment, and letting go), but like several of the other questionnaires it provides only one total score. Each item begins with "Usually when I have distressing thoughts or images" and continues with a mindfulness-related statement, such as "they take over my mind for quite a while afterwards" (reverse scored) or "I am able to just notice them without reacting."

The Kentucky Inventory of Mindfulness Skills (KIMS; Baer, Smith, & Allen, 2004), based largely on the conceptualization of mindfulness found in DBT, provides separate subscale scores for each of four mindfulness skills: observing, describing, acting with awareness, and accepting without judgment. Items include "I notice when my moods begin to change" (observing), "I'm good at finding the words to describe my feelings" (describing), "When I do things, my mind wanders off and I'm easily distracted" (acting with awareness, reverse scored), and "I tell myself that I shouldn't be feeling the way I'm feeling" (accepting without judging, reverse scored).

The Philadelphia Mindfulness Scale (PHLMS; Cardaciotto, Herbert, Forman, Moitra, & Farrow, 2007) includes two factors that are scored separately: awareness of ongoing internal and external experiences, and acceptance of these experiences, which includes nonjudging and openness toward them while refraining from attempts to avoid or escape them. Items include "I'm aware of thoughts I'm having when my mood changes" (awareness) and "I try to distract myself when I feel unpleasant emotions" (acceptance, reverse scored).

An Integrated Measure of Mindfulness

Several authors have argued that it is important to define and measure complex constructs at the level of facets or components; this allows researchers to clarify relationships between the construct and other variables (Hough & Schneider, 1995; Paunonen & Ashton, 2001; Smith, Fischer, & Fister, 2003; Smith & McCarthy, 1995). In the case of mindfulness, a multifacet conceptualization may also help clarify exactly what is changing when people participate in mindfulness-based interventions and how these treatments lead to beneficial outcomes. A facet-based conceptualization may be especially useful in clinical practice. The ability to assess the elements of mindfulness separately may aid in tailoring mindfulness training to individuals with particular strengths and weaknesses. In addition, empirically based information about the components of mindfulness may provide useful information for clinicians about how to describe mindfulness to clients. As noted by Santorelli and Kabat-Zinn (2002), the ability to describe mindfulness in ordinary language is essential for providers of mindfulness-based stress reduction (MBSR).

In a recent study of facets of mindfulness, Baer, Smith, Hopkins, Krietemeyer, and Toney (2006) administered five of the mindfulness questionnaires just described (all but the PHLMS, which had not been developed at the time) to a large sample of undergraduate students and conducted exploratory factor analysis. This method allowed items from different instruments to combine to form factors and provided an empirical analysis of components of mindfulness based on the thinking of five research teams who had made independent efforts to operationalize mindfulness by writing questionnaire items to assess it. This analysis yielded five clearly identifiable factors: observing, describing, acting with awareness, nonjudging of inner experience, and nonreactivity to inner experience.

The *observing* factor consists of noticing or attending to a variety of internal or external phenomena (e.g., bodily sensations, cognitions, emotions, sounds) and includes items originally written for the KIMS. The *describing* factor refers to applying words or labels to observed phenomena and includes items from the KIMS and the CAMS-R. The *acting with awareness* factor involves engaging fully in one's present activity rather than functioning on automatic pilot and includes items from the MAAS and the KIMS. The *nonjudging of inner experience* factor refers to taking a non-evaluative stance toward thoughts and feelings and includes items from the KIMS and the SMQ. Finally, the *nonreactivity to inner experience* factor involves accepting thoughts and feelings and allowing them to come and go without getting caught up in or carried away by them. All of these items came from the FMI and the SMQ. The items that most clearly represented each factor in this analysis (those with the strongest factor loadings) were combined to form the Five Facet Mindfulness Questionnaire (FFMQ; Baer et al., 2006) which has a total of thirty-nine items representing all five of the questionnaires included in the analysis. The FFMQ is included as an appendix to this chapter.

All five of the facets measured by the FFMQ are internally consistent and appear to be conceptually consistent with elements of mindfulness that have been described in the published literature. The five facets have also been shown to be significantly correlated with numerous other variables that should theoretically be related to aspects of mindfulness, such as emotional intelligence, self-compassion, and openness to experience (positive correlations) and experiential avoidance and thought suppression (negative correlations). Because the FFMQ allows elements of mindfulness to be measured separately and reliably, it has been used in several studies examining whether increased mindfulness is a mechanism by which the practice of mindfulness leads to healthy psychological functioning, and whether some facets are more important than others in explaining these changes.

Mindfulness as a Mechanism of Change in Mindfulness-Based Stress Reduction

MBSR (Kabat-Zinn, 1982, 1990) is an eight-week group program that cultivates mindfulness through the intensive practice of meditation-based exercises. Carmody and Baer (2008) studied 121 MBSR participants with complaints of stress, anxiety, and pain. Their average age was forty-seven years, 63 percent were women, and most worked in white-collar settings. Before and after MBSR, they completed the FFMQ and several measures of symptoms and well-being. They also used home practice logs to record the number of minutes they practiced mindfulness exercises each day. Mindfulness scores increased significantly over the eight-week course. This effect was largest for the facets of observing and nonreactivity to inner experience, and smallest for the facet of describing. This latter finding is not surprising, because MBSR doesn't emphasize verbal labeling of experience to the extent seen in other mindfulness-based treatments, such as DBT and acceptance and commitment therapy (ACT; Hayes et al., 1999), which incorporate exercises to cultivate labeling of cognitions, emotions, and sensations.

In Carmody and Baer's 2008 study, symptoms and well-being also changed significantly. The total number of minutes spent in home practice of mindfulness exercises was significantly related to the extent of change in mindfulness, symptoms, and well-being. The more participants practiced, the more improvement they reported. The most interesting finding was that the change in mindfulness scores mediated the relationship between total home practice time and degree of improvement in psychological functioning. That is, the results were consistent with the idea that practicing mindfulness meditation improves psychological functioning because it increases people's ability to observe their internal experiences nonjudgmentally and nonreactively and bring awareness to their daily activities.

Mindfulness as a Mechanism of Change in Long-Term Meditators

Baer and colleagues (2008) studied relationships between long-term meditation experience, self-reported mindfulness (as measured by the FFMQ), and psychological well-being among 176 adults who had practiced meditation in a Buddhist-based tradition for an average of seven years. Their average age was forty-nine years, 68 percent were women, and most had high levels of education. Many were mental health or medical professionals. A control group of adults of similar age, educational background, and professional experience but with no regular meditation practice was also included. All completed the FFMQ and the Scales of Psychological Well-Being (SPWB; Ryff, 1989), a well-known measure of healthy psychological functioning. Total meditation experience, expressed as the number of months of regular practice, was significantly correlated with both mindfulness scores and psychological well-being. That is, those who had more meditation experience also had higher levels of self-reported mindfulness and well-being, even after controlling for age, education, and professional experience in the mental health field. The most interesting finding was that three of the processes assessed by a subscale of the FFMQ (describing, nonjudging of inner experience, and nonreactivity to inner experience) were significant mediators of the relationship between meditation experience and well-being. This pattern of results suggests that long-term meditation practice is associated with an increased ability to label one's internal experiences and be nonjudgmental and nonreactive toward them. In turn, the ability to respond to internal experiences in these ways is associated with greater psychological health.

Why It's Beneficial to Be Mindful in Daily Life

The findings just reviewed are consistent with a long-standing assumption in Buddhist meditation traditions and in contemporary mindfulness-based treatments: that the regular practice of mindfulness meditation will lead to increased ability to respond mindfully to the experiences of daily life, and that this in turn will encourage healthy psychological functioning. However, it isn't entirely clear why responding mindfully to the experiences of daily life is adaptive. Several authors have discussed the potential benefits of consistent mindful observation, especially of internal experiences such as cognitions, emotions, and sensations. For example, nonreactively observing thoughts as they appear and labeling them as thoughts, rather than becoming absorbed in their content, is believed to cultivate the skill of decentering, in which cognitions are observed and labeled as transitory mental events rather than as aspects of the self or important truths that must dictate behavior. Decentering, which is considered in greater detail later in this chapter, prevents rumination, a prominent style of thinking in many psychological disorders. Rumination is a form of repetitive thought that involves passively and unproductively thinking about and analyzing unpleasant symptoms and internal experiences and their causes, consequences, and implications (Nolen-Hoeksema, Wisco, & Lyubomirsky, 2008). Mindful observation of thoughts encourages noticing them as they come and go without getting caught up in rumination. Thus, cultivating mindfulness of thoughts should be beneficial for people suffering from any of the psychological disorders in which rumination is an important factor.

These include mood and anxiety disorders, substance use disorders, and eating disorders, among others (Harvey, Watkins, Mansell, & Shafran, 2004; Nolen-Hoeksema et al., 2008). Reduced rumination is believed to be a central mechanism of change in mindfulness-based cognitive therapy, and preliminary evidence suggests that participants report less rumination after completing the program (Kingston, Dooley, Bates, Lawlor, & Malone, 2007; Ramel, Goldin, Carmona, & McQuaid, 2004).

Other authors have suggested that the process of emotional exposure is important in helping explain the benefits of mindfulness practice (Linehan, 1993; Kabat-Zinn, 1982). Engaging in sustained, nonjudgmental, and non-reactive observation of internal experiences, some of which may be very unpleasant, without trying to avoid or escape them, probably constitutes a form of exposure. If so, reductions in emotional reactivity and avoidance behaviors should occur through a process of desensitization in which participants become less fearful of their own inner experiences. Linehan (1993) suggests that this process may be especially important for people suffering from borderline personality disorder (BPD) because they are often phobic of their own intense negative emotions. The effect of mindfulness training on fear of emotion in BPD hasn't been studied. However, in a study of experienced meditators, Lykins and Baer (2009) found that fear of emotion partially mediated the relationship between meditation experience and well-being. That is, participants who had been meditating longer had lower self-reported fear of emotion and better psychological health.

Limitations of some of this research must be recognized. Mediation analyses are more convincing if change in the proposed mediator (mindfulness) can be shown to precede changes in the dependent variables (symptoms and well-being). Without this temporal sequence, we can't be sure that increased mindfulness leads to improved psychological health. It could be that improved psychological health leads to increased mindfulness. In addition, the research described here has relied on self-report measures, which can be subject to biases. In particular, people who have meditated for years are probably well aware of the expected benefits and may respond accordingly to questionnaire items. On the other hand, maintaining a regular meditation practice requires daily discipline, making it unlikely that people who don't perceive significant benefits will continue to practice. Thus, although long-term meditators probably have a lot of positive things to say about meditation, if they didn't, they probably would have stopped meditating. In addition, some aspects of mindfulness may be difficult to report on, especially for people with no mindfulness training. Future work should investigate alternative methods of assessing mindfulness.

DECENTERING

Decentering has been defined as the ability to observe one's thoughts and feelings as transitory events in the mind that do not necessarily reflect reality, truth, or self-worth, are not necessarily important, and do not require particular behaviors in response (Fresco, Moore, et al., 2007). It includes taking a present-focused, nonjudgmental, and accepting stance toward thoughts and feelings (Fresco, Segal, Buis, & Kennedy, 2007). In cognitive therapy, decentering has been discussed primarily in relation to thoughts. Observation and identification of thoughts is described as critical to cognitive therapy (Hollon & Beck, 1979) because it enables clients to recognize their negative thoughts as mental phenomena or ideas to be tested, rather than as facts. Thus, repeatedly asking clients to observe and identify their thoughts, and often to write them down, provides practice in decentering.

Theoretical Importance of Decentering

In the early days of cognitive therapy, it was widely assumed that preventing relapse of depression required changing the content of depressive thinking. For this reason, identifying and decentering from thoughts was seen as only a first step and was typically followed by strategies designed to change the content of thoughts, such as identifying evidence for and against specific thoughts and generating more rational or balanced alternative thoughts. However, the empirical literature increasingly suggested that changing the content of thoughts isn't the central ingredient in cognitive therapy's beneficial effects on relapse rates. For example, studies showed that antidepressant medication was equally effective in changing the content of depressive cognitions yet was associated with much higher relapse rates (Barber & DeRubeis, 1989; Simons, Garfield, & Murphy, 1984). Clearly, some other element of cognitive therapy was providing the enhanced protection against relapse. Several authors suggested that the early steps in cognitive therapy, in which people identify and observe their thoughts in order to evaluate their accuracy, cultivated a decentered perspective on thoughts, and that this was the critical skill providing protection against future episodes (Ingram & Hollon, 1986; Teasdale et al., 2002).

This idea became the basis for the theoretical model that underlies mindfulness-based cognitive therapy (MBCT), which was developed for the prevention of relapse in adults with a history of recurrent episodes of major depression. According to this model, people with a history of depressive episodes have developed strong associations between sadness and negative thought patterns. In these individuals, the ordinary sad moods of daily life trigger the same depressive thinking patterns that occurred during previous episodes. These patterns typically include global negative judgments about themselves and the world and a ruminative style of thinking in which problems and inadequacies are repeatedly but unproductively analyzed in an attempt to gain insight about how to solve them. These negative thinking patterns tend to be self-perpetuating and may escalate into a new depressive episode. Rather than teaching participants to change the content of depressive thoughts and attitudes, MBCT uses mindfulness practices to teach decentering from thoughts, sensations, and emotions. Mindfulness skills enable the recognition of sad moods when they occur and encourage decentering from depressive thoughts. This prevents reactivated negative thinking patterns from escalating into rumination, which may lead to relapse. It also allows time for choosing more adaptive responses to the occurrence of a sad mood. Depressive thinking is thereby nipped in the bud, forestalling relapse.

In MBCT, decentering is defined both more broadly and more specifically than in traditional cognitive therapy (Segal et al., 2002). Whereas cognitive therapy emphasizes decentering specifically from thoughts, MBCT teaches a decentered relationship to bodily sensations and emotional states, as well as cognitions. All of these phenomena are seen as transitory experiences that don't necessarily reflect reality or self-worth and don't require particular responses. MBCT's definition of decentering is also more specific than cognitive therapy's because it explicitly encourages an attitude of openness, acceptance, and curiosity toward the experiences to which it is applied, even when they are unpleasant or unwanted. Terms such as "allowing," "embracing," and "welcoming" are used to describe this attitude toward present-moment experiences.

Decentering as defined in MBCT appears to be synonymous with reperceiving, a term introduced by Shapiro, Carlson, Astin, and Freedman (2006), who describe it as the primary mechanism of change in mindfulness-based treatment. They propose that reperceiving facilitates other mechanisms, including self-regulation, values clarification, and cognitive and emotional flexibility, which in turn lead to the reduction of symptoms and improvements in well-being. Decentering is also closely related to defusion, a term used in ACT to describe a very similar stance toward internal experience. Defusion is discussed in greater detail in chapter 2.

Assessment of Decentering

Two recently developed tools can be used to measure decentering. The Measure of Awareness and Coping in Autobiographical Memory (MACAM; Teasdale et al., 2002) is a vignette-based, semistructured interview in which participants are asked to imagine themselves in several mildly distressing situations and to feel the feelings that would be elicited in each situation. Then they are asked to remember specific occasions from their own lives that are brought to mind by the vignettes and to describe these occasions in detail, including their feelings in the situation and how they responded to them. Responses are recorded and coded by trained raters for the presence of decentering, defined as awareness of thoughts and feelings as separate from the self. Teasdale and colleagues (2002) found that decentering scores were higher for a group of adults who had never been depressed than for a previously depressed group, and that baseline decentering scores predicted risk of relapse in the previously depressed group. In addition, lower baseline levels of decentering predicted earlier relapse following treatment for depression with either cognitive therapy or medication. Overall, these findings support the idea that the ability to adopt a decentered perspective on thoughts and feelings is centrally related to recovery from depression and prevention of relapse.

Although these findings suggest that the MACAM has good psychometric properties, it is difficult and time-consuming to use. Respondents must listen to several vignettes, and the administrator must be trained to conduct the interview and code the responses. To provide a more easily usable instrument, Teasdale designed the Experiences Questionnaire (EQ; unpublished), which was further developed and investigated by Fresco, Moore, and colleagues (2007). The EQ was originally designed to have two subscales, one measuring decentering and the other measuring rumination. The rumination items weren't psychometrically sound and haven't been used in recent studies. However, an eleven-item decentering factor was identified, which includes items such as "I can observe unpleasant feelings without being drawn into them" and "I can separate myself from my thoughts and feelings." The decentering factor showed good internal consistency in both clinical and nonclinical samples, a positive correlation with cognitive reappraisal, and significant negative correlations (as expected) with experiential avoidance, rumination, emotion suppression, anxiety, and depression. Depressed patients in remission showed lower decentering scores than a healthy control group, and levels of decentering were significantly correlated with current self-reported and clinician-rated levels of depressive symptoms. Thus, the decentering subscale of the EQ appears to have good psychometric properties. The EQ is included as an appendix to this chapter.

Evidence That Decentering Is Related to Mindfulness Training

The study just described (Teasdale et al., 2002) also investigated whether treatment with MBCT would lead to changes in decentering scores on the MACAM. Results showed that previously depressed people who completed MBCT had larger increases in decentering than a control group who received treatment available in the community (e.g., from their family doctor). MBCT also led to significantly reduced relapse rates. This pattern of results suggests that increased ability to decenter from thoughts and feelings may be the mechanism through which MBCT leads to reductions in depressive relapse. However, the design of the study did not permit a full mediational analysis.

Carmody, Baer, Lykins, and Olendzki (2009) measured both mindfulness and decentering in a group of 309 participants in MBSR. Participants reported a variety of pain and stress-related complaints and were either self-referred to MBSR or referred by their physicians. Mindfulness was measured with the FFMQ and decentering was measured with the decentering subscale from the EQ. Both instruments were completed before and after the eight-week intervention, along with measures of symptoms and stress. Mindfulness and decentering both increased significantly from pre- to post-treatment, and symptoms and stress were significantly reduced. The degree of change in both mindfulness and decentering was significantly correlated with the degree of change in symptoms and stress. Because there was no control group, the design of this study did not permit a full analysis of whether changes in decentering mediated the effects of MBSR on psychological symptoms and stress. However, the results are consistent with this idea. Results also suggested that mindfulness and decentering, when considered in combination, led to increases in values clarification and flexible responding to environmental demands, which in turn were related to reduced symptoms and stress.

How Distinct Are Mindfulness and Decentering?

Several authors have suggested that mindfulness training is a way of teaching decentering skills (Shapiro et al., 2006; Teasdale et al., 2002). Shapiro and colleagues (2006) proposed that increased mindfulness should lead to increases in decentering, which in turn would lead to other proposed mechanisms of change (such as increased self-regulation and clarity of values) and improvements in psychological health. Fresco, Moore, and colleagues (2007) suggested that the EQ wasn't designed to be a measure of mindfulness and that mindfulness and decentering are related but distinct constructs.

On the other hand, published definitions of decentering are very similar to definitions of mindfulness, and the empirical evidence suggests that the distinction between mindfulness and decentering requires further clarification. Carmody and colleagues (2009) found that these two variables, as measured by the FFMQ and EQ, were very highly correlated both before MBSR ($r = 0.81$) and after MBSR ($r = 0.74$). They also tested the mediational model proposed by Shapiro and colleagues (2006) and found no evidence for a sequential process in which improvement in mindfulness leads to improvement in decentering. Instead, the findings suggested that mindfulness and decentering are highly overlapping constructs that both increase substantially with participation in MBSR. Overall, this research suggests that the tendencies to be mindful and decentered in daily life, as measured by the FFMQ and EQ, are very similar, and that both increase with mindfulness training. Future refinements in definitions and measurements of mindfulness and decentering may help to clarify the extent to which they are distinct and whether they develop simultaneously or sequentially over the course of a regular mindfulness practice.

CONCLUSIONS

Although mindfulness-based interventions are associated with positive changes in psychological adjustment, the mechanisms leading to these beneficial outcomes are not yet clear. In order to understand these mechanisms, it is necessary to assess the processes believed to be responsible for therapeutic changes. The five-facet conceptualization of mindfulness (Baer et al., 2006) appears to be clinically useful because it encompasses the qualities of mindfulness thought to be important by leading scholars in this field. These authors stress the importance of observing and describing experiences occurring in the present moment in a nonjudgmental, nonreactive manner and participating with awareness in the activities of daily life. Each of these qualities of mindfulness can be reliably and separately measured using the FFMQ (Baer et al., 2006). A similar point can be made about decentering. Although the EQ was developed quite recently, its psychometric properties are promising and it seems likely to yield important information about the effects of mindfulness training. Research with the FFMQ and EQ suggests that mindfulness and decentering are likely to be important mechanisms through which mindfulness- and acceptance-based treatments lead to beneficial outcomes.

REFERENCES

Baer, R. A. (2003). Mindfulness training as a clinical intervention: A conceptual and empirical review. *Clinical Psychology: Science and Practice, 10*, 125-143.

Baer, R. A., Smith, G. T., & Allen, K. B. (2004). Assessment of mindfulness by self-report: The Kentucky Inventory of Mindfulness Skills. *Assessment, 11*, 191-206.

Baer, R. A., Smith, G. T., Hopkins, J., Krietemeyer, J., & Toney, L. (2006). Using self-report assessment methods to explore facets of mindfulness. *Assessment, 13*, 27-45.

Baer, R. A., Smith, G. T., Lykins, E., Button, D., Krietemeyer, J., Sauer, S. E., et al. (2008). Construct validity of the five facet mindfulness questionnaire in meditating and nonmeditating samples. *Assessment, 15*, 329-342.

Barber, J. P., & DeRubeis, R. J. (1989). On second thought: Where the action is in cognitive therapy for depression. *Cognitive Therapy and Research, 13*, 441-457.

Bishop, S. R., Lau, M., Shapiro, S., Carlson, L., Anderson, N. C., Carmody, J., et al. (2004). Mindfulness: A proposed operational definition. *Clinical Psychology: Science and Practice, 11*, 230-241.

Block-Lerner, J., Salters-Pedneault, K., & Tull, M. T. (2005). Assessing mindfulness and experiential acceptance: Attempts to capture inherently elusive phenomena. In S. M. Orsillo & L. Roemer (Eds.), *Acceptance- and mindfulness-based approaches to anxiety: Conceptualization and treatment.* New York: Springer.

Brown, K. W., & Ryan, R. M. (2003). The benefits of being in the present: Mindfulness and its role in psychological well-being. *Journal of Personality and Social Psychology, 84*, 822-848.

Brown, K. W., & Ryan, R. M. (2004). Perils and promise in defining and measuring mindfulness: Observations from experience. *Clinical Psychology: Science and Practice, 11*, 242-248.

Buchheld, N., Grossman, P., & Walach, H. (2001). Measuring mindfulness in insight meditation (vipassana) and meditation-based psychotherapy: The development of the Freiburg Mindfulness Inventory (FMI). *Journal for Meditation and Meditation Research, 1*, 11-34.

Cardaciotto, L., Herbert, J. D., Forman, E. M., Moitra, E., & Farrow, V. (2007). The assessment of present-moment awareness and acceptance: The Philadelphia Mindfulness Scale. *Assessment, 15*, 204-223.

Carmody, J., & Baer, R. A. (2008). Relationships between mindfulness practice and levels of mindfulness, medical and psychological symptoms and well-being in a mindfulness- based stress reduction program. *Journal of Behavioral Medicine, 31*, 23-33.

Carmody, J., Baer, R. A., Lykins, E. L. B., & Olendzki, N. (2009). An empirical study of the mechanisms of mindfulness in a mindfulness-based stress reduction program. *Journal of Clinical Psychology, 65*, 613-626.

Chadwick, P., Hember, M., Symes, J., Peters, E., & Kuipers, E. (2008). *Responding mindfully to unpleasant thoughts and images: Reliability and validity of the Southampton Mindfulness Questionnaire (SMQ). British Journal of Clinical Psychology, 47,* 451-455.

Clark, L. A., & Watson, D. (1995). Constructing validity: Basic issues in objective scale development. *Psychological Assessment, 7,* 309-319.

Eifert, G. H., & Forsyth, J. P. (2005). *Acceptance and commitment therapy for anxiety disorders.* Oakland, CA: New Harbinger.

Feldman, G. C., Hayes, A. M., Kumar, S. M., Greeson, J. G., & Laurenceau, J. P. (2007). Mindfulness and emotion regulation: The development and initial validation of the Cognitive and Affective Mindfulness Scale-Revised (CAMS-R). *Journal of Psychopathology and Behavioral Assessment, 29,* 177-190.

Fresco, D. M., Moore, M. T., van Dulmen, M., Segal, Z. V., Ma, S. H., Teasdale, J. D. et al. (2007). Initial psychometric properties of the Experiences Questionnaire: Validation of a self-report measure of decentering. *Behavior Therapy, 38,* 234-246.

Fresco, D. M., Segal, Z. V., Buis, T., & Kennedy, S. (2007). Relationship of posttreatment decentering and cognitive reactivity to relapse in major depression. *Journal of Consulting and Clinical Psychology, 75,* 447-455.

Goldstein, J. (2002). *One dharma: The emerging Western Buddhism.* New York: Harper Collins.

Grossman, P., Neimann, L., Schmidt, S., & Walach, H. (2004). Mindfulness-based stress reduction and health benefits: A meta-analysis. *Journal of Psychosomatic Research, 57,* 35-43.

Harvey, A., Watkins, E., Mansell, W, & Shafran, R. (2004). *Cognitive behavioural processes across psychological disorders: A transdiagnostic approach to research and treatment.* Oxford, UK: Oxford University Press.

Hayes, S. C., Luoma, J., Bond, F., Masuda, A., & Lillis, J. (2006). Acceptance and commitment therapy: Model, processes and outcomes. *Behaviour Research and Therapy, 44,* 1-25.

Hayes, S. C., Strosahl, K. D., & Wilson, K. G. (1999). *Acceptance and commitment therapy: An experiential approach to behavior change.* New York: Guilford.

Hollon, S. D., & Beck, A. T. (1979). Cognitive therapy of depression. In P. C. Kendall & S. D. Hollon (Eds.), *Cognitive-behavioral interventions: Theory, research, and procedures.* New York: Academic Press.

Hough, L. M., & Schneider, R. J. (1995). Personality traits, taxonomies, and applications in organizations. In K. R. Murphy (Ed.), *Individuals and behavior in organizations.* San Francisco: Jossey-Bass.

Ingram, R. E., & Hollon, S. D. (1986). Cognitive therapy for depression from an information processing perspective. In R. E. Ingram (Ed.), *Information processing approaches to clinical psychology*. Orlando, FL: Academic Press.

Kabat-Zinn, J. (1982). An outpatient program in behavioral medicine for chronic pain patients based on the practice of mindfulness meditation: Theoretical considerations and preliminary results. *General Hospital Psychiatry, 4*, 33-47.

Kabat-Zinn, J. (1990). *Full catastrophe living: Using the wisdom of your mind and body to face stress, pain, and illness.* New York: Delacorte.

Kabat-Zinn, J. (1994). *Wherever you go, there you are.* New York: Hyperion.

Kabat-Zinn, J. (2003). Mindfulness-based interventions in context: Past, present, and future. *Clinical Psychology: Science and Practice, 10*, 144-156.

Kingston, T., Dooley, B., Bates, A., Lawlor, E., & Malone, K. (2007). Mindfulness-based cognitive therapy for residual depressive symptoms. *Psychology and Psychotherapy: Theory, Research, and Practice, 80*, 193-203.

Kristeller, J. L., & Hallett, C. B. (1999). An exploratory study of a meditation-based intervention for binge eating disorder. *Journal of Health Psychology, 4*, 357-363.

Leahey, T., Crowther, J., & Irwin, S. (2008). A cognitive-behavioral mindfulness group therapy intervention for the treatment of binge eating in bariatric surgery patients. *Cognitive and Behavioral Practice, 15*, 364-375.

Linehan, M. (1993). *Cognitive-behavioral treatment of borderline personality disorder.* New York: Guilford.

Lykins, E. L., & Baer, R. A. (2009). Psychological functioning in a sample of long-term practitioners of mindfulness meditation. *Journal of Cognitive Psychotherapy, 23*, 226-241.

Lynch, T. R., Trost, W. T., Salsman, N., & Linehan, M. M. (2007). Dialectical behavior therapy for borderline personality disorder. *Annual Review of Clinical Psychology, 3*, 181-205.

Marlatt, G. A., & Kristeller, J. L. (1999). Mindfulness and meditation. In W. R. Miller (Ed.), *Integrating spirituality into treatment*. Washington, DC: American Psychological Association.

Nolen-Hoeksema, S., Wisco, B. E., & Lyubomirsky, S. (2008). Rethinking rumination. *Perspective on Psychological Science, 3*, 400-424.

Paunonen, S. V., & Ashton, M. C. (2001). Big five factors and facets and the prediction of behavior. *Journal of Personality and Social Psychology, 81*, 524-539.

Ramel, W., Goldin, P. R., Carmona, P. E., & McQuaid, J. R. (2004). The effects of mindfulness meditation on cognitive processes and affect in patients with past depression. *Cognitive Therapy and Research, 28*, 433-455.

Robins, C. J., & Chapman, A. L. (2004). Dialectical behavior therapy: Current status, recent developments, and future directions. *Journal of Personality Disorders, 18*, 73-89.

Ryff, C. (1989). Happiness is everything, or is it? Explorations on the meaning of psychological well-being. *Journal of Personality and Social Psychology, 57*, 1069-1081.

Santorelli, S., & Kabat-Zinn, J. (2002). *Mindfulness-based stress reduction professional training: MBSR curriculum guide and supporting materials.* Worcester: University of Massachusetts Medical School.

Segal, Z. V., Williams, J. M., & Teasdale, J. D. (2002). *Mindfulness-based cognitive therapy for depression: A new approach to preventing relapse.* New York: Guilford.

Shapiro, S. L., Carlson, L. E., Astin, J. A., & Freedman, B. (2006). Mechanisms of mindfulness. *Journal of Clinical Psychology, 62*, 373-386.

Simons, A., Garfield, S. L., & Murphy, G. E. (1984). The process of change in cognitive therapy and pharmacotherapy for depression. *Archives of General Psychiatry, 41*, 45-51.

Smith, G. T, Fischer, S., & Fister, S. M. (2003). Incremental validity principles in test construction. *Psychological Assessment, 15*, 467-477.

Smith, G. T., & McCarthy, D. M. (1995). Methodological considerations in the refinement of clinical assessment instruments. *Psychological Assessment, 7*, 300-308.

Teasdale, J. D., Moore, R. G., Hayhurst, H., Pope, M., Williams, S., & Segal, Z. V. (2002). Metacognitive awareness and prevention of relapse in depression: Empirical evidence. *Journal of Consulting and Clinical Psychology, 68*, 615-623.

Walach, H., Buchheld, N., Buttenmuller, V., Kleinknecht, N., & Schmidt, S. (2006). Measuring mindfulness: The Freiburg Mindfulness Inventory (FMI). *Personality and Individual Differences, 40*, 1543-1555.

Witkiewitz, K., Marlatt, G. A., & Walker, D. (2005). Mindfulness-based relapse prevention for alcohol and substance use disorders. *Journal of Cognitive Psychotherapy, 19*, 211-228.

APPENDIX A: FIVE FACET MINDFULNESS QUESTIONNAIRE (FFMQ)

Please rate each of the following statements using the scale provided. Write the number in the blank that best describes *your own opinion* of what is *generally true for you*.

1	2	3	4	5
Never or very rarely true	Rarely true	Sometimes true	Often true	Very often or always true

_______ 1. When I'm walking, I deliberately notice the sensations of my body moving.

_______ 2. I'm good at finding words to describe my feelings.

_______ 3. I criticize myself for having irrational or inappropriate emotions.

_______ 4. I perceive my feelings and emotions without having to react to them.

_______ 5. When I do things, my mind wanders off and I'm easily distracted.

_______ 6. When I take a shower or bath, I stay alert to the sensations of water on my body.

_______ 7. I can easily put my beliefs, opinions, and expectations into words.

_______ 8. I don't pay attention to what I'm doing because I'm daydreaming, worrying, or otherwise distracted.

_______ 9. I watch my feelings without getting lost in them.

_______ 10. I tell myself I shouldn't be feeling the way I'm feeling.

_______ 11. I notice how foods and drinks affect my thoughts, bodily sensations, and emotions.

_______ 12. It's hard for me to find the words to describe what I'm thinking.

_______ 13. I am easily distracted.

_______ 14. I believe some of my thoughts are abnormal or bad and I shouldn't think that way.

_______ 15. I pay attention to sensations, such as the wind in my hair or sun on my face.

_______ 16. I have trouble thinking of the right words to express how I feel about things.

_______ 17. I make judgments about whether my thoughts are good or bad.

_______ 18. I find it difficult to stay focused on what's happening in the present.

_______ 19. When I have distressing thoughts or images, I "step back" and am aware of the thought or image without getting taken over by it.

_______ 20. I pay attention to sounds, such as clocks ticking, birds chirping, or cars passing.

_______ 21. In difficult situations, I can pause without immediately reacting.

_______ 22. When I have a sensation in my body, it's difficult for me to describe it because I can't find the right words.

_______ 23. It seems I am "running on automatic" without much awareness of what I'm doing.

_______ 24. When I have distressing thoughts or images, I feel calm soon after.

_______ 25. I tell myself that I shouldn't be thinking the way I'm thinking.

_______ 26. I notice the smells and aromas of things.

_______ 27. Even when I'm feeling terribly upset, I can find a way to put it into words.

_______ 28. I rush through activities without being really attentive to them.

_______ 29. When I have distressing thoughts or images, I am able just to notice them without reacting.

_______ 30. I think some of my emotions are bad or inappropriate and I shouldn't feel them.

_______ 31. I notice visual elements in art or nature, such as colors, shapes, textures, or patterns of light and shadow.

_______ 32. My natural tendency is to put my experiences into words.

_______ 33. When I have distressing thoughts or images, I just notice them and let them go.

_______ 34. I do jobs or tasks automatically without being aware of what I'm doing.

_______ 35. When I have distressing thoughts or images, I judge myself as good or bad depending what the thought or image is about.

_______ 36. I pay attention to how my emotions affect my thoughts and behavior.

_______ 37. I can usually describe how I feel at the moment in considerable detail.

_______ 38. I find myself doing things without paying attention.

_______ 39. I disapprove of myself when I have irrational ideas.

SCORING THE FFMQ

(Note: R = reverse-scored item)

Observing: Sum responses to items 1, 6, 11, 15, 20, 26, 31, and 36.

Describing: Sum responses to items 2, 7, 12R, 16R, 22R, 27, 32, and 37.

Acting with Awareness: Sum responses to items 5R, 8R, 13R, 18R, 23R, 28R, 34R, and 38R.

Nonjudging of inner experience: Sum responses to items 3R, 10R, 14R, 17R, 25R, 30R, 35R, and 39R.

Nonreactivity to inner experience: Sum responses to items 4, 9, 19, 21, 24, 29, and 33.

First published in Baer, R. A., Smith, G. T., Hopkins, J., Krietemeyer, J., & Toney, L. (2006). Using self-report assessment methods to explore facets of mindfulness. *Assessment, 13,* 27–45.

APPENDIX B: EXPERIENCES QUESTIONNAIRE (EQ)

We are interested in your recent experiences. Below is a list of things that people sometimes experience. Please write the number in the blank that indicates how much you currently have experiences similar to those described. Please do not spend too long on each item—it is your first response we are interested in. Please be sure to answer every item. Use the following scale:

1	2	3	4	5
Never	Rarely	Sometimes	Often	All the time

_______ 1. I think about what will happen in the future.

_______ 2. I remind myself that thoughts aren't facts.

_______ 3. I am better able to accept myself as I am.

_______ 4. I notice all sorts of little things and details in the world around me.

_______ 5. I am kinder to myself when things go wrong.

_______ 6. I can slow my thinking at times of stress.

_______ 7. I wonder what kind of person I really am.

_______ 8. I am not so easily carried away by my thoughts and feelings.

_______ 9. I notice that I don't take difficulties so personally.

_______ 10. I can separate myself from my thoughts and feelings.

_______ 11. I analyze why things turn out the way they do.

_______ 12. I can take time to respond to difficulties.

_______ 13. I think over and over again about what others have said about me.

_______ 14. I can treat myself kindly.

______ 15. I can observe unpleasant feelings without being drawn into them.

______ 16. I have the sense that I am fully aware of what is going on around me and inside me.

______ 17. I can actually see that I am not my thoughts.

______ 18. I am consciously aware of a sense of my body as a whole.

______ 19. I think about the ways in which I am different from other people.

______ 20. I view things from a wider perspective.

To score the decentering factor, sum responses to items 3, 6, 9, 10, 12, 14, 15, 16, 17, 18, and 20.

Items reprinted with permission from Elsevier.

CHAPTER 2

Psychological Flexibility as a Mechanism of Change in Acceptance and Commitment Therapy

Joseph Ciarrochi, Linda Bilich, and Clair Godsell, University of Wollongong, Australia

In psychology, the last several decades of clinical research have focused on evaluating the efficacy of entire intervention packages. A wide range of therapies have been rated as at least probably efficacious, including various forms of cognitive behavioral therapy (CBT), stress inoculation training, interpersonal therapy, parent training, behavioral marital therapy, eye movement desensitization and reprocessing, brief dynamic therapy, self-control therapy, social problem-solving therapy, dialectical behavior therapy (DBT), and many others (Chambless & Ollendick, 2001). While the package approach has been useful in obtaining empirical validation for clinical interventions, it does have its limitations (Rosen & Davison, 2003). Essentially, this approach doesn't help identify which components of the package are effective and which are inert or possibly even harmful. It doesn't help identify how packages are similar and how they differ. And it doesn't prevent people from creating an endless number of therapy packages that are really just repackages of currently existing therapies.

One way forward is to focus on processes of change rather than entire therapy packages (Rosen & Davison, 2003), using research to identify the active ingredients that might cut across therapy packages. This chapter focuses on processes of change in acceptance and commitment therapy

(ACT). The goal is to examine the mediational evidence concerning why ACT works. The central mechanism of change in the ACT model is psychological flexibility, which includes six subprocesses (discussed below). In this chapter we examine whether ACT works in the theoretically expected way, by increasing psychological flexibility. We also examine whether the processes elicited in ACT are distinctive from other therapies.

WHAT IS ACT?

Before we discuss mediators of change, it is important to consider the philosophical underpinnings of ACT and how ACT theorists use terms like "mediator." ACT is somewhat different from other forms of CBT in that it comes from the radical behaviorist wing of psychology (Ciarrochi & Bailey, 2008; Hayes, Hayes, & Reese, 1988). Researchers within ACT don't view internal constructs as causes of behavior (Hayes, 1995). Rather, the causes are located in the external environment and, in principle, can be directly manipulated. For example, individual differences in psychological acceptance are conceptualized as patterns of behaving rather than mechanisms in the mind. In this view, low acceptance wouldn't be seen as a cause of psychological distress. Rather, the cause would be located in the environmental factors that promote low acceptance behavior. Although low acceptance is part of a behavioral chain that temporally proceeds symptoms, it doesn't cause these symptoms. The main goal of the ACT researcher is to understand how to predict and influence acceptance and other processes, rather than to understand how those processes are represented in the mind and interact with other internal phenomena, such as emotions, beliefs, and personality.

ACT theorists utilize terms like "acceptance" only insomuch as they are functional. Specifically, ACT theorists talk about processes of change because it helps them understand what aspects of their intervention are working and why and guides them toward what might be missing in the intervention. For example, one may discover that an ACT intervention increases commitment to valued activity but doesn't increase mindfulness. This may guide the intervener to develop better mindfulness components in the intervention.

ACT is based on relational frame theory (RFT), a modern behavioral account of language (Hayes, Barnes-Holmes, & Roche, 2001). RFT treats language as a kind of behavior that is under operant control. It seeks to identify the contexts that give rise to language and its ability to dominate people's lives, such as the contexts that lead people to experience disturbance about past events (even if they never occurred) or future events (even if they will never occur). RFT inquires into how people become so controlled by their internal dialogues that they become insensitive to environmental contingencies. In sum, RFT seeks to identify the contexts in which language dominates and promotes suffering, and also contexts that undermine the dominance of language.

With this perspective, ACT emphasizes that language-based suffering is normal for humans (Hayes, Strosahl, & Wilson, 1999). What prolongs suffering are the psychological processes of experiential avoidance and cognitive fusion (Hayes et al., 1999; Hayes, Strosahl, Bunting, Twohig, & Wilson, 2005). Experiential avoidance is a process whereby an individual deliberately attempts to change the form or frequency of private experiences (such as bodily sensations, emotions, thoughts, memories, and behavioral predispositions) and the contexts in which they occur, regardless of the social, emotional, cognitive, and behavioral consequences that may result (Blackledge & Hayes, 2001; Hayes, 2004; Hayes et al., 1999; Wilson & Murrell, 2003). Cognitive fusion, which supports experiential avoidance, occurs when an individual's verbal processes (i.e., thoughts) markedly regulate overt behavior in ineffective ways due to an inability or failure to notice the process of thinking, or context, over the products of thinking, or content (Hayes, Luoma, Bond, Masuda, & Lillis, 2006; Pierson, Gifford, Smith, Bunting, & Hayes, 2004). When these processes dominate an individual's experience, psychological inflexibility can result.

Psychological inflexibility can be thought of as being excessively entangled in experiential avoidance and cognitive fusion and having difficulties connecting with the context of a situation and choosing behavior in line with identified values and goals (Hayes et al., 1999). In order to control or remove unpleasant experiences, individuals may engage in behavior that's damaging to their physical, emotional, and psychological well-being, such as drinking excessively or avoiding certain situations. To make matters worse, attempts to control private experiences can lead to a paradoxical increase in the intensity and frequency of those experiences and may even result in psychopathology (Hayes, 2004; Hayes et al., 1999; Hayes et al., 2005; Wegner, Erber, & Zanakos, 1993; Wenzlaff & Wegner, 2000).

One of the main goals of ACT is to increase psychological flexibility, which refers to an individual's ability to connect with the present moment fully and consciously and to change or persist in behavior that's in line with the person's identified values (Hayes et al., 1999). Assisting clients in increasing psychological flexibility involves helping them disentangle themselves from the cycle of experiential avoidance and cognitive fusion, not by challenging or changing private experiences such as thoughts and emotions, but by learning to react more mindfully to such experiences so that they no longer seem to be barriers (Ciarrochi & Blackledge, 2006). Clients are encouraged to shift their energies away from experiential control and toward valued activity, and to consistently choose to act effectively, even in the presence of difficult private events. For a detailed and comprehensive account of ACT, readers are referred to Hayes and colleagues (1999).

WHAT PROCESSES DOES ACT TARGET?

The ACT treatment model consists of six subprocesses that are organized into a hexaflex, illustrated in the following figure. The hexaflex can be divided into two overarching (and slightly overlapping) processes: The first includes acceptance and mindfulness processes (acceptance, defusion, contact with the present moment, and a transcendent sense of self, or self-as-context), and the second reflects commitment and behavior change processes (values, committed action, contact with the present moment, and self-as-context). Contact with the present moment and self-as-context are considered elements of both groups. The ACT practitioner targets these six processes in order to build psychological flexibility.

Acceptance. The focus of this ACT process is to develop and enhance people's willingness to have and accept their private experiences. Treatment involves exploring the futility of emotional control and avoidance, which can often paradoxically increase people's levels of distress and deter them from engaging in purposeful, vital, and values-driven behavior. Instead, clients are encouraged to accept their private experiences when doing so helps them engage in valued behavior.

Defusion. This process involves weakening the language processes that promote fusion (Hayes et al., 1999; Strosahl, Hayes, Wilson, & Gifford, 2004). People learn to see thoughts for what they are and not what they say they are (Hayes et al., 1999), for example, as symbols of one's experience rather than descriptions of reality or reality itself. Defusion exercises help people notice their language processes as they unfold and watch their thoughts come and go from the perspective of a neutral observer. Defusion

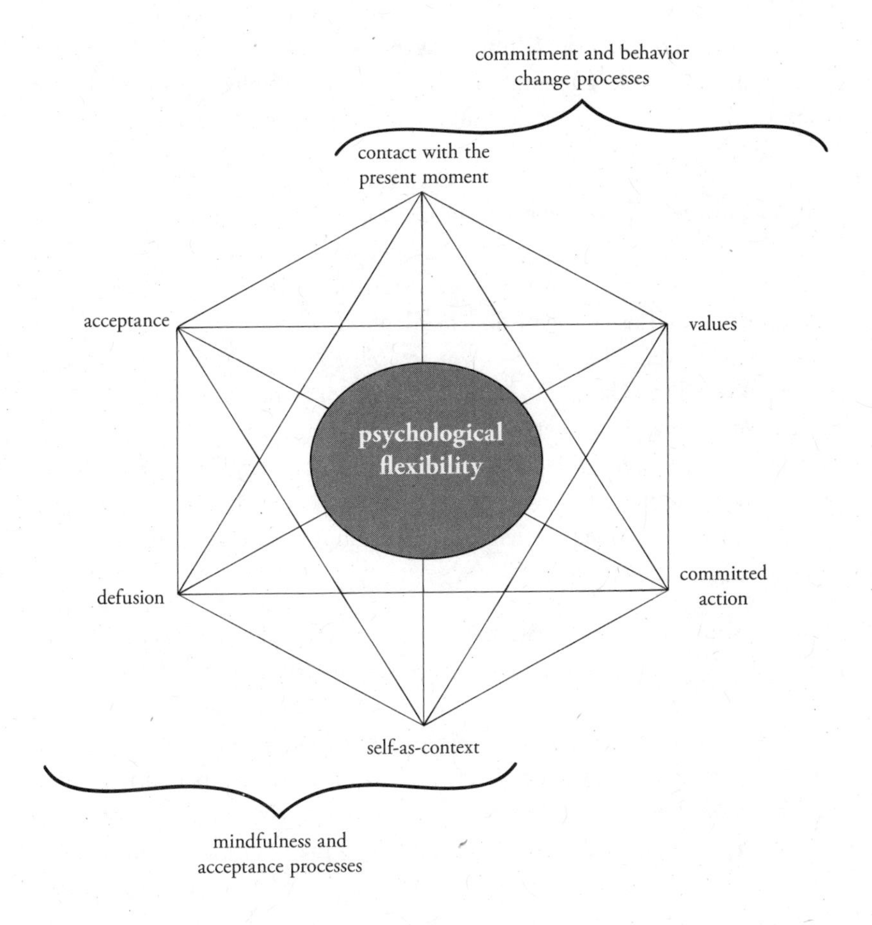

thus involves a radical shift in context where thoughts become observed events, rather than literal truths that must dictate behavior.

Contact with the present moment. In this ACT process, which is often equated with mindfulness, clients are taught to build their awareness of their private experiences and be fully open to whatever is happening in the present moment. This involves experiencing thoughts as what they are, events that come and go, rather than what they often seem to be: barriers or binding truths. For example, a self-critical thought such as "I'm useless" can be viewed as a passing event rather than something that must control behavior. Contact with the present moment also connects to the values and committed action components of ACT in that it allows action to be informed and regulated by needs, feelings, and values and how they fit with the current situation (Brown, Ryan, & Creswell, 2007). According to Strosahl and colleagues (2004) and Hayes and colleagues (1999), the qualities that reflect this process are vitality, spontaneity, connection, and creativity.

Self-as-context. To develop this process, clients are taught to build their awareness of their observing self, or self-as-context, and work on letting go of their attachment to a conceptualized self (for example, "I'm boring" or "I'm useless"). Self-as-context is independent of content: It is the place where content is observed. No matter how many self-statements we generate about who we are ("I'm a father," "I'm an athlete," or "I'm not good enough"), there is an "I" that can observe these self-statements. This "I" is experienced as constant and stable, whereas self-evaluations come and go (Hayes et al., 1999). From the perspective of self-as-context, people come to realize that they can let go of unhelpful self-evaluations and still retain a sense of self (Pierson et al., 2004).

Values. Values are the directions in life that individuals choose to guide their behavior. Thus, values are never really achieved or obtained (Hayes et al., 1999; Pierson et al., 2004). (Goals, on the other hand, are concrete actions that can be achieved or obtained, often undertaken in the service of values.) Individuals who are entangled in fusion and experiential avoidance are more likely to engage in behaviors that are inconsistent with their values. For example, even though an individual may value a relationship, he may engage in destructive social behavior because he's afraid of intimacy. In ACT, people learn to be open to experiencing difficult thoughts and feelings in order to engage in valued behavior (Strosahl et al., 2004).

Committed action. Engaging in values-directed behavior can often produce difficult experiences, such as distress and failure. ACT helps people see that choosing actions in keeping with a valued direction isn't a permanent thing. The choice must be made again and again. ACT helps prepare people for the difficult feelings and thoughts that will show up due to striving in valued directions, particularly after perceived failure, and also helps them be more willing to carry those feelings and thoughts in order to do what it takes to move in a valued direction.

The hexaflex illustrates that these processes are all connected and support each other. There is no correct order for focusing on the processes, and not all individuals need to concentrate extensively on all of them (Hayes et al.,

2005; Strosahl et al., 2004). The ultimate goal is to help people to persist in or change their behavior, as appropriate, in order to move toward what they value. ACT clinicians use a number of exercises for each process to enhance adoption and understanding of relevant skills (for more detail see Hayes et al., 1999; Strosahl et al., 2004). These include metaphor, paradox, and experiential exercises that aim to undermine the power of experiential avoidance and cognitive fusion.

MEASURING PSYCHOLOGICAL FLEXIBILITY

Psychological flexibility is a construct that captures the overarching ACT model in its most current rendition (Bond et al., 2009; Hayes et al., 2006; Hayes, Strosahl, et al., 2004; Hayes, Wilson, Gifford, Follette, & Strosahl, 1996). Accordingly, assessment of individual differences in psychological flexibility has been a central focus of ACT research. A generic self-report measure of psychological flexibility, the Acceptance and Action Questionnaire (AAQ) has been developed for this purpose (Bond et al., 2009; Hayes, Strosahl, et al., 2004). The current form of this instrument is the AAQ-II (Bond et al., 2009), which is designed to evaluate the extent to which an individual exhibits psychological flexibility, that is, the ability to fully contact the present moment and the thoughts and feelings it contains without needless defense, and to persist in or change behavior, depending on the situation, in the pursuit of goals and values (Hayes et al., 2006). Both positive and negative manifestations of psychological flexibility are reflected in the various AAQ-II items. As such, this measure is deemed suitable for application in a wide and divergent range of contexts, for example, in both organizational and clinical psychology settings that differentially emphasize positive and negative aspects of psychological flexibility (Bond et al., 2009). The AAQ-II is included as an appendix to this chapter.

The AAQ-II is derived from an earlier version of the AAQ (Hayes, Strosahl, et al., 2004). The original instrument, developed particularly for use in adult population-based studies, is said to be a general measure of several ACT processes that are markers of psychological flexibility (Hayes et al., 2006). Several versions of the original AAQ exist, two of which have demonstrated adequate criterion-related, predictive, and convergent validity (Bond & Bunce, 2003; Hayes, Bissett, et al., 2004): The first is a two-dimensional sixteen-item version that measures acceptance and mindfulness as well as values-based action; these dimensions have been shown to load onto a second-order factor labeled "psychological flexibility" (Bond & Bunce, 2003; Hayes, Strosahl, et al., 2004). The second is a nine-item version that has been shown to be unidimensional (Hayes et al., 2006). These two versions have been found to significantly correlate at 0.89 (Hayes, Strosahl, et al., 2004). Norms have been obtained for these instruments using both clinical and nonclinical populations, and a number of versions of the AAQ have been developed in languages other than English.

The AAQ has demonstrated moderate to high correlations in the expected direction with general markers of emotional well-being, such as stress and negative affect, as well as perceived physical health, work-related well-being, and quality of life (Hayes, Strosahl, et al., 2004). It has been shown to be distinctive from other, related measures (Feldner, Zvolensky, Eifert, & Spira, 2003; Hayes, Strosahl, et al., 2004; Hayes, Wilson, et al., 2004). Additionally, it has shown modest correlations with measures of specific aspects of experiential avoidance, including thought suppression, dissociation, self-deceptive positivity, and avoidant coping, indicating that it is related to these processes yet taps into something unique, most likely the overarching facet of experiential avoidance (Hayes, Strosahl, et al., 2004).

Longitudinal research suggests that the AAQ predicts future mental health (Bond & Bunce, 2003) and objectively measures work performance (Bond & Flaxman, 2006). In addition, psychological flexibility as measured by the AAQ has been shown to mediate the link between ACT and improvements in well-being and values-consistent behavior (Bond & Bunce, 2000; Dalrymple & Herbert, 2007; Forman, Herbert, Moitra, Yeomans, & Geller, 2007; Kocovski, Fleming, & Rector, 2009; Roemer, Orsillo, & Salters-Pedneault, 2008; Varra, Hayes, Roget, & Fisher, 2008; Woods, Wetterneck, & Flessner, 2006).

However, the AAQ has some problems with internal consistency levels and item complexity (Bond et al., 2009; Godsell & Ciarrochi, 2009), which the AAQ-II seeks to remedy. This ten-item instrument has been described as an internally consistent measure of ACT's model of mental health and behavioral effectiveness (Bond et al., 2009). The AAQ-II consists of both positively worded items, such as "My thoughts and feelings do not get in the way of how I want to live my life," and negatively worded items, which are reverse scored, such as "My painful experiences and memories make it difficult for me to live a life that I would value" and "Emotions cause problems in my life."

Although the AAQ-II is in the early stages of development, preliminary results from a validation study across seven samples involving 3,280 participants are promising (Bond et al., 2009). Specifically, findings indicate that the measure has adequate structure, reliability, and validity and reveals the presence of a single factor, namely "psychological flexibility," thought to reflect the degree of acceptance of negatively evaluated private experiences (Bond et al., 2009). The AAQ-II has also demonstrated good internal consistency. Values for Cronbach's index of internal consistency (α) range between 0.76 and 0.87 across the samples tested, with an average α coefficient of 0.83 overall. It has also shown good test retest reliability in a community sample over both a three-month period ($\alpha = 0.80$) and a twelve-month period ($\alpha = 0.78$) and significantly correlates with the AAQ ($\alpha = 0.82$).

The AAQ-II has been found to relate to variables to which it is theoretically tied. For instance, higher levels of psychological flexibility as measured by the AAQ-II have been associated with lower levels of depression, anxiety, and overall psychological distress. Longitudinally, higher scores on the AAQ-II have been shown to predict self-reported mental health (Bond et al., 2009) and objectively measured workplace absenteeism, success at sales, and ability to learn new workplace skills (Bond et al., 2009). The AAQ-II has also been shown to be unrelated to measures to which it is not theoretically linked, such as social desirability (Bond et al., 2009).

In addition to the AAQ and AAQ-II, which are designed for general populations, other versions of the AAQ have been designed for populations with specific problems, including the Chronic Pain Acceptance Questionnaire (CPAQ; Vowles, McCracken, & Eccleston, 2008), the Avoidance and Inflexibility Scale (AIS) for smoking behaviors (Gifford et al., 2004), the Acceptance and Action Diabetes Questionnaire (AADQ; Gregg, Callaghan, Hayes, & Glenn-Lawson, 2007), the Acceptance and Action Questionnaire for Weight-Related Difficulties (AAQW; Lillis, Hayes, Bunting, & Masuda, 2009), and the Acceptance and Action Questionnaire for Prejudice (AAQP; Lillis & Hayes, 2007).

In addition to these specific measures based on the AAQ, there are also measures that emphasize the fusion/defusion component of the hexaflex. Fusion is said to be present to the extent that a verbal-based event, such as a thought, has a controlling role over behavior and dominates other sources of control, such as environmental contingencies. Fusion measures typically ask people to indicate the extent to which they believe certain dysfunctional thoughts (Blackledge & Hayes, 2006; Varra et al., 2008; Zettle & Hayes,

1986; Zettle, Rains, & Hayes, in press) or hallucinations (Bach & Hayes, 2002; Gaudiano & Herbert, 2006a).

Although the AAQ and AAQ-II are purported to measure psychological flexibility, they do so only indirectly, by measuring processes correlated with psychological flexibility. That is, they don't directly assess the ability to persist or change in behavior, depending on the situation, in the pursuit of goals and values. Rather, they appear to measure ACT subprocesses, including experiential acceptance ("It's okay if I remember something unpleasant") and beliefs (fused thoughts) that private experience interferes with valued activity ("Worries get in the way of my success"). Similarly, measures of the believability of thoughts map primarily to the fusion component of the hexaflex. We will use the term "psychological flexibility" to refer to the aggregate of all ACT subprocesses and will return to definitional issues at the end of the chapter.

RESEARCH ON PSYCHOLOGICAL FLEXIBILITY AS A MEDIATOR OF ACT OUTCOMES

A substantial body of research has developed around what we refer to as ACT's core mediational hypotheses, in which psychological inflexibility is expected to be a precursor to suffering across a wide variety of diagnoses and populations (e.g., clinical and nonclinical).

1. ACT is expected to improve psychological flexibility.

2. Psychological flexibility is expected to lead to well-being, reduced clinical symptoms, and increased values-based activity.

A considerable number of cross-sectional studies have evaluated the first part of the core mediational hypothesis, namely that low psychological flexibility is important in understanding a wide variety of problems and symptoms. Almost without fail, these studies find significant mediational effects and suggest that low psychological flexibility may be a significant component in the development of a wide range of symptoms, including distress, anxiety, depression, hair pulling, post-traumatic stress disorder, and self-harm. For example, Marx and Sloan (2002) found that psychological flexibility mediated the relationship between a history of childhood sexual abuse and current psychological distress in young adults. Similar findings were reported by Reddy, Pickett, and Orcutt (2006) and Rosenthal, Rasmussen Hall, Palm, Batten, and Follette (2005). These findings are important because they suggest that childhood abuse alone does not entirely account for later psychological distress; rather, experiential avoidance following such experiences plays an important role in exacerbating the distress. Many other studies with a wide range of populations have shown a similar pattern of findings (Kashdan & Breen, 2007; Kashdan, Morina, & Priebe, 2009; Masuda, Price, Anderson, Schmertz, & Calamaras, in press; Orcutt, Pickett, & Pope, 2005).

All of these studies have used cross-sectional designs, in which all variables were measured at a single point in time. Cross-sectional designs have advantages, in that they are usually less expensive to conduct than other designs and allow one to test whether the mediational model is feasible. If the mediational model fails to fit the cross-sectional data, then more expensive designs may be unnecessary. However, cross-sectional designs also suffer from confounds, or unplanned factors that may affect the results, and cannot determine the direction of causality. Although these studies suggest that psychological inflexibility contributes to the development of symptoms, the opposite relationship is also possible (that symptoms contribute to the development of inflexibility). This problem can be addressed, at least in part, by studying ACT interventions and measuring the relevant variables before and after treatment, and perhaps also at a follow-up point. ACT intervention studies fall into two broad categories: those studying nonclinical and behavioral medicine populations and those studying mental health and substance abuse problems.

Studies of Nonclinical and Behavioral Medicine Interventions

Studies of nonclinical and behavioral medicine interventions have encompassed substantial breadth in target populations, including people who work in organizational settings, work as counselors, have chronic pain and other health problems, have cancer, have a history of smoking, or have a child with autism (Bilich & Ciarrochi, 2009; Blackledge & Hayes, 2006; Bond & Bunce, 2000; Branstetter, Wilson, Hildebrandt, & Mutch, 2004; Flaxman, 2006; Gifford et al., 2004; Gregg et al., 2007; Hayes, Bissett, et al., 2004; Hesser, Westin, Hayes, & Andersson, 2009; Lillis et al., 2009; Lundgren, Dahl, & Hayes, 2008; Varra et al., 2008; Vowles & McCracken, 2008). ACT has been shown to improve mental health and well-being and promote a broad range of values-consistent behaviors, such as increased innovativeness, reduced taking of sick days and utilization of medical resources, reduced cigarette smoking, improved diabetes self-care, nonprejudiced actions, better weight maintenance, behavioral activity despite pain, and willingness of professional counselors to use empirically supported treatments.

The issue of mediation, or of how these interventions work, has been studied with the general AAQ as a measure of psychological flexibility, or with the adaptations of the AAQ for specific populations. In addition, measures of believability of thoughts have occasionally been used. Of studies that used the general AAQ, three showed evidence that increases in psychological flexibility were at least partially responsible for the positive outcomes observed. For example, Bond and Bunce (2000) showed that changes in psychological flexibility as measured by the AAQ mediated improvements in the general mental health of employees of a media organization who completed an ACT intervention. Flaxman (2006) reported similar findings in government employees. Varra and colleagues (2008) found that changes in psychological flexibility (measured by the AAQ) and in believability of particular thoughts mediated the impact of ACT on professional counselors' willingness to use empirically supported interventions. In contrast, two studies using the AAQ didn't find evidence of mediation. Bilich and Ciarrochi (2009) reported that ACT led to significant improvements in mental health and in values-based living in members of the police force, but AAQ scores didn't change during the intervention. And although Blackledge and Hayes (2006) found that ACT led to improved mental health in parents of children with autism, AAQ scores were only marginally changed by the intervention; however, believability of dysfunctional thoughts changed more substantially and mediated the effects of the intervention. Overall, this group of studies provides mixed evidence that increased psychological flexibility is responsible for the positive outcomes of ACT interventions.

In contrast to studies that used the general AAQ, all eight studies that focused on population-specific measures of psychological flexibility found significant evidence of mediation. ACT improved acceptance and flexibility related to smoking cessation (Gifford et al., 2004), self-care in diabetes (Gregg et al., 2007), prejudice (Lillis & Hayes, 2007), weight-related issues (Lillis et al., 2009), seizures and quality of life in epilepsy (Lundgren et al., 2008), and adaptive functioning in chronic pain patients (McCracken, Vowles, &

Eccleston, 2005; Vowles & McCracken, 2008; Wicksell, Ahlqvist, Bring, Melin, & Olsson, 2008). In addition, there was evidence that ACT influenced population-specific measures of the believability of negative thoughts (Hayes, Bissett, et al., 2004; Varra et al., 2008).

The majority of studies involving nonclinical and behavioral medicine samples assessed psychological flexibility and outcomes at two time points: pre- and post-treatment. That is, the studies predominantly found changes in psychological flexibility occurring at the same time as changes in the outcome variables (both at post-treatment). Thus, there is no way to know if improved psychological flexibility caused the observed positive outcomes or vice versa. There were three notable exceptions: Gifford and her colleagues (2004) and Zettle and Hayes (1986) found that psychological flexibility changed before outcome variables changed. And Hesser and colleagues (2009) reliably coded in-session behaviors reflecting either acceptance or cognitive defusion. They found that the peak level and frequency of cognitive defusion behaviors and peak level of acceptance rated in session 2 predicted symptom reduction six months after treatment. They showed that these relationships couldn't be accounted for by improvements that occurred prior to the measurement of defusion and acceptance. These findings suggest that psychological flexibility is likely to be influencing the outcome variables, rather than exclusively vice versa.

Studies of Mental Health and Substance Abuse Problems

We now turn to a consideration of ACT interventions for mental health and substance abuse. ACT has shown some efficacy in treating a wide variety of disorders, including psychosis, social anxiety, anxiety and depression, borderline personality disorder (BPD), obsessive-compulsive disorder (OCD), and substance abuse. Many studies have examined whether increased psychological flexibility, as measured by the AAQ, is responsible for these outcomes. Only two failed to find evidence of mediation (Block, 2002; Hayes, Wilson, et al., 2004), whereas ten studies reported that increased flexibility mediated the observed improvements (Dalrymple & Herbert, 2007; Forman et al., 2007; Gratz & Gunderson, 2006; Kocovski et al., 2009; Lappalainen et al., 2007; Luoma, Kohlenberg, Hayes, Bunting, & Rye, 2008; Roemer et al., 2008; Twohig, 2009; Woods et al., 2006; Zettle, 2003). ACT has also been shown to reduce believability of hallucinations (Bach & Hayes, 2002;

Gaudiano & Herbert, 2006b) and dysfunctional thoughts (Zettle et al., in press; Zettle & Hayes, 1986).

Although many of these studies showed changes in psychological flexibility occurring at the same time as changes in the outcome (both at post-treatment), three studies provided evidence that changes in flexibility preceded changes in outcomes: Dalrymple and Herbert (2007) and Kocovski and colleagues (2009) showed that earlier changes in the AAQ predicted later changes in symptom severity, even after controlling for earlier changes in symptoms. And Twohig (2009) collected session data on believability of obsessions and willingness to have obsessions without reacting to them. Time lag correlations suggested that the ACT processes were more likely to predict obsessive symptoms than vice versa. This study, along with the other two, suggests that acceptance and defusion are likely to be precursors of outcomes, rather than merely concomitants or consequences.

Comparing Mechanisms in ACT to Those in Other Interventions

Several studies allow us to examine whether ACT works by different mechanisms than other interventions. There are two general classes of studies relevant to this issue: those that compare ACT to a variety of educational or supportive interventions, and those that compare ACT to a form of cognitive therapy. Four studies have shown that ACT works differently than educational lectures for reducing prejudice (Hayes, Bissett, et al., 2004; Lillis & Hayes, 2007), increasing willingness among counselors to use empirically supported treatments (Varra et al., 2008), and improving self-care in diabetes (Gregg et al., 2007). Two other studies suggest that ACT works by different processes than supportive therapy (Lundgren et al., 2008) and different processes than an intervention that teaches people to modify workplace stressors (Bond & Bunce, 2000). These studies generally show that ACT increases psychological flexibility, whereas educational lectures and supportive interventions do not.

Seven studies have compared ACT to a form of cognitive therapy. ACT was better than cognitive therapy at decreasing avoidant coping among cancer patients (Branstetter et al., 2004) and has been shown (via the AAQ) to be better than cognitive therapy at improving psychological flexibility among government employees (Flaxman, 2006), university students with anxiety or depression (Forman et al., 2007), people from the general public with mood and interpersonal problems (Lappalainen et al., 2007), and people with clinical depression (Zettle et al., in press; Zettle & Hayes, 1986). One possible explanation for the general pattern of differences between ACT and cognitive therapy is that ACT is simply better at influencing any process measure, regardless of whether it is consistent or inconsistent with ACT. However, three studies appear to be inconsistent with this hypothesis. Dalrymple and Herbert (2007) showed that ACT improved psychological flexibility but didn't improve skill at controlling private experience, a process that's incongruent with ACT. Forman and colleagues (2007) showed that CBT, but not ACT, improved observing and describing components of mindfulness. Lappalainen and colleagues (2007) showed that ACT improved psychological flexibility, whereas CBT improved self-confidence.

The results of Flaxman (2006) are somewhat more complicated but generally support the notion that ACT and cognitive therapy work by distinct processes. Both the ACT group and the group participating in stress inoculation training (SIT, a form of cognitive therapy) produced improvements in measures consistent with ACT (psychological flexibility) and measures consistent with cognitive therapy (dysfunctional attitudes). Flaxman (2006) conducted mediational analyses that looked at the unique influence of psychological flexibility and dysfunctional attitudes and found that psychological flexibility was the primary mediator in the ACT condition but didn't mediate the SIT outcomes. In addition, and there was some evidence that dysfunctional cognitions mediated the effect of SIT between pretreatment and six-month follow-up (but not between pretreatment and three-month follow-up).

CONCLUSIONS

Although more research is needed to compare the influence of ACT on general versus specific measures of the AAQ, this review suggests that increased psychological flexibility is likely to be an important mechanism through which ACT leads to beneficial outcomes for a wide variety of populations and clinical symptoms. The majority of intervention studies show that participating in ACT leads to changes in flexibility and changes in outcomes at the same time (post-treatment), and that these changes are correlated. This is consistent with the core ACT mediational hypothesis, but it doesn't rule out an alternative hypothesis that reductions in symptoms lead to improvement in psychological flexibility, rather than vice versa. For example, reduced anxiety symptoms may lead people to become more accepting of anxiety.

However, several lines of research suggest that changes in psychological flexibility occur prior to changes in symptoms and therefore are not mere correlates or consequences of reduced symptoms. First, a number of ACT intervention studies have shown that changes in psychological flexibility occurred prior to changes in symptoms (Dalrymple & Herbert, 2007; Gifford et al., 2004; Hesser et al., 2009; Kocovski et al., 2009; Twohig, 2009; Zettle & Hayes, 1986). Second, experimental studies show that individuals high in experiential avoidance (or low in psychological flexibility) as measured by the AAQ demonstrate greater distress and lower endurance of pain during laboratory-induced physical stress (Feldner et al., 2003; Feldner et al., 2006). Thus, high scores on avoidance occur prior to physical stress and moderate people's reactions to that stress, rather than being merely the consequence of stress. Third, longitudinal research suggests that psychological flexibility predicts future levels of mental health and positive workplace behaviors, even when controlling for baseline measures of these variables (Bond & Bunce, 2003; Bond & Flaxman, 2006; Supavadeeprasit & Ciarrochi, 2009).

Perhaps no form of psychotherapy has as inspired as much mediational research as ACT. We identified over fifty studies, many of them completed in the last five years. The evidence suggests that ACT improves three markers of psychological flexibility: It reduces believability of dysfunctional thoughts, increases acceptance of private experience, and reduces believability that private experience acts as a barrier to action. More research is needed to evaluate the other components of the hexaflex. Does ACT improve the extent to which people contact self-as-context? Does ACT increase commitment to valued actions? To what extent are the dimensions within the hexaflex distinctive? That is, can interventions improve some aspects of the hexaflex but not others? Do some clients struggle with some dimensions, such as fusion and avoidance, but not others, such as mindfulness and self-as-context? Answers to these questions could have practical value. If, for example, the dimensions are distinctive, this would allow one to identify the particular dimensions that a client was struggling with and customize the intervention accordingly.

A somewhat broader issue with the current ACT conceptualization of psychological flexibility is that none of the current measures assess it. They could be said to assess markers or correlates of psychological flexibility, but none assess people's tendency to persist in or change behavior depending on the situation (a core aspect of psychological flexibility). Research is needed to develop more direct measures of psychological flexibility. It will be especially important to evaluate the extent to which each of the six ACT subprocesses is correlated with flexible behavior.

There is some evidence that dimensions of the hexaflex correlate with, and therefore might be influenced by, a single common factor. At present, research suggests that experiential avoidance correlates with both mindfulness (Baer, Smith, & Allen, 2004; Baer, Smith, Hopkins, Krietemeyer, & Toney, 2006) and fusion with dysfunctional thoughts (Godsell & Ciarrochi, 2009). However, this does not indicate that the common factor—psychological flexibility—is what is primarily measured by all six process variables, or that it's what is targeted by ACT interventions. For example, there might be substantial variance in mindfulness that isn't directly related to psychological flexibility but is related to mental health (Baer et al., 2004). It is clear that further psychometric research is needed.

The ACT researcher works within a functional framework, which means the ultimate test of a measure is its utility—whether a measure helps guide an intervention and make it more effective. The current state of evidence suggests that ACT produces a number of beneficial outcomes across a wide variety of populations, and that it does so by improving several indices of psychological flexibility. The practitioner can feel reasonably confident that ACT will improve a client's level of experiential acceptance and ability to defuse from difficult thoughts. More research is needed to examine other processes that might be active in ACT.

REFERENCES

Bach, P. B., & Hayes, S. C. (2002). The use of acceptance and commitment therapy to prevent the rehospitalization of psychotic patients: A randomized controlled trial. *Journal of Consulting and Clinical Psychology, 70*, 1129-1139.

Baer, R. A., Smith, G. T., & Allen, K. B. (2004). Assessment of mindfulness by self-report: The Kentucky Inventory of Mindfulness Skills. *Assessment, 11*, 191-206.

Baer, R. A., Smith, G. S., Hopkins, J., Krietemeyer, J., & Toney, L. (2006). Using self-report assessment methods to explore facets of mindfulness. *Assessment, 13*, 27-45.

Bilich, L., & Ciarrochi, J. (2009). *Evaluating acceptance and commitment therapy in the police force.* Unpublished manuscript, Wollongong, NSW, Australia.

Blackledge, J. T., & Hayes, S. C. (2001). Emotion regulation in acceptance and commitment therapy. *Journal of Clinical Psychology, 57*, 243-255.

Blackledge, J. T., & Hayes, S. C. (2006). Using acceptance and commitment training in the support of parents of children diagnosed with autism. *Child and Family Behavior Therapy, 28*, 1-18.

Block, J. (2002). Acceptance and change of private experiences: A comparative analysis in college students with public speaking anxiety. Doctoral dissertation, University of Albany, State University of New York, Albany.

Bond, F. W., & Bunce, D. (2000). Mediators of change in emotion-focused and problem-focused worksite stress management interventions. *Journal of Occupational Health Psychology, 5*, 156-163.

Bond, F. W., & Bunce, D. (2003). The role of acceptance and job control in mental health, job satisfaction, and work performance. *Journal of Applied Psychology, 88*, 1057-1067.

Bond, F. W., & Flaxman, P. E. (2006). The ability of psychological flexibility and job control to predict learning, job performance, and mental health. *Journal of Organizational Behavior Management, 26*, 113-130.

Bond, F. W., Hayes, S. C., Baer, R. A., Carpenter, K. M., Orcutt, H. K., Waltz, T., et al. (2009). *Preliminary psychometric properties of the Acceptance and Action Questionnaire II: A revised measure of psychological flexibility and acceptance.* Unpublished manuscript.

Branstetter, A. D., Wilson, K. G., Hildebrandt, M., & Mutch, D. (2004, November). *Improving psychological adjustment among cancer patients: ACT and CBT.* Paper presented at the annual meeting of the Association for Advancement of Behavior Therapy, New Orleans, LA.

Brown, K. W., Ryan, R. M., & Creswell, J. D. (2007). Mindfulness: Theoretical foundations and evidence for its salutary effects. *Psychological Inquiry, 18*, 211-237.

Chambless, D. L., & Ollendick, T. H. (2001). Empirically supported psychological interventions: Controversies and evidence. *Annual Review of Psychology, 52*, 685-716.

Ciarrochi, J., & Bailey, A. (2008). *A CBT-practitioner's guide to ACT: How to bridge the gap between cognitive behavioral therapy and acceptance and commitment therapy.* Oakland, CA: New Harbinger.

Ciarrochi, J., & Blackledge, J. T. (2006). Mindfulness-based emotional intelligence training: A new approach to reducing human suffering and promoting effectiveness. In J. Ciarrochi, J. P. Forgas, & J. D. Mayer (Eds.), *Emotional intelligence in everyday life* (2nd ed.). New York: Psychology Press.

Dalrymple, K. L., & Herbert, J. D. (2007). Acceptance and commitment therapy for generalized social anxiety disorder: A pilot study. *Behavior Modification, 31*, 543-568.

Feldner, M. T., Hekmat, H., Zvolensky, M., Vowles, K. E., Secrist, Z., & Leen-Feldner, E. (2006). The role of experiential avoidance in acute pain tolerance: A laboratory test. *Journal of Behavior Therapy and Experimental Psychiatry, 37*, 146-158.

Feldner, M. T., Zvolensky, M. J., Eifert, G. H., & Spira, A. P. (2003). Emotional avoidance: An experimental test of individual differences and response suppression using biological challenge. *Behaviour Research and Therapy, 41*, 403-411.

Flaxman, P. E. (2006). *Acceptance-based and traditional cognitive-behavioural stress management in the workplace: Investigating the mediators and moderators of change.* Unpublished Ph.D. dissertation, Goldsmiths College, University of London.

Forman, E. M., Herbert, J. D., Moitra, E., Yeomans, P. D., & Geller, P. A. (2007). A randomized controlled effectiveness trial of acceptance and commitment therapy and cognitive therapy for anxiety and depression. *Behavior Modification, 31*, 772-799.

Gaudiano, B. A., & Herbert, J. D. (2006a). Acute treatment of inpatients with psychotic symptoms using acceptance and commitment therapy: Pilot results. *Behaviour Research and Therapy, 44*, 415-437.

Gaudiano, B. A., & Herbert, J. D. (2006b). Believability of hallucinations as a potential mediator of their frequency and associated distress in psychotic inpatients. *Behavioural and Cognitive Psychotherapy, 34*, 497-502.

Gifford, E. V., Kohlenberg, B. S., Hayes, S. C., Antonuccio, D. O., Piasecki, M. M., Rasmussen-Hall, M. L., et al. (2004). Acceptance theory-based treatment for smoking cessation: An initial trial of acceptance and commitment therapy. *Behavior Therapy, 35*, 689-706.

Godsell, C., & Ciarrochi, J. (2009). *A psychometric evaluation of process measures in cognitive behavioral therapy.* Unpublished manuscript, Wollongong, Australia.

Gratz, K. L., & Gunderson, J. G. (2006). Preliminary data on an acceptance-based emotion regulation group intervention for deliberate self-harm among women with borderline personality disorder. *Behavior Therapy, 37*, 25-35.

Gregg, J. A., Callaghan, G. M., Hayes, S. C., & Glenn-Lawson, J. L. (2007). Improving diabetes self-management through acceptance, mindfulness, and values: A randomized controlled trial. *Journal of Consulting and Clinical Psychology, 75*, 336-343.

Hayes, S. C. (1995). Why cognitions are not causes. *Behavior Therapist, 18*, 59-64.

Hayes, S. C. (2004). Acceptance and commitment therapy, relational frame theory, and the third wave of behavioral and cognitive therapies. *Behavior Therapy, 35*, 639-665.

Hayes, S. C., Barnes-Holmes, D., & Roche, B. (Eds.). (2001). *Relational frame theory: A post-Skinnerian account of human language and cognition.* New York: Kluwer.

Hayes, S. C., Bissett, R., Roget, N., Kohlenberg, B. S., Fisher, G., Masuda, A., et al. (2004). The impact of acceptance and commitment training and multicultural training on the stigmatizing attitudes and professional burnout of substance abuse counselors. *Behavior Therapy, 35*, 821-835.

Hayes, S. C., Hayes, L. J., & Reese, H. W. (1988). Finding the philosophical core: A review of Stephen C. Pepper's world hypotheses. *Journal of Experimental Analysis of Behavior, 50*, 97-111.

Hayes, S. C., Luoma, J. B., Bond, F. W., Masuda, A., & Lillis, J. (2006). Acceptance and commitment therapy: Model, processes and outcomes. *Behaviour Research and Therapy, 44*, 1-25.

Hayes, S. C., Strosahl, K. D., Bunting, K., Twohig, M., & Wilson, K. G. (2005). What is acceptance and commitment therapy? In S. C. Hayes & K. D. Strosahl (Eds.), *A practical guide to acceptance and commitment therapy*. New York: Springer.

Hayes, S. C., Strosahl, K. D., & Wilson, K. G. (1999). *Acceptance and commitment therapy: An experiential approach to behavior change*. New York: Guilford.

Hayes, S. C., Strosahl, K. D., Wilson, K. G., Bissett, R. T., Pistorello, J., Toarmino, D., et al. (2004). Measuring experiential avoidance: A preliminary test of a working model. *Psychological Record, 54*, 553-578.

Hayes, S. C., Wilson, K. G., Gifford, E. V., Bissett, R., Piasecki, M., Batten, S. V., et al. (2004). A randomized controlled trial of twelve-step facilitation and acceptance and commitment therapy with polysubstance abusing methadone maintained opiate addicts. *Behavior Therapy, 35*, 667-688.

Hayes, S. C., Wilson, K. G., Gifford, E. V., Follette, V. M., & Strosahl, K. D. (1996). Experiential avoidance and behavioral disorders: A functional dimensional approach to diagnosis and treatment. *Journal of Consulting and Clinical Psychology, 64*, 1152-1168.

Hesser, H., Westin, V., Hayes, S. C., & Andersson, G. (2009). Clients' in-session acceptance and cognitive defusion behaviors in acceptance-based treatment of tinnitus distress. *Behaviour Research and Therapy, 47*, 523-528.

Kashdan, T. B., & Breen, W. E. (2007). Materialism and diminished well-being: Experiential avoidance as a mediating mechanism. *Journal of Social and Clinical Psychology, 26*, 521-539.

Kashdan, T. B., Morina, N., & Priebe, S. (2009). Post-traumatic stress disorder, social anxiety disorder, and depression in survivors of the Kosovo War: Experiential avoidance as a contributor to distress and quality of life. *Journal of Anxiety Disorders, 23*, 185-196.

Kocovski, N. L., Fleming, J. E., & Rector, N. A. (2009). Mindfulness and acceptance-based group therapy for social anxiety disorder: An open trial. *Cognitive and Behavioral Practice, 16*, 276-289.

Lappalainen, R., Lehtonen, T., Skarp, E., Taubert, E., Ojanen, M., & Hayes, S. C. (2007). The impact of CBT and ACT models using psychology trainee therapists. *Behavior Modification, 31*, 488-511.

Lillis, J., & Hayes, S. C. (2007). Applying acceptance, mindfulness, and values to the reduction of prejudice: A pilot study. *Behavior Modification, 31*, 389-411.

Lillis, J., Hayes, S. C., Bunting, K., & Masuda, A. (2009). Teaching acceptance and mindfulness to improve the lives of the obese: A preliminary test of a theoretical model. *Annals of Behavioral Medicine, 37*, 58-69.

Lundgren, T., Dahl, J. C., & Hayes, S. C. (2008). Evaluation of mediators of change in the treatment of epilepsy with acceptance and commitment therapy. *Journal of Behavior Medicine, 31*, 225-235.

Luoma, J. B., Kohlenberg, B. S., Hayes, S. C., Bunting, K., & Rye, A. K. (2008). Reducing self-stigma in substance abuse through acceptance and commitment therapy: Model, manual development, and pilot outcomes. *Addiction Research and Theory, 16*, 149-165.

Marx , B. P., & Sloan, D. M. (2002). The role of emotion in the psychological functioning of adult survivors of childhood sexual abuse. *Behavior Therapy, 33*, 563-577.

Masuda, A., Price, M., Anderson, P., Schmertz, S., & Calamaras, M. (in press). The role of psychological flexibility in mental health stigma and psychological distress for the stigmatizer. *Journal of Social and Clinical Psychology.*

McCracken, L. M., Vowles, K. E., & Eccleston, C. (2005). Acceptance-based treatment for persons with complex, long standing chronic pain: A preliminary analysis of treatment outcome in comparison to a waiting phase. *Behavior Research and Therapy, 43*, 1335-1346.

Orcutt, H. K., Pickett, S. M., & Pope, E. B. (2005). Experiential avoidance and forgiveness as mediators in the relation between traumatic interpersonal events and posttraumatic stress disorder symptoms. *Journal of Social and Clinical Psychology, 24*, 1003-1029.

Pierson, H., Gifford, E. V., Smith, A. A., Bunting, K., & Hayes, S. C. (2004). *Functional Acceptance and Commitment Therapy Scale.* Unpublished manuscript, University of Nevada, Reno.

Reddy, M. K., Pickett, S. M., & Orcutt, H. K. (2006). Experiential avoidance as a mediator in the relationship between childhood psychological abuse and current mental health symptoms in college students. *Journal of Emotional Abuse, 6*, 67-85.

Roemer, L., Orsillo, S., & Salters-Pedneault, K. (2008). Efficacy of an acceptance-based behavior therapy for generalized anxiety disorders: Evaluation in a randomized controlled trial. *Journal of Consulting and Clinical Psychology, 76*, 1083-1089.

Rosen, G. M., & Davison, G. C. (2003). Psychology should list empirically supported principles of change (ESPs) and not credential trademarked therapies or other treatment packages. *Behavior Modification, 27*, 300-312.

Rosenthal, M. Z., Rasmussen Hall, M. L., Palm, K., Batten, S. V., & Follette, V. M. (2005). Chronic avoidance helps explain the relationship between severity of childhood sexual abuse and psychological distress in adulthood. *Journal of Child Sexual Abuse, 14*, 25-41.

Strosahl, K., Hayes, S. C., Wilson, K. G., & Gifford, E. V. (2004). An ACT primer: Core therapy processes, intervention strategies, and therapist competencies. In S. C. Hayes & K. D. Strosahl (Eds.), *A practical guide to acceptance and commitment therapy.* New York: Springer.

Supavadeeprasit, S., & Ciarrochi, J. (2009). *The role of experiential avoidance in predicting future social and emotional well-being amongst adolescents: A one-year longitudinal study.* Unpublished manuscript, University of Wollongong, Australia.

Twohig, M. (2009). *A randomized clinical trial of acceptance and commitment therapy vs. progressive relaxation training in the treatment of obsessive compulsive disorder.* Unpublished Ph.D. dissertation, University of Nevada, Reno.

Varra, A. A., Hayes, S. C., Roget, N., & Fisher, G. (2008). A randomized control trial examining the effect of acceptance and commitment training on clinician willingness to use evidence-based pharmacotherapy. *Journal of Consulting and Clinical Psychology, 76*, 449-458.

Vowles, K. E., & McCracken, L. M. (2008). Acceptance and values-based action in chronic pain: A study of treatment effectiveness and process. *Journal of Consulting and Clinical Psychology, 76*, 397-407.

Vowles, K. E., McCracken, L. M., & Eccleston, C. (2008). Patient functioning and catastrophizing in chronic pain: The mediating effects of acceptance. *Health Psychology, 27*, S136-143.

Wegner, D. M., Erber, R., & Zanakos, S. (1993). Ironic processes in the mental control of mood and mood-related thought. *Journal of Personality and Social Psychology, 65*, 1093-1104.

Wenzlaff, R. M., & Wegner, D. M. (2000). Thought suppression. *Annual Review of Psychology, 51*, 59-91.

Wicksell, R. K., Ahlqvist, J., Bring, A., Melin, L., & Olsson, G. (2008). Can exposure and acceptance strategies improve the functioning and life satisfaction in people with chronic pain and whiplash-associated disorders (WAD)? A randomized controlled trial. *Cognitive Behaviour Therapy, 37*, 1-14.

Wilson, K. G., & Murrell, A. R. (2003). Values-centered interventions: Setting a course for behavioral treatment. In S. C. Hayes, V. M. Follette, & M. Linehan (Eds.), *The new behavior therapies: Expanding the cognitive behavioral tradition*. New York: Guilford.

Woods, D. W., Wetterneck, C. T., & Flessner, C. A. (2006). A controlled evaluation of acceptance and commitment therapy plus habit reversal for trichotillomania. *Behavior Research and Therapy, 44*, 639-656.

Zettle, R. D. (2003). Acceptance and commitment therapy (ACT) vs. systematic desensitization in treatment of mathematics anxiety. *Psychological Record, 53*, 197-215.

Zettle, R. D., & Hayes, S. (1986). Dysfunctional control by client verbal behavior: The context of reason giving. *Analysis of Verbal Behavior, 4*, 30-38.

Zettle, R. D., Rains, J., & Hayes, S. C. (in press). Processes of change in acceptance and commitment therapy and cognitive therapy for depression: A mediational reanalysis of Zettle and Rains (1989). *Behavior Modification*.

APPENDIX: ACCEPTANCE AND ACTION QUESTIONNAIRE–II (AAQ-II)

Below you will find a list of statements. Please rate how true each statement is for you by writing the appropriate number in each blank.

1	2	3	4	5	6	7
Never true	Very seldom true	Seldom true	Sometimes true	Frequently true	Almost always true	Always true

_____ 1. It's okay if I remember something unpleasant.

_____ 2. My painful experiences and memories make it difficult for me to live a life that I would value.

_____ 3. I'm afraid of my feelings.

_____ 4. I worry about not being able to control my worries and feelings.

_____ 5. My painful memories prevent me from having a fulfilling life.

_____ 6. I am in control of my life.

_____ 7. Emotions cause problems in my life.

_____ 8. It seems like most people are handling their lives better than I am.

_____ 9. Worries get in the way of my success.

_____ 10. My thoughts and feelings do not get in the way of how I want to live my life.

Items 2, 3, 4, 5, 7, 8, and 9 are reverse scored.

CHAPTER 3

Understanding, Assessing, and Treating Values Processes in Mindfulness- and Acceptance-Based Therapies

Kelly Wilson, Emily K. Sandoz, Maureen K. Flynn, and Regan M. Slater, University of Mississippi; and Troy DuFrene, OneLife Education and Training

Behavior therapy is undergoing a shift in focus. Instead of making symptom reduction the primary goal in treatment, these therapies are focusing on the development of broader, more flexible patterns of activity in clients. This is particularly true of the emerging mindfulness- and acceptance-based treatments (Hayes, 2004). While this is a major shift, it would be too facile to think of this change as a complete about-face. Traditional cognitive behavioral therapy (CBT) has, of course, been committed to general improvement in clients' lives all along. Setting goals toward this end has always been part of CBT, but protocols have been more focused on interventions aimed directly at reducing clients' problematic ways of thinking and excessive and maladaptive emotional responses. Third-wave behavior therapy interventions, in contrast, directly target acceptance, mindfulness, openness to experience, and valued living and don't primarily structure treatments specifically to diminish symptoms.

Openness to experience has always been a focus of third-wave treatments. Recently, though, valued living as a focus of treatment has received increasing attention (Hayes, Wilson, Gifford, Follette, & Strosahl, 1996). In some ways, values were always at the crux of these treatments, since openness to experience was itself really openness in the service of valued living (Hayes, Strosahl, & Wilson, 1999). Nevertheless, this shift in both the goals and the putative processes of therapy has created a need for accurate ways to assess both openness to experience and values. Assessment of openness to experience has most obviously moved ahead, in the form of measures of mindfulness (e.g., Baer, Smith, & Allen, 2004) and measures of experiential avoidance (e.g., Hayes, Strosahl, et al., 2004). Empirical validation of values processes are much needed, both as a guide to intervention and as a psychometric instrument for evaluating these treatments. In this chapter, we examine values in behavioral terms and describe an iterative approach to the development of values interventions and assessment, and we also take a look at some of the current and emerging means for treating and assessing values processes.

OUTCOMES OF TARGETING BREADTH AND FLEXIBILITY OF LIVING

Early data supporting the shift to flexibility-focused therapy are encouraging. In a randomized trial, Bach and Hayes (2002) compared treatment as usual to a brief acceptance-based intervention plus treatment as usual in a state mental hospital in a sample of residential patients experiencing psychotic symptoms. After the intervention, patients who spent an average of three hours focused on accepting positive psychotic symptoms while making contact with chosen life directions were half as likely to have been rehospitalized at a four-month follow-up. This finding has since been replicated in an independent study with better experimental control (Gaudiano & Herbert, 2006). Success of the acceptance-based treatment was not attributable to reduction of psychotic symptoms. In fact, patients in the acceptance group reported more symptoms at follow-up.

Another randomized controlled trial compared a ten-week acceptance-based intervention with a multidisciplinary treatment in a sample of children and adolescents with chronic pain (Wicksell, Melin, Lekander, & Olsson, 2009). Although both groups showed improvement, the acceptance group reported statistically significant improvement in quality of life, fear of reinjury, discomfort related to pain, and perceived ability to function regardless of pain intensity.

Researchers have demonstrated similar preliminary findings in a wide range of populations, such as those with work-related stress (Bond & Bunce, 2000), polysubstance abuse (Hayes, Wilson, et al., 2004), depression (Zettle & Hayes, 1986; Zettle & Rains, 1989), and social phobia (Block, 2002), to name just a few. Acceptance-based treatments show promising outcomes in nonpsychiatric samples as well as psychiatric samples (e.g., Hayes, Luoma, Bond, Masuda, & Lillis, 2006; cf. Öst, 2008). In some of these studies, symptoms were reduced in the acceptance and commitment therapy (ACT) group relative to controls (e.g., Gregg, Callaghan, Hayes, & Glenn-Lawson, 2007). In others, changes in symptoms were equivalent (e.g., Dahl, Wilson, & Nilsson, 2004). And in still other instances, such as Bach and Hayes (2002), reports of psychotic symptoms actually went down less in the ACT group than in the control group. In all of these studies, however, acceptance-based treatments led to significant changes in socially important outcomes, such as medical and sick leave utilization (Dahl et al., 2004), rehospitalization (Bach & Hayes, 2002), and diabetic control (Gregg et al., 2007). This general finding is consistent with the intent of these treatments, since the model suggests the importance of unlinking painful aspects of experience from one's ability to take action in valued life directions.

Meta-analyses have not always taken these somewhat odd outcomes into account. They often focus on the presenting concern, at times to the exclusion of broader outcomes. For example, Dahl and colleagues (2004) suggest that even though pain remained equivalent between groups, medical and sick leave utilization were impacted dramatically. However, in Powers, Vörding, and Emmelkamp's meta-analysis (2009), group differences in pain intensity were used to calculate an effect size for primary outcomes, rather than sick leave and medical utilization. So the treatments end up looking equivalent even though the treatment as usual group took ten times more sick leave than the ACT group (the primary outcome variable identified by Dahl and colleagues) and utilized medical services over seven times more often.

We have only just begun to examine the processes that may account for such changes in acceptance-based treatments. However, a series of studies seem to support the virtues of expanding the processes targeted in treatment, and the call for expanded treatment targets isn't limited to proponents of these emerging treatments. For example, an editor of the journal *Pain* commented on the study by Wicksell and colleagues (2009) and discussed the potential importance of emphasizing goals broader than mere pain relief: "In considering whether psychological treatment can affect nonpain outcomes in children, acceptance and commitment therapy (ACT), as an extension of traditional CBT, offers several strategies that may be particularly useful. Because traditional behavioral and CBT interventions center on children's development of pain coping skills (e.g., relaxation, etc.), they may be biased toward a primary focus on pain relief. In contrast, ACT through its emphasis on the importance of accepting pain symptoms and working toward valued goals, using interventions such as exposure, cognitive defusion, and mindfulness, de-emphasizes pain relief and introduces in a more focused way goals directed towards enhancing daily functioning" (Palermo, 2009, p. 189).

ACCOUNTING FOR PROCESSES TARGETED

Demonstrating the kinds of improvements targeted in acceptance- and mindfulness-based therapies—valued living and increased breadth and flexibility of living—has proved challenging. A pilot study recently showed that an intervention focused on acceptance of the thoughts, feelings, and sensations that precede epileptic seizures resulted in shorter durations of seizures and self-reported higher quality of life than supportive therapy by increasing action in chosen life directions (Lundgren, Dahl, & Hayes, 2008; Lundgren, Dahl, Melin, & Kies, 2006). Yet researchers rarely collect this sort of data, and there are few assessments available to measure the data. The vast majority of clinical assessments available measure the frequency or intensity of symptoms, or both, because they were developed to measure the effectiveness of therapies targeting symptom reduction. Outcome variables like rehospitalization (Bach & Hayes, 2002) or improved self-care (Gregg et al., 2007) serve as proxies for significant life change but say little about the processes that precipitate the change. To adequately evaluate processes and outcomes of acceptance- and mindfulness-based approaches, researchers need more measures that assess breadth and flexibility in living and positive action in valued directions.

VALUED LIVING IN EXPERIMENTAL PSYCHOLOGY

A variety of findings in experimental psychology suggest ways that direct values interventions might benefit clients. For example, Creswell and colleagues (2005) had subjects respond to a series of questions about their thoughts and feelings regarding either their top-ranked value or their fifth-ranked value. Subjects who answered questions about their top-ranked value showed significantly lower cortisol response to a subsequent highly stressful task. Values-centered writing about high- versus low-value issues has produced better grades among African-American students (Cohen, Garcia, Apfel, & Master, 2006). In another study, people writing about highly rated values report greater feelings of love, connectedness, empathy, and giving (Crocker, Niiya, & Mischkowski, 2008) as compared to those writing about a low-rated value. In a separate study using the same high-values versus low-values writing exercise, Crocker and colleagues (2008) demonstrated that smokers had an increased openness to an article on the health risks of smoking and that these effects were mediated by increased feelings of love and connectedness.

Although findings are not entirely uniform across the literature, Creswell and colleagues suggest that clients may benefit from the introduction of "value affirmation tasks prior to stressful events or in chronically stressful environments" (Creswell et al., 2005, p. 850). Taken together, these data suggest the importance for empirical clinical psychology of developing interventions and measurement in a domain that is highly important to the client.

VALUED LIVING IN APPLIED PSYCHOLOGY

Although valued living has long been a feature of existential psychology, most of that tradition hasn't been particularly attentive to empiricism. Valued living as a primary purpose of empirically oriented therapy has been most recently proposed, elaborated, and investigated within the approach known as acceptance and commitment therapy (ACT) (Hayes et al., 1999; Wilson & Murrell, 2004). Several developments have emerged from this approach: a behavioral definition of values, techniques for direct intervention on valued patterns of living, and, most recently, methods for the assessment of change in patterns of valued living.

A BEHAVIORAL DEFINITION OF VALUES

Although values have been conceptualized in a number of ways in psychology generally (e.g., Allport, Vernon, & Lindzey, 1960; Rokeach, 1973) this area has been most recently and extensively elaborated within the context of acceptance- and mindfulness-based therapies, and especially within ACT. As a therapy within the behavioral tradition, ACT relies on basic behavioral principles to establish technical analyses of values. To fully understand values from an ACT perspective, a brief discussion of the development and maintenance of psychological difficulties from a behavioral perspective is necessary.

Considering Psychological Difficulties in Context

Behavior analysis is based on the relatively uncontroversial idea that behavior is influenced by immediate and historical context. This position doesn't ignore biological or genetic anomalies as causes; it simply focuses on the analysis of contextual causes. Presumably, even when the biological causes are quite clear, as in Down syndrome, contextual causes remain important in facilitating effective living and learning. In fact, the history of psychological intervention is littered with examples of times when biological difficulties, including Down syndrome, were thought to impose far greater limits on learning and living than proved to be the case.

The only way we can truly know the limits imposed by biology is to explore the impact of context. When we look at potential biological determinants of difficulties such as depression, psychosis, and anxiety, we simply do not know the limits these conditions biologically impose on behavior. Some malleability certainly exists. How much is a matter for empirical investigation.

Aversive Control

Psychological difficulties can be conceptualized from a behavioral perspective as the dominance of aversive control in the organization of behavior.

Aversive stimuli are events that an organism will work to end, delay, or attenuate. An example would be the shriek of a small child. The mother might engage in a great number of behaviors to end, delay, or reduce this kind of stimulation. The shape the resulting behavior takes might vary. For example, she might buy the child a candy bar because it causes the child's shrieking to cease, or she might tell the child she will get a spanking if she doesn't stop shrieking.

The behaviors that characterize psychological difficulties are frequently the result of the dominance of aversive control and its three side effects: conditioned elicitation, avoidance or escape (or both), and conditioned suppression. *Conditioned elicitation* is heightened arousal in the presence of aversive stimuli. *Avoidance and escape* are behaviors that result in the cessation, delay, or attenuation of aversive stimuli. *Conditioned suppression* is the general inhibiting effect of the aversive stimuli on behavior that might otherwise occur if the stimuli were absent.

Consider a man who experiences social phobia. For him, social contexts are aversive. When people are around, his heart pounds and his hands shake (conditioned elicitation). He organizes much of his life around avoiding or escaping situations in which others are present, skipping parties and leaving meetings early. When he can't avoid these situations and finds himself stuck in others' presence, behaviors like telling a joke, describing a new project, or noticing the food or music at a party are highly unlikely (conditioned suppression).

Behavior patterns dominated by aversive control are relatively narrow and inflexible. The man with social phobia could perhaps benefit from telling a joke, describing a new project, or appreciating the food or music at the party. In fact, behavioral principles suggest that engaging in these behaviors is precisely what will alleviate the dominance of aversive control exerted by social situations, along with its side effects. However, as long as his behavior remains too inflexible for him to contact the consequences that could allow for new experiences and a broadening of behavior, the pattern is perpetuated.

A similar situation can result when thoughts, feelings, perceptions, memories, beliefs, or other private events have aversive functions. A woman may experience the same narrowness and inflexibility in intimate relationships when she remembers being raped as a teenager. Whether the aversive stimulus is something external or an aspect of a person's psychology, such as a memory, the effect on behavior and repertoire is similar: significant reduction in all behavior except arousal and avoidance.

Abundant Appetitive Control

Appetitive stimuli are events that work as positive reinforcers—events that people will work to obtain or sustain. Introduction of freely available appetitive stimuli into the environment has very interesting effects on behavior. Just as aversive stimuli tend to have a general suppressing effect on behavior, an abundance of appetitive control tends to broaden behavioral repertoire. In some respects, behavioral activation therapy relies on just this impact (Martell, Addis, & Jacobson, 2001). ACT addresses the issue of appetitive control directly and explicitly through values work. Some of the experimental work described above makes it abundantly clear that values can be made present psychologically through the use of simple experimental instructions.

A TECHNICAL DEFINITION OF VALUES

From an ACT perspective, "values are freely chosen, verbally constructed consequences of ongoing, dynamic, evolving patterns of activity, which establish predominant reinforcers for that activity that are intrinsic in engagement in the valued behavioral pattern itself" (Wilson & DuFrene, 2009, p. 64). For the purposes of this chapter, we can simplify this somewhat technical and dense definition of values to five essential components:

- Freely chosen
- Constructed
- Dynamic and evolving
- Ongoing patterns of activity
- Establish intrinsic reinforcers

Values Are Freely Chosen

People sometimes experience values as "shoulds" or something they have to do, implying aversive consequences for choosing otherwise. As conceived in ACT, however, values are the orientations we would choose in a world with no "shoulds." These are not necessarily mutually exclusive categories. For example, a father might sometimes experience conscientious parenting as a freely chosen value, and other times experience it as a burden. ACT interventions involve highlighting the freely chosen aspect of the value as a context for action.

Values Are Constructed

When people refer to finding meaning or purpose, it is often as if their values are preexisting—out there in the world to be discovered. We speak of finding meaning in the way we speak of finding our car keys or finding rare gems. If values are conceived as existing out in the world, identifying them becomes a process of discovery or clarification.

ACT takes a different approach, being interested in an individual's capacity to engage in the ongoing process of constructing a valued life. For example, a woman's parents may have had opinions about how she ought to raise her children, but ultimately she raises her children in her own world, in her own moment in time and not in theirs. Her approach may draw from theirs, but ultimately she constructs her own pattern for parenting.

In ACT, we sometimes describe this process using the metaphor of building a house—a values house, if you will. Imagine building a house of valued patterns of activity. What sort of house would you build? Would it contain rooms for family? What sorts of activities would fill that room? What would you look like as a partner or a parent? In ACT, values work involves client and therapist collaborating in the ongoing construction or authorship of the client's valued life.

Values Are Dynamic and Evolving

Values as defined in ACT are distinguished from goals. Goals involve particular achievable aims or results. Values, on the other hand, involve patterns of behavior that, while they imply potential goals, are not defined by them. In the domain of intimate relationships, for example, one goal may be to get married. Once the marriage license is issued, the act of being a spouse doesn't just stop.

If a man values being a loving husband, this establishes a long-term pattern defined not by immediate outcomes, but by its consistency with his sense of meaning in this area. More goals are established along the way. Being a loving husband in the first month of marriage might involve a very different pattern from being a husband in the fifth, fifteenth, or fiftieth month—though all might be recognizable as a pattern of being a loving husband. Likewise, being a loving husband in times of joy and prosperity may look very different from being a husband in a time of despair and loss, yet all are part of the same pattern.

Values Are Ongoing Patterns of Activity

When we speak of values in ACT, we are less interested in any particular action than in the qualities of the ongoing pattern of activity. For example, being a loving husband might be exemplified by a particular act, such as buying one's wife a single rose. However, doing so after a week of abuse is an altogether different act than offering a single rose as a part of a larger pattern of love and kindness. And as described above, the patterns itself is likely to evolve over time. Again, in ACT, collaboration with the therapist supports the client in cultivating the qualities and identifying the small acts that might populate such a pattern.

Values Establish Intrinsic Reinforcers

Reinforcers for nonhumans, with very few exceptions, involve evolutionary imperatives like food, water, shelter, and sex. Further, these typically have to be available relatively immediately following the behavior that produces them. However, because of verbal conditioning processes, humans can be sensitive to reinforcers that are removed in time or place from their immediate experience. An elaborated account of these processes can be found in *Relational Frame Theory* (Hayes, Barnes-Holmes, & Roche, 2001; cf. Wilson & DuFrene, 2009, for an elaborated clinical description).

In ACT, we are interested in a particular subset of reinforcers; namely, those reinforcers that are intrinsic to engagement in the valued pattern. Consider parenting. There are many reinforcing outcomes that might emerge from conscientious parenting, including, for example, good social and economic outcomes. However, many people value conscientious parenting even when a child's terminal illness or profound disability precludes these outcomes. In these instances, we see clearly that conscientious parenting can be sufficient in and of itself. The reinforcers for a hand laid to a child's fevered brow or kind attention to a child's acrobatic lessons are intrinsic in the acts themselves.

These acts don't rely on outcomes as an essential reinforcer. In fact, ACT places far greater emphasis on the *process* of valuing, and too tight an attachment to outcome can potentially undermine the process. For example, sometimes parents become so attached to particular education or career for their child that they entirely alienate the child. The ACT conception of values also leaves the door open to valued living even when the world doesn't cooperate with desired outcomes. Mother Teresa could work for the poor even though the world didn't cooperate with her mission and the plight of the poor wasn't universally relieved. Comforting a single person in distress can be sufficient to the moment and unto itself.

VALUES AND VULNERABILITIES

Although values in therapeutic contexts have most frequently been elaborated theoretically and clinically from the ACT perspective, contact with values is an important mechanism of change across many mindfulness- and acceptance-based therapies. Although mindfulness- and acceptance-based interventions might not directly target values construction and valued living, mindful acceptance and increases in valued living are intimately connected, at least in theory.

Acceptance- and mindfulness-based therapies share a focus on openness to psychological experience. Clients are asked to embrace those experiences that are most difficult for them. In making this request, clinicians may be giving clients the skills to pursue that which is most meaningful to them. This exchange shows that mindful acceptance and valued living seem to be interdependent, making valued living implicit in many, if not all, mindfulness- and acceptance-based therapies (Wilson & Sandoz, 2008). People are most vulnerable in the areas that are most precious to them. As soon as people mindfully acknowledge that something truly matters to them, the risk of failure or disappointment reveals itself. Ask for a date and you might be rejected. Answer a question in class and you might sound stupid. The instant a mother brings to mind her children simply because she loves them, she also contacts an awareness of the possibilities of what could go wrong for them. Without openness to experiencing those risks, we cannot fully experience being a partner, a student, or a parent. When those domains of life are deemed highly important, turning away from those possibilities means turning away from values.

ASSESSING VALUES WITH THE VALUED LIVING QUESTIONNAIRE (VLQ AND VLQ-2)

In the context of therapy, the purpose of assessment of values isn't merely to gather information about what clients value and the extent to which they are living in accordance with those values. Rather, there should be a tight connection between assessment and treatment. This sensibility emerges from the behavioral tradition. The earliest behavioral assessment for phobia was the behavioral approach task. In its simplest form, this assessment involves having the client walk toward a phobic object and measuring the distance between the client and the object when the client can walk no closer. Treatment is a natural extension of assessment and consists of the client walking closer and otherwise becoming engaged with the object. Indeed the only real distinction between treatment and assessment is duration and articulation; treatment lasts longer than assessment and involves a greater variety of behaviors than assessment.

Early developers of ACT observed that clients often couldn't even speak about valued domains of living, especially when they had experienced significant losses in those areas. In some respects, these therapists faced a problem similar to those faced by therapists who treat phobias. Their clients approached values with difficulty: those with panic disorder had missed children's dance recitals, those with substance-abuse problems had lost marriages, and those with depression had turned their backs on career and education. As therapists had long done when treating phobias; early developers of ACT asked their clients to engage with this difficult material and then observed the extent to which they were able to do so. This initial assessment indicated the direction of treatment and, indeed, became the basis for treatment.

The Valued Living Questionnaire

The values interventions illustrated in the original ACT text (Hayes et al., 1999) asked clients to describe and sometimes record valued directions and values-consistent goals. These early methods of facilitating choosing valued directions and evaluating progress in living in accordance with values were eventually shortened and adapted into the Valued Living Questionnaire (VLQ; Wilson, Sandoz, Kitchens, & Roberts, in press). Both the VLQ and the values interventions in the original ACT book (Hayes et al., 1999) were developed initially as guides to intervention and then secondarily as potential measurements.

THE VLQ AS A GUIDE TO INTERVENTION

The domains assessed on the VLQ are slightly modified from the version in the original ACT book (Hayes et al., 1999). That volume asked for ratings of values in nine domains:

1. Couples/intimate relationships
2. Family relations
3. Social relations
4. Employment
5. Education and training
6. Recreation
7. Spirituality
8. Citizenship
9. Health/physical well-being

These domains are a reasonable summary of those likely to emerge directly from clinical work on valued living. To these, the VLQ adds the domain of parenting because some clients showed a very different response to parenting than to the more general category of family. For example, some people have little investment in working on relationships within their family of origin but feel very strongly about values connected to their role as parents. When completing the VLQ, clients rate each of these ten domains of living on two ten-point scales. The first scale reflects how important each domain is to them. The second rates how consistent their actions have been with their values in each domain during the past week.

The VLQ facilitates a clinical conversation and establishes a direction for treatment. Therapists interview clients about the domains on the VLQ one valued domain at a time. In treatment, clients sometimes respond to items in very idiosyncratic ways. For example, a client might assign the lowest importance to the intimate relations domain, genuinely reflecting that this area holds no particular interest for him. More often, however, low ratings have other meanings. In this example, the low rating may mean that the client has been badly hurt in an intimate relationship and feels as if intimacy is hopeless for him. Alternatively, clients may feel that a value is extremely important in a long-term sense, but not at the time they're completing the VLQ. A common example is college students who value parenting overall but aren't invested in that value while still in school. Some students who hold parenting as a strong long-term value give it a high rating, responding as if the question inquired about long-term values, whereas others, equally invested over the long term, give parenting a low rating, thinking the question inquires about the short term.

Inquiring about low ratings is fruitful, since such inquiry often points us directly at treatment targets. For a client who has been hurt in a relationship, for example, these conversations might point toward potential targets for acceptance, defusion, and mindfulness, which might make intimate relations possible. For a client who says the area genuinely isn't all that important at the present time, other domains might be more fruitful targets of early session work.

THE VLQ AS A PSYCHOMETRIC INSTRUMENT

The VLQ can be evaluated as a psychometric instrument by multiplying the importance rating by the consistency rating for each domain and then summing the cross products and dividing that sum by 10 to obtain a composite valued living score with a potential range from 0 to 100. Examination of reliability and validity has shown promise (Wilson et al., in press). The VLQ was found to have adequate internal consistency at three different administrations (Cronbach's $\alpha = 0.77$ to 0.83) and adequate test-retest reliability with a one- to three-week delay between administrations ($r = 0.75$). The VLQ composite score was positively correlated with psychological flexibility, life satisfaction, social functioning, mental health, and action despite difficulties. The composite score negatively correlated with depression, anxiety, hostility, and interpersonal difficulties (Wilson et al., in press).

In the referenced study, valued living did not, as it was measured, account for a large proportion of the variability in measures of psychological well-being or of distress. This could be attributable to a significant amount of error in the measurement of valued living. Although these correlations were disappointing, they were not entirely surprising, given the idiosyncratic ways clients sometimes answered questions.

These idiosyncratic answers don't present a problem clinically, since interviewing clients on an item-by-item basis will produce treatment targets and clarify the source of their ratings. However, when the VLQ is used as a psychometric instrument, idiosyncratic answers are highly problematic. Diversity in how the questions are interpreted limit the validity of conclusions based solely upon initial scores. While the overall pattern of correlations is consistent with theory, the measurement error makes the VLQ less useful as an assessment instrument than as a treatment tool.

ADDITIONAL PROBLEMS WITH THE VLQ AS AN ASSESSMENT

Presenting the VLQ as a clinical tool to clinicians worldwide has revealed several other concerns about its use as an assessment. Many clinicians suggested virtues like honesty and courage as values. Though these could be presented as values, we have found in a clinical setting that these virtues are reliably linked to domains already present on the VLQ. For example, courage is almost always expressed as courage in relationships, at work, or in some other domain, and honesty generally appears as honesty in relationships, at work, and so forth.

Some domains didn't translate well into other cultural contexts. For example, the VLQ domain citizenship/community life is meant to suggest a sense of commitment to community involvement. However, when the VLQ is used in northern European countries, this domain has been almost universally interpreted as something like nationalism or perhaps even jingoism. Naturally, this failure in translation has a negative impact on the psychometrics.

In addition, two domains that don't fit the existing categories have emerged repeatedly as holding important values for clients. First is what might be called sustainability or green sensibilities: a concern for the environment and our roles as stewards of the planet. The second might be called aesthetics, which broadly includes an appreciation of art, music, literature, and so on, and also extends to nature and other realms. Again, the emergence of new domains isn't problematic in a clinical context, where the therapist might simply add them to the VLQ. However, these omissions are problematic when using the VLQ as a psychometric instrument.

The Valued Living Questionnaire–2

The revision of the Valued Living Questionnaire, the Valued Living Questionnaire–2 (VLQ-2; Wilson & DuFrene, 2009), was developed primarily to clarify ratings and add domains for the environment and aesthetics. In addition, the wording of the ninth domain was changed to "community life" to avoid the nationalism interpretation. As a result, the VLQ-2 assesses valued living across the following twelve domains:

1. Family (other than marriage or parenting)
2. Marriage, couples, or intimate relations
3. Parenting
4. Friends and social life
5. Work
6. Education and training
7. Recreation and fun
8. Spirituality
9. Community life
10. Physical self-care (diet, exercise, and sleep)
11. The environment (caring for the planet)
12. Aesthetics (art, literature, music, beauty)

The original two rating scales were expanded to clarify sources of variability in answers to the original VLQ. The VLQ-2 includes six rating scales:

1. Possibility
2. Current importance
3. Overall importance
4. Action
5. Satisfaction with level of action
6. Concern

Clients rate all twelve domains on each of the six rating scales. Ratings are provided on a ten-point scale (1 = not at all possible, important, concerned, etc.; 10 = very possible, important, concerned, etc.).

Possibility. In the area of possibility, the instructions ask, "How possible is it that something very meaningful could happen in this area of your life?" This is an important question, since people often regard aspects of their current circumstances or past history as limitations to what they might achieve. The goal in ACT is not to raise ratings of possibility by convincing the client that all things are possible. Rather, the goal is to change the relationship between thoughts about possibility, importance, and action such that thoughts about possibility don't unnecessarily constrain importance or action. In this case, clients may have the thought that vitality in a certain domain isn't possible for them and still engage in acts in the service of that value. The core sensibility is that thinking something is impossible need not necessarily change in order for related behavior to change.

Current and overall importance. Unlike the original VLQ, the VLQ-2 asks clients about both current importance ("How important is this area at this time in your life?") and overall importance ("How important is this area in your life as a whole?") of valued areas. Clients are often very clear about what's important to them but find themselves holding back from pursuing it. This might be reflected in a large discrepancy between importance and action or satisfaction, such that importance ratings are higher than action and satisfaction ratings. Clients may also find themselves using many personal resources to pursue things that aren't important to them. This might be reflected in a discrepancy wherein action ratings are significantly higher than importance ratings. The goal in ACT is not necessarily to raise importance ratings in all domains or to lessen the discrepancy between current and overall importance. Rather, the goal is to change the relationship between importance and action so that importance better predicts action.

Action and satisfaction with level of action. These scales ask clients to rate how much they have acted in the service of each area in the past week and whether they are satisfied with their level of action in each area during the past week. Sometimes clients choose to focus on one or several domains while still holding important values in other domains. Sometimes this is deliberate, but other times important things slip away gradually and without the person being aware of it. Sometimes clients are surprised to discover how the distribution of their actions varies from what is truly important to them.

Once again, the goal in ACT is to change the relationship between action and importance such that importance predicts action or, when it doesn't predict action, that this is chosen with awareness and intention.

Concern. The final scale on the VLQ-2 asks clients, "How concerned are you that this area won't progress as you want?" In some respects, this overlaps with the rating of possibility. Although clients sometimes give lower importance ratings to painful areas, they more often assign high importance ratings and also express high concern. Concerns are explored in an attempt to find potential experiential barriers to committed action. These barriers, in turn, present potential targets for defusion and acceptance interventions.

THE VLQ-2 AS A GUIDE TO INTERVENTION

To develop robust, testable intervention strategies directly aimed at values, we need to systematize intervention. To that end, the VLQ-2 more directly orients the clinician toward potential points of intervention. For example, by systematically asking about both the importance of a domain and the client's sense of possibility or level of concern within that domain, we are less likely to overlook important ACT treatment targets, such as fused beliefs about the impossibility of some valued direction or fused beliefs about self, such as "I'm just unlovable." Identifying such targets leads quite directly to ACT interventions.

The overall goal of the VLQ-2 is clinical utility. Exploration of the client's responses may serve to generate patterns of valued activity in session. The client and therapist may discuss commitments that are consistent with the client's personal valued directions. Homework assignments in line with valued domains may be similar to behavioral activation. One example of this would be a valued events schedule, which could be used in the same manner as the Pleasant Events Schedule (MacPhillamy & Lewinsohn, 1982). This would give clients more opportunities to come into contact with reinforcers related to their values.

THE VLQ-2 AS A PSYCHOMETRIC INSTRUMENT

Though the modifications to the original VLQ that led to the VLQ-2 were largely an attempt to systematize the clinical interview about values, to remove some of the original instrument's ambiguities, and to make it a more reliable psychometric tool, we are only just beginning to examine the psychometric properties of the VLQ-2. Ratings are considered to be most meaningful when taken in the context of other ratings. Full scoring results in a number of potential composite scores related to different patterns of interactions with values. Exploration of scoring methods and relationships between the scales has begun and is the subject of ongoing development. Although the full scoring protocol is outside of the scope of this article, the preceding overview of the six rating scales may suggest possible relationships between them, examples of presentations to which they might be sensitive, and examples of patterns that might reflect ACT-consistent goals being met. For example, among agoraphobic clients, low ratings on possibility coupled with high ratings on current importance may serve as a guide to values-directed exposure, acceptance, and defusion work. Likewise, depressed clients with low levels of satisfaction with action but high current importance ratings may be encouraged to select among highly rated values for behavioral activation targets. The VLQ-2 is included as an appendix to this chapter.

OTHER VALUES ASSESSMENTS

In addition to the VLQ, several other assessment and treatment tools have been developed: the Personal Values Questionnaire, the Bull's-Eye Instrument, and the Values Compass. Each offers different advantages and may be more or less relevant for use in different populations, presentations, clinical settings, or research projects.

The Personal Values Questionnaire

The Personal Values Questionnaire (PVQ; Blackledge & Ciarrochi, 2006) assesses nine values domains: family relationships, friendships/social relationships, couples/romantic relationships, work/career, education-schooling/personal growth and development, recreation/leisure/sports, spirituality/religion, community/citizenship, and health/physical well-being. For each domain, the instructions ask respondents to consider aspects and qualities that are meaningful to them personally, and then to write down what they value in that domain. Keeping their personal value in mind, respondents then assign nine ratings to each domain on a five-point, Likert-type scale. These ratings assess reasons for valuing, importance, consistency, commitment, and progress. Preliminary examinations show good internal consistency among items on the PVQ and promising concurrent validity (Blackledge, Spencer, & Ciarrochi, 2007). Additional investigation of the reliability and validity of this measure is needed, with larger sample sizes.

The PVQ combines a personal values narrative, or values statement, with prompts designed to facilitate clients or subjects in contacting their chosen values as they are personally meaningful, with a focus on ways clients can take action. For example, some clients might refer to specific goals or outcomes that are outside of their control, such as "I value my spouse being more loving and caring." The instructions for writing out personal values in each domain are intended to guide respondents away from a focus on specific goals or outcomes, especially outcomes over which they have no direct control, and toward engagement in valuing as a process. Using questions like "What kind of relationships would you most like to build?" with examples of appropriate responses, the PVQ can facilitate this shift from values as goals to values as process. Some clients might refer to values that are held under aversive control. For example, people might respond based on standards held by society in general or people who are important to them. They might also respond based on values that they hold or pursue to defend against negative evaluation. Elements of the PVQ are aimed at identifying pseudovaluing that is excessively influenced by perceived social desirability.

Because its primary purpose is to facilitate ACT-consistent contact with values and to assess for aversive versus appetitive control, the PVQ would be particularly advantageous in research or clinical contexts where assessment occurs outside of the therapeutic context. It might also be useful early in the course of therapy, before values have been specifically explored with the therapist.

The Bull's-Eye Instrument

The Bull's-Eye Instrument (Lundgren, 2006) is a two-part measure assessing behavioral consistency with respect to valued directions and persistence of valuing in the face of barriers. The domains assessed by the Bull's-Eye Instrument are parenting, education/personal development, leisure time, spiritual life, health, work, social relations, intimate relations, family, and community. The measure also provides examples of valued directions in each of these domains. Respondents then write what the value means to them, how they would like to be in this area, and why it's important to them. The measure also uses an illustration of a dartboard on which clients place X's to represent their consistency and persistence. The distance of the X from the bull's-eye is a measure of valued living. The Bull's-Eye has a test-retest reliability of 0.86 and good criterion validity (Lundgren, 2006).

The Bull's-Eye was created for use with poor South Africans with drug-refractory epilepsy to serve as a means of assessing consistency and persistence in living in accord with values using a visual representation. The visual format allows respondents to see, on an ongoing basis, how their actions in a given domain correspond to their rating of the importance of that domain. One benefit of this format is that it can be helpful in overcoming communication difficulties attributable to language deficits or barriers. In a similar vein, a variant of the Bull's-Eye has been clinically useful with children, where its more visual representation can assist in values interventions and assessment with these less verbally adept clients (Murrell, Coyne, & Wilson, 2004). And because of its emphasis on action in valued domains, the Bull's Eye can easily lead to conversations about committed action—another important component of ACT. In addition, it may be more useful than other measures for ongoing assessment of degree of valued action.

The Values Compass

The Values Compass (Dahl, Wilson, Luciano, & Hayes, 2005) is a measure originally used in studies of chronic pain to assess eight valued domains: family relations, leisure activities, education/development, intimate relations, spiritual development, work, social life, and physical health. The measure also asks the client to describe barriers within those valued domains. To date, there are no psychometric data available on this measure.

The Values Compass is unique in that it asks respondents not only to think about a valued direction, but also to describe perceived obstacles to valued living. People often think, "I'll do ________________ after ________________ happens [or goes away, or is solved]." Assessing obstacles specifically allows for a conversation in which the therapist aims to loosen the rigidity with which those events are perceived as obstacles and explore valued action in the context of hardship. The Values Compass may be particularly useful with individuals whose behavior is under strong aversive control or who seem particularly resistant to treatment.

ALTERNATIVE APPROACHES LINKING ASSESSMENT AND INTERVENTION

The Hexaflex Functional Dimensional Experiential Interview (HFDEI; Wilson & DuFrene, 2009) is a clinical diagnostic tool designed to help conceptualize client difficulties and establish therapeutic objectives based on valued living rather than symptoms. The HFDEI is comprised of a values-centered mindfulness exercise, a values writing exercise, and a systematic interview regarding valued domains, including use of the VLQ-2. The purpose of the interview is to facilitate assessment and quantification of mindfulness processes in the context of particular valued domains. A full description of the HFDEI, including mindfulness and interviewing scripts and worksheets to guide assessment, is available in *Mindfulness for Two* (Wilson & DuFrene, 2009).

The HFDEI systematizes the intimacy between assessment and intervention in regard to values. During the interview, the clinician invites the client to contact possible valued directions in the context of mindfulness and acceptance. This involves extended probes of the very behaviors the intervention is targeting. These probes are included to allow for both direct observation of behaviors related to mindfulness processes and exposure to those experiences that are most precious, and therefore often most defended.

The worksheets and elaborated rating scales included in the HFDEI allow for research into the interview as a psychometric instrument. For example, utility of the rating scales for quantifying mindfulness processes will require inter-rater reliability; that is, two people who observe an interview should rate the individual's behavior similarly. In addition, conclusions based on the HFDEI should demonstrate convergent validity, wherein ratings on the HFDEI correlate with scores on other measures of mindfulness, acceptance, psychological flexibility, and valued living. Another possibility is to examine the consistency between symptoms reported in a typical symptom-focused clinical interview and those reported in the HFDEI. After the HFDEI's psychometric properties are established, there are many other ways its utility might be evaluated. For example, clinicians might rate the utility of a traditional interview versus an HFDEI with respect to case conceptualization, making traditional diagnoses, creating treatment objectives, or facilitating therapeutic alliance.

CONCLUSIONS

ACT is part of a larger body of psychological science that has been called contextual behavioral science (Hayes, Strosahl, & Wilson, in press). The developmental trajectory of the VLQ in particular and values assessments generally is an example of a contextual approach to intervention and assessment development. The process has been iterative, as we've moved freely between clinical applications and measurement sensibilities. The development process has been inclusive and horizontal, as we've persistently sought feedback from clients, researchers, and clinicians worldwide and turned this feedback into useful modifications to the instrument. The development process has been pragmatic, and we hope that further development of the VLQ in the context of clinical work, research, and a wide variety of applied settings will result in instrumentation that is well connected with intervention and broadly applicable across settings and cultures.

Among other characteristics, the currently developing mindfulness- and acceptance-based therapies share an emphasis on increasing the breadth and flexibility of living as a primary treatment goal. ACT offers valued living as a functional conceptualization of what is being targeted in mindfulness- and acceptance-based therapies. This general approach has produced promising outcomes, but changes in breadth and flexibility of living have typically been inferred by clinicians rather than being directly demonstrated by assessment instruments. Tools and methods for assessing valued living are emerging from the therapy room as ways of facilitating values construction. This is somewhat disadvantageous in that these intervention tools rarely involve the same level of standardization as psychometric tools. Clinicians say and do things to ensure that the questions being asked are fully understood and answered with intention. Gradually, though, more sensitive instruments are being created that attempt to anticipate the challenges observed in values construction interventions and that systematize responsiveness to these challenges.

The various assessments described above serve as examples of how interventions can shape assessment and how assessment can facilitate the continued development of interventions. Psychometric evaluations of these assessments are in their infancy, but initial findings suggest that valued living can be measured reliably. Continued adaptation of these instruments to minimize their limitations with regard to moving values construction forward in session seems to be a promising method of developing assessment tools. It would be beneficial to see how these and other instruments might develop if they were used more widely in the context of other acceptance- and mindfulness-based interventions. The HFDEI and other alternatives to pencil-and-paper measures draw even less of a distinction between assessment and intervention and offer particularly interesting possible future directions for this work.

This shift to a more holistic view of assessment and intervention is consistent with the behavioral perspective, in which treatment involves creating conditions relevant to the presenting problem, observing the client's behavior, and manipulating the conditions until the target behavior is observed. In ACT, clinicians probe mindfulness processes and attempt to manipulate the context such that client behavior approaches those processes. How the data collected from this type of assessment compare to those collected from more traditional approaches remains an empirical question, but findings in regard to efficacy and effectiveness are promising.

REFERENCES

Allport, G. W., Vernon, P. E., & Lindzey, G. (1960). *Study of values: A scale for measuring the dominant interests in personality* (3rd ed.). Boston: Houghton Mifflin.

Bach, P., & Hayes, S. C. (2002). The use of acceptance and commitment therapy to prevent the rehospitalization of psychotic patients: A randomized controlled trial. *Journal of Consulting and Clinical Psychology, 70*, 1129-1139.

Baer, R. A., Smith, G. T., & Allen, K. B. (2004). Assessment of mindfulness by self-report: The Kentucky Inventory of Mindfulness Skills. *Assessment, 11*, 191-206.

Blackledge, J. T., & Ciarrochi, J. (2006). Personal Values Questionnaire. Presentation at Association for Behavior Analysis annual conference in Atlanta, GA.

Blackledge, J. T., Spencer, R., & Ciarrochi, J. (2007, May). *Initial validation of the Personal Values Questionnaire.* Presentation at the annual conference of the Association for Behavior Analysis, San Diego, CA.

Block, J. A. (2002). *Acceptance or change of private experiences: A comparative analysis in college students with public speaking anxiety.* Doctoral dissertation, University at Albany, State University of New York.

Bond, F. W., & Bunce, D. (2000). Mediators of change in emotion-focused and problem-focused worksite stress management interventions. *Journal of Occupational Health Psychology, 5*, 156-163.

Cohen, G. L., Garcia, J., Apfel, N., & Master, A. (2006). Reducing the racial achievement gap: A social-psychological intervention. *Science, 313*, 1307-1310.

Creswell, J. D., Welch, W. T., Taylor, S. E., Sherman, D. K., Gruenewald, T. L., & Mann, T. (2005). Affirmation of personal values buffers neuroendocrine and psychological stress responses. *Psychological Science, 16*, 846-851.

Crocker, J., Niiya, Y., & Mischkowski, D. (2008). Why does writing about values reduce defensiveness? Self-affirmation and the role of positive other-directed feelings. *Psychological Science, 19*, 740-747.

Dahl, J., Wilson, K. G., Luciano, C., & Hayes, S. C. (2005). *ACT for chronic pain*. Reno, NV: Context Press.

Dahl, J., Wilson, K. G., & Nilsson, A. (2004). Acceptance and commitment therapy and the treatment of persons at risk for long-term disability resulting from stress and pain symptoms: A preliminary randomized trial. *Behavior Therapy, 35*, 785-801.

Gaudiano, B. A., & Herbert, J. D. (2006). Acute treatment of inpatients with psychotic symptoms using acceptance and commitment therapy: Pilot results. *Behaviour Research and Therapy, 44*, 415-437.

Gregg, J. A., Callaghan, G. M., Hayes, S. C., & Glenn-Lawson, J. L. (2007). Improving diabetes self-management through acceptance, mindfulness, and values: A randomized controlled trial. *Journal of Consulting and Clinical Psychology, 75*, 336-343.

Hayes, S. C. (2004). Acceptance and commitment therapy, relational frame theory, and the third wave of behavior therapy. *Behavior Therapy, 35*, 639-665.

Hayes, S. C., Barnes-Holmes, D., & Roche, B. (Eds.). (2001). *Relational frame theory: A post-Skinnerian account of human language and cognition*. New York: Plenum Press.

Hayes, S. C., Luoma, J. B., Bond, F. W., Masuda, A., & Lillis, J. (2006). Acceptance and commitment therapy: Model, processes, and outcomes. *Behaviour Research and Therapy, 44*, 1-25.

Hayes, S. C., Strosahl, K. D., & Wilson, K. G. (1999). *Acceptance and commitment therapy: An experiential approach to behavior change*. New York: Guilford.

Hayes, S. C., Strosahl, K. D., & Wilson, K. G. (in press). *Acceptance and commitment therapy: An experiential approach to behavior change* (2nd ed.). New York: Guilford.

Hayes, S. C., Strosahl, K. D., Wilson, K. G., Bissett, R. T., Pistorello, J., Toarmino, D., et al. (2004). Measuring experiential avoidance: A preliminary test of a working model. *Psychological Record, 54*, 553-578.

Hayes, S. C., Wilson, K. G., Gifford, E. V., Bissett, R., Piasecki, M., Batten, S. V., et al. (2004). A preliminary trial of twelve-step facilitation and acceptance and commitment therapy with polysubstance-abusing methadone-maintained opiate addicts. *Behavior Therapy, 35*, 667-688.

Hayes, S. C., Wilson, K. G., Gifford, E. V., Follette, V. M., & Strosahl, K. (1996). Experiential avoidance and behavioral disorders: A functional dimensional approach to diagnosis and treatment. *Journal of Consulting and Clinical Psychology, 64*, 1152-1168.

Lundgren, T. (2006, July). *Validation and reliability data of the Bull's-Eye.* Presentation at the Second World Conference on ACT, RFT, and Contextual Behavioral Science, London.

Lundgren, T., Dahl, J., & Hayes, S. C. (2008). Evaluation of mediators of change in the treatment of epilepsy with acceptance and commitment therapy. *Journal of Behavioral Medicine, 31*, 225-235.

Lundgren, T., Dahl, J., Melin, L., & Kies, B. (2006). Evaluation of acceptance and commitment therapy for drug refractory epilepsy: A randomized controlled trial in South Africa—A pilot study. *Epilepsia, 47*, 2173-2179.

MacPhillamy, D. J., & Lewinsohn, P. M. (1982). The Pleasant Events Schedule: Studies on reliability, validity, and scale intercorrelation. *Journal of Consulting and Clinical Psychology, 50*, 363-375.

Martell, C. R., Addis, M. E., & Jacobson, N. S. (2001). *Depression in context: Strategies for guided action.* New York: W. W. Norton.

Murrell, A. R., Coyne, L., & Wilson, K. G. (2004). Treating children with acceptance and commitment therapy. In S. C. Hayes & K. D. Strosahl (Eds.), *A practical guide to acceptance and commitment therapy.* New York: Springer.

Öst, L. (2008). Efficacy of the third wave of behavioral therapies: A systematic review and meta-analysis. *Behaviour Research and Therapy, 46*, 296-321.

Palermo, T. M. (2009). Enhancing daily functioning with exposure and acceptance strategies: An important stride in the development of psychological therapies for pediatric chronic pain. *Pain, 141*, 189-190.

Powers, M. B., Vörding, M. B., & Emmelkamp, P. M. (2009). Acceptance and commitment therapy: A meta-analytic review. *Psychotherapy and Psychosomatics, 78*, 73-80.

Rokeach, M. (1973). *The nature of human values.* New York: Free Press.

Wicksell, R. K., Melin, L., Lekander, M., & Olsson, G. L. (2009). Evaluating the effectiveness of exposure and acceptance strategies to improve functioning and quality of life in longstanding pediatric pain: A randomized controlled trial. *Pain, 141*, 248-257.

Wilson, K. G., & DuFrene, T. (2009). *Mindfulness for two: An acceptance and commitment therapy approach to mindfulness in psychotherapy.* Oakland, CA: New Harbinger.

Wilson, K. G., & Murrell, A. R. (2004). Values work in acceptance and commitment therapy: Setting a course for behavioral treatment. In S. C. Hayes, V. M. Follette, & M. M. Linehan (Eds.), *Mindfulness and acceptance: Expanding the cognitive-behavioral tradition.* New York: Guilford.

Wilson, K. G., & Sandoz, E. K. (2008). Mindfulness, values, and the therapeutic relationship in acceptance and commitment therapy. In S. Hick & T. Bein (Eds.), *Mindfulness and the therapeutic relationship.* New York: Guilford.

Wilson, K. G., Sandoz, E. K., Kitchens, J., & Roberts, M. E. (in press). The Valued Living Questionnaire: Defining and measuring valued action within a behavioral framework. *Psychological Record.*

Zettle, R. D., & Hayes, S. C. (1986). Dysfunctional control by client verbal behavior: The context of reason giving. *Analysis of Verbal Behavior, 4*, 30-38.

Zettle, R. D., & Rains, J. C. (1989). Group cognitive and contextual therapies in treatment of depression. *Journal of Clinical Psychology, 45*, 438-445.

APPENDIX: VALUED LIVING QUESTIONNAIRE–2 (VLQ-2)

Below are areas of life that are valued by some people. We are concerned with your quality of life in each of these areas. There are several aspects that we ask you to rate. Ask yourself the following questions when you rate each area. Not everyone will value all of these areas or value all areas the same. Rate each according to your own personal view of that area.

Possibility: How possible is it that something very meaningful could happen in this area of your life? Rate how possible you think it is on a scale of 1 to 10, where 1 means it is not at all possible and 10 means it is very possible.

Current importance: How important is this area at this time in your life? Rate the importance on a scale of 1 to 10, where 1 means the area is not at all important and 10 means the area is very important.

Overall importance: How important is this area in your life as a whole? Rate the importance on a scale of 1 to 10, where 1 means the area is not at all important and 10 means the area is very important.

Action: How much have you acted in the service of this area during the past week? Rate your level of action on a scale of 1 to 10, where 1 means you have not been active at all with this value and 10 means you have been very active with this value.

Satisfaction with your level of action: How satisfied are you with your level of action in this area during the past week? Rate your satisfaction with your level of action on a scale of 1 to 10, where 1 means you are not at all satisfied and 10 means you are completely satisfied with your level of action in this area.

Concern: How concerned are you that this area will not progress as you want? Rate your level of concern on a scale of 1 to 10, where 1 means you are not at all concerned and 10 means you are very concerned.

	Possibility	Current Importance	Overall Importance	Action	Satisfaction with Action	Concern
1. Family (other than couples or parenting)						
2. Marriage, couples, or intimate relations						
3. Parenting						
4. Friends and social life						
5. Work						
6. Education and training						
7. Recreation and fun						
8. Spirituality						
9. Community life						
10. Physical self-care (diet, exercise, and sleep)						
11. The environment (caring for the planet)						
12. Aesthetics (art, music, literature, beauty)						

If you could choose five of these twelve areas to work on, which would they be?

1. ______________________________

2. ______________________________

3. ______________________________

4. ______________________________

5. ______________________________

If you could choose just three areas to work on, which would they be?

1. ______________________________

2. ______________________________

3. ______________________________

If you could choose just one area to work on, which would it be?

1. ______________________________

CHAPTER 4

Emotion Regulation as a Mechanism of Change in Acceptance- and Mindfulness-Based Treatments

Kim L. Gratz and Matthew T. Tull,
University of Mississippi Medical Center

Over the past decade, emotion regulation has received increasing attention as a potentially unifying function of diverse symptom presentations, and growing evidence suggests that difficulties in emotion regulation underlie many of the clinically relevant behaviors and psychological difficulties for which clients seek treatment, including deliberate self-harm (Gratz & Chapman, 2007; Gratz & Roemer, 2008), substance use (Fox, Axelrod, Paliwal, Sleeper, & Sinha, 2007; Fox, Hong, & Sinha, 2008), binge eating (Leahey, Crowther, & Irwin, 2008; Whiteside et al., 2007), depression and anxiety (Roemer et al., 2009; Tull, Stipelman, Salters-Pedneault, & Gratz, 2009; Vujanovic, Zvolensky, & Bernstein, 2008), worry (Salters-Pedneault, Roemer, Tull, Rucker, & Mennin, 2006; Vujanovic et al., 2008), generalized anxiety disorder (Mennin, Heimberg, Turk, & Fresco, 2005; Roemer et al., 2009; Salters-Pedneault et al., 2006), post-traumatic stress disorder (PTSD: McDermott, Tull, Gratz, Daughters, & Lejuez, 2009; Tull, Barrett, McMillan, & Roemer, 2007), and borderline personality disorder (Gratz, Rosenthal, Tull, Lejuez, & Gunderson, 2006). In response, treatments for a variety of difficulties are increasingly incorporating a focus on emotion regulation and seeking to promote adaptive emotion regulation skills (Gratz & Gunderson, 2006; Linehan, 1993; Mennin, 2006).

Yet despite the interest in emotion regulation as a mechanism underlying various forms of psychopathology and an important target of treatment, there is no consistent or agreed-upon definition of this construct (see Putnam & Silk, 2005), and there remains a great deal of disagreement regarding the definition that is most clinically relevant. However, clinical applications of the emerging research on the role of emotion dysregulation in various psychological difficulties require an understanding of the precise conceptualization of emotion regulation that is most applicable to these difficulties.

EXTANT CONCEPTUALIZATIONS OF EMOTION REGULATION

This section describes extant approaches to the conceptualization of emotion regulation and seeks to clarify the conceptualization of emotion regulation that may be most clinically useful, particularly with regard to the development of new interventions and modification of existing interventions. Although numerous conceptual definitions of emotion regulation currently exist, two particular areas of disagreement are most relevant to developing a clinically useful definition of emotion regulation: whether emotion regulation refers to the control of negative emotions or the control of behavior when experiencing negative emotions, and the relationship between emotion regulation and emotional vulnerability.

Control of Emotions vs. Control of Behavior When Experiencing Emotions

There is a great deal of disagreement as to whether emotion regulation refers to the control of negative emotions or the control of behavior when experiencing negative emotions. One approach has been to equate emotion regulation with the control and reduction of negative emotions (e.g., Kopp, 1989; Zeman & Garber, 1996), implying that experiencing negative emotions is a sign of emotion dysregulation. Although the assumption that negative emotions are disruptive, problematic, or should be carefully controlled is widespread in psychology (and throughout our society as a whole), recent research provides evidence that efforts to control negative emotions may not always be effective or healthy. For example, there has been a great deal of research in the past decade indicating that efforts to control, suppress, or avoid unwanted internal experiences (including emotions) may actually have paradoxical effects, increasing the frequency, severity, and accessibility of these experiences (Hayes, Luoma, Bond, Masuda, & Lillis, 2006; Salters-Pedneault, Tull, & Roemer, 2004). The classic studies in this area focused on thought suppression (deliberately trying not to think about something) and involved instructing study participants not to think of a white bear (Wegner, Schneider, Carter, & White, 1987). These studies provided the first experimental evidence that attempts to avoid or suppress internal experiences may have paradoxical effects (referred to as ironic processes; Wegner, 1994). More recently, researchers have extended this line of inquiry to emotions and have found similar results (for a review, see Salters-Pedneault et al., 2004). All in all, these findings suggest that conceptualizations of emotion regulation that equate regulation with the control or avoidance of certain emotions may confound processes that undermine regulation with those that promote emotion regulation.

Another approach to emotion regulation emphasizes the functionality of all emotions (see Cole, Michel, & Teti, 1994; Thompson & Calkins, 1996) and suggests that adaptive emotion regulation involves the ability to control one's behaviors (for example, by inhibiting impulsive behaviors and engaging in goal-directed behaviors) when experiencing negative emotions, rather than the ability to directly control one's emotions per se (see Linehan, 1993; Melnick & Hinshaw, 2000). This approach distinguishes emotion regulation from emotional control and defines regulation as the control of behavior in the face of emotional distress. According to this approach, although adaptive regulation may involve efforts to modulate the intensity or duration of an emotion (Thompson, 1994; Thompson & Calkins, 1996), these efforts are in the service of reducing the urgency associated with the emotion in order to control one's behavior, rather than the emotion itself. In other words, this approach suggests the potential utility of efforts to take the edge off an emotion or self-soothe when distressed, provided that the individual is not trying to get rid of the emotion or escape it altogether. Moreover, attachment to the outcome of efforts to modulate the intensity or duration of an emotion is thought to have paradoxical effects, as directly trying to reduce emotional arousal to a particular level or make an emotion end after a certain amount of time is considered to reflect an emotional control agenda indicative of emotional avoidance. As such, this functional approach may be considered an acceptance-based approach, conceptualizing both positive and negative emotions as functional and encouraging the awareness, understanding, and acceptance of all emotions.

Relationship Between Emotion Regulation and Emotional Vulnerability

The second area of disagreement within the literature on emotion regulation concerns the relationship between emotion regulation and a temperamental emotional vulnerability. Specifically, some researchers equate emotion regulation with a particular temperament: low emotional intensity and reactivity (e.g., Livesley, Jang, & Vernon, 1998). This approach implies that intense, reactive emotional responses are problematic and inherently dysregulated. Although there is evidence to suggest that individuals who are more emotionally intense and reactive may be at greater risk for emotion dysregulation (Flett, Blankstein, & Obertynski, 1996), this relationship is not direct, and most research indicates that emotional intensity and reactivity in and of themselves are not associated with negative psychological outcomes (Gratz, 2006; Larsen & Diener, 1987; Larsen, Diener, & Emmons, 1986).

Other researchers define emotion regulation as separate from the nature or quality of the emotional response (Linehan, 1993; Mennin et al., 2005; Thompson & Calkins, 1996), implying that there is a difference between emotion regulation and one's emotional temperament. According to this conceptualization, emotional intensity and reactivity do not preclude adaptive regulation; one can be emotionally intense or reactive and not dysregulated. Instead, this approach conceptualizes emotion regulation as any adaptive way of responding to one's emotions, regardless of their intensity or reactivity (thereby distinguishing responses to emotions from the nature or quality of emotions). Providing some support for the utility and practicality of this approach, an ongoing longitudinal study of borderline personality disorder (BPD) has found that BPD symptoms associated with a temperamental emotional vulnerability decrease the least over time, whereas symptoms associated with behavioral dyscontrol, such as self-harm, improve the most (Zanarini, Frankenburg, Hennen, & Silk, 2003).

These findings suggest that characteristics of an individual's temperament or personality, such as emotional intensity and reactivity, may be both less likely to change and less amenable to treatment. As such, the clinical utility of trying to change these characteristics is unclear. Thus, conceptualizations of emotion regulation that distinguish emotion regulation from emotional temperament may arguably direct attention to clinical difficulties that are amenable to change, as opposed to those that are not. Moreover, given that emotional intensity and reactivity are not pathological in and of themselves, one could argue that there is no reason to try to change them, even if they were in some way amenable to treatment. Instead, it might make more sense to focus attention on behaviors that are both within an individual's control and directly associated with risk for clinical difficulties, such as the way individuals respond to and manage their emotions when they experience distress.

A CLINICALLY USEFUL CONCEPTUALIZATION OF EMOTION REGULATION

Based on the research reviewed above, a clinically useful conceptual definition of emotion regulation may arguably focus on adaptive ways of responding to emotional distress, rather than on the control of emotions or dampening of emotional arousal in general. One such conceptualization (see Gratz & Roemer, 2004) emphasizes the functionality of emotions and defines emotion regulation as a multidimensional construct involving the awareness, understanding, and acceptance of emotions; ability to engage in goal-directed behaviors and inhibit impulsive behaviors when experiencing negative emotions; flexible use of situationally appropriate strategies to modulate the intensity or duration of emotional responses, rather than to eliminate emotions entirely; and willingness to experience negative emotions as part of pursuing meaningful activities in life. Conversely, deficits in any of these areas are considered indicative of emotion regulation difficulties.

Of note, this conceptualization of emotion regulation overlaps with some of the other processes of change examined in this book. For example, emotion regulation involves being accepting of one's internal experience (in particular, emotions), as well as being compassionate toward oneself when experiencing emotions. Emotion regulation also overlaps with mindfulness in its emphasis on observing and describing emotions (without necessarily acting on those emotions) and participating in present-moment activities even in the context of emotional distress (i.e., engaging in goal-directed behavior when distressed). Thus, treatments that emphasize mindfulness, acceptance, and self-compassion should in theory also facilitate improvements in emotion regulation.

Indeed, the acceptance-based nature of this conceptualization of emotion regulation is consistent with theories underlying acceptance- and mindfulness-based approaches to the treatment of psychopathology, suggesting that these types of treatments may be particularly useful for effectively targeting emotion regulation. In particular, given evidence that many individuals who engage in maladaptive behaviors struggle with their emotions (see Chapman, Gratz, & Brown, 2006; Whiteside et al., 2007), treatments that focus on teaching these individuals ways to avoid or control their emotions may not be useful and may inadvertently reinforce a nonaccepting, judgmental, and unhealthy stance toward emotions. Instead, the fact that such individuals may be caught in a struggle with their emotions suggests that they may benefit from learning another (more adaptive) way of approaching and responding to their emotions, such as emotional acceptance, willingness, and mindfulness.

THEORIZED EFFECTS OF MINDFULNESS- AND ACCEPTANCE-BASED INTERVENTIONS ON EMOTION REGULATION

As mentioned above, acceptance- and mindfulness-based treatments may be particularly useful for promoting emotion regulation and facilitating the development of more adaptive ways of responding to emotions. For example, the process of observing and describing one's emotions (an element common across many mindfulness- and acceptance-based treatments, including dialectical behavior therapy [DBT], acceptance and commitment therapy [ACT], mindfulness-based cognitive therapy [MBCT], mindfulness-based stress reduction [MBSR], and acceptance-based behavioral therapy [ABBT] for generalized anxiety disorder; see Linehan, 1993; Hayes, Strosahl, & Wilson, 1999; Segal, Williams, & Teasdale, 2002; Kabat-Zinn, 2005; and Roemer, Orsillo, & Salters-Pedneault, 2008; respectively) is expected to promote emotional awareness and clarity, as clients are encouraged to observe their emotions as they occur in the moment and label them objectively. Through this process, clients increase their contact with these emotions and focus attention on the different components of their emotional responses, which is expected to increase their emotional awareness. Further, the process of describing emotions is expected to facilitate the ability to identify, label, and differentiate between emotional states.

Moreover, the emphasis on letting go of evaluations, such as "good" or "bad," and taking a nonjudgmental and nonevaluative stance toward one's emotions is expected to facilitate emotional acceptance and increase the willingness to experience these emotions. Specifically, given that the evaluation of emotions as bad or wrong likely both motivates attempts to avoid emotions and leads to the development of secondary emotional responses (such as fear or shame; Greenberg & Safran, 1987), learning to approach emotions in a nonjudgmental way is expected to increase the willingness to experience emotions and decrease secondary emotional reactions. Indeed, it is likely this nonevaluative stance, in which stimuli are described as simply what is, rather than as bad or good, that underlies many of the potential benefits of observing and describing one's emotions.

Mindfulness training may also promote the decoupling of emotions and behaviors, teaching clients that emotions can be experienced and tolerated without necessarily acting on them. As such, these skills may facilitate the ability to control one's behaviors in the context of emotional distress (one of the dimensions of emotion regulation as defined here). One factor thought to interfere with this ability is the experience of emotions as inseparable from behaviors, such that the emotion and the behavior that occurs in response to that emotion are experienced as one (e.g., anger and throwing things, or anxiety and taking an anxiolytic). Thus, the process of observing one's emotions and their associated action urges is thought to increase awareness of the separateness of emotions and the behaviors that often accompany them, facilitating the ability to control one's behaviors when distressed.

Another element of some acceptance-based treatments that is expected to promote a more adaptive approach to emotional experience is the emphasis on the function of emotions. Specifically, several treatments include psychoeducation on the fact that emotions are evolutionarily adaptive and provide important information about the environment that can be used to guide behavior and inform an appropriate course of action (e.g., Gratz & Gunderson, 2006; Linehan, 1993; Roemer & Orsillo, 2005, 2007). These treatments teach clients that connecting with and acting on the information provided by their emotions in an adaptive way facilitates more effective engagement with and responses to their environment. This emphasis on the functionality of emotions is expected to increase emotional acceptance.

Finally, the emphasis on emotional willingness (defined as an active process of being open to emotional experiences as they arise) within several acceptance-based treatments (including DBT, ACT, ABBT for generalized anxiety disorder, and acceptance-based emotion regulation group therapy; see Linehan, 1993; Hayes et al., 1999; Roemer et al., 2008; and Gratz & Gunderson, 2006; respectively) is also expected to promote emotion regulation. In particular, given that emotional nonacceptance and avoidance may amplify emotions and contribute to the experience of emotions as undesirable and negative, practicing emotional acceptance and willingness is expected to increase emotion regulation and reduce emotional suffering (which includes secondary emotional responses and failed attempts at the control or avoidance of emotions). Further, emotional willingness likely serves as a form of nonreinforced exposure to emotions, increasing tolerance for previously avoided and feared emotions.

Despite the theoretical links between adaptive emotion regulation and these commonly targeted processes within acceptance- and mindfulness-based interventions (as well as the clear relevance of these treatments to various dimensions of emotion regulation), few studies have examined whether and to what extent these treatments do indeed affect emotion regulation. One factor that may have contributed to the lack of research in this area was the absence (until recently) of comprehensive measures of emotion regulation based on a conceptualization of this construct that is theoretically consistent with the treatments of interest. Indeed, only by identifying and utilizing measures based on an acceptance-based conceptualization of emotion regulation that emphasizes the functionality of emotions can the potential mediating role of emotion regulation as a process of change in acceptance- and mindfulness-based treatments be examined.

AN ACCEPTANCE-BASED MEASURE OF EMOTION REGULATION DIFFICULTIES

One measure that may be useful in this regard is the Difficulties in Emotion Regulation Scale (DERS; Gratz & Roemer, 2004), a comprehensive measure of difficulties in emotion regulation based on the conceptualization of emotion regulation described above. The DERS (included as an appendix to this chapter) is a thirty-six-item self-report measure that assesses individuals' typical levels of emotion regulation difficulties both in general and across a number of specific dimensions. Individuals are asked to indicate how often the items apply to them, with responses ranging from 1 to 5, where 1 is almost never (0 to 10 percent), 2 is sometimes (11 to 35 percent), 3 is about half the time (36 to 65 percent), 4 is most of the time (66 to 90 percent), and 5 is almost always (91 to 100 percent). The DERS is scored so that the overall score, as well as all subscale scores, reflect greater difficulties in emotion regulation. It provides a total score (ranging from 36 to 180) that represents overall difficulties in emotion regulation, as well as scores on six subscales:

1. Nonacceptance of emotional responses; e.g., "When I'm upset, I feel ashamed with myself for feeling that way." (Scores range from 6 to 30.)

2. Difficulties engaging in goal-directed behaviors when distressed; e.g., "When I'm upset, I have difficulty getting work done." (Scores range from 5 to 25.)

3. Difficulties controlling impulsive behaviors when distressed; e.g., "When I'm upset, I lose control over my behaviors." (Scores range from 6 to 30.)

4. Lack of emotional awareness; e.g., "I pay attention to how I feel [reverse scored]." (Scores range from 6 to 30.)

5. Limited access to emotion regulation strategies perceived as effective; e.g., "When I'm upset, I know that I can find a way to eventually feel better [reverse scored]." (Scores range from 8 to 40.)

6. Lack of emotional clarity; e.g., "I have difficulty making sense out of my feelings." (Scores range from 5 to 25.)

In terms of reliability, the overall DERS score as well as the subscale scores have been found to have high internal consistency within both clinical populations (e.g., Fox et al., 2007; Gratz, Tull, Baruch, Bornovalova, & Lejuez, 2008; McDermott et al., 2009) and nonclinical populations (e.g., Gratz & Roemer, 2004; Johnson et al., 2008). In addition, the DERS has demonstrated good test-retest reliability over a period of four to eight weeks (with an intraclass correlation coefficient of 0.88; Gratz & Roemer, 2004).

In support of the construct validity of this measure, scores on the DERS have been found to be significantly associated with a variety of behaviors thought to serve an emotion-regulating function, including deliberate self-harm (Gratz & Chapman, 2007; Gratz & Roemer, 2008), chronic worry

(Salters-Pedneault et al., 2006; Vujanovic et al., 2008), intimate partner abuse perpetration by men (Gratz, Paulson, Jakupcak, & Tull, 2009), binge eating (Whiteside et al., 2007), and cocaine dependence (Fox et al., 2007). Further, scores on the DERS have been found to be heightened among individuals with psychiatric disorders thought to be characterized by emotion regulation difficulties, including BPD (vs. outpatients without a personality disorder; Gratz, Rosenthal, et al., 2006); co-occurring BPD and substance dependence (vs. substance users without BPD; Gratz et al., 2008); probable PTSD (vs. trauma-exposed individuals without PTSD; Tull, Barrett, et al., 2007); and panic attacks (vs. nonpanickers; Tull & Roemer, 2007). Finally, the DERS demonstrates significant associations with a number of factors thought to be related to emotion regulation difficulties, including positive associations with negative affect (Cisler, Olatunji, & Lohr, 2009; Johnson et al., 2008; Vujanovic et al., 2008), depression and anxiety symptoms (Roemer et al., 2009; Tull et al., 2009; Vujanovic et al., 2008), anxiety sensitivity (Johnson et al., 2008; McDermott et al., 2009; Tull, 2006; Tull et al., 2009; Vujanovic et al., 2008), and experiential avoidance (Gratz & Roemer, 2004; Tull & Gratz, 2008; Tull & Roemer, 2007); and negative associations with emotional expression and processing (Johnson et al., 2008), mindfulness (see Baer, Smith, Hopkins, Krietemeyer, & Toney, 2006; Roemer et al., 2009), and self-compassion (Roemer et al., 2009).

The DERS and its subscales have also been found to be associated with behavioral, neurological, and experimental measures of related constructs. For example, the emotional nonacceptance subscale of the DERS has been found to predict performance on two behavioral measures of the willingness to experience emotional distress (Gratz, Bornovalova, Delany-Brumsey, Nick, & Lejuez, 2007), as well as a behavioral measure of the ability to engage in goal-directed behaviors when distressed (Gratz, Rosenthal, et al., 2006). Further, scores on the DERS subscale of difficulties controlling impulsive behaviors when distressed have been found to be negatively associated with activation of the rostral anterior cingulate cortex (an area of the brain thought to be associated with inhibitory control) among cocaine-dependent patients (Li et al., 2008). Finally, the overall DERS score has been found to be strongly correlated with an experimental measure of emotion regulation among patients with BPD ($r = -0.63$; see Gratz, Rosenthal, et al., 2006). Finally, and of particular relevance to this chapter, DERS scores have been found to be sensitive to change over time (i.e., following short-term treatments). For example, Gratz, Lacroce, and Gunderson (2006) found significant and progressive improvements in emotion dysregulation (as assessed with the DERS) following one and three months of treatment in an integrative, step-down treatment program for BPD. Further, Fox and colleagues (2008) found significant improvements in scores on the emotional awareness and clarity subscales over the course of inpatient treatment for alcohol-dependent individuals. Finally, Fox and colleagues (2007) found that inpatient treatment for cocaine-dependent patients resulted in significant improvements in overall DERS scores, as well as the subscales of difficulties engaging in goal-directed behavior when distressed, limited access to emotion regulation strategies perceived as effective, and lack of emotional clarity.

Of note, as the literature on the DERS continues to grow, there is emerging evidence of standard average scores on the DERS within different clinical and nonclinical populations. Specifically, evidence suggests that nonclinical samples of college students and adults from the community average 75 to 80 on the DERS (Gratz & Roemer, 2004; Salters-Pedneault et al., 2006; Vujanovic et al., 2008), self-harming college students average 85 to 90 (Gratz & Chapman, 2007; Gratz & Roemer, 2008), treatment-seeking substance users average 85 to 90 (Fox et al., 2007; Gratz et al., 2008; Gratz & Tull, in press), individuals with panic attacks average 89 to 95 (Tull, 2006; Tull et al., 2009), individuals with generalized anxiety disorder (GAD) and probable GAD average 95 to 100 (Roemer et al., 2009; Salters-Pedneault et al., 2006), individuals with PTSD symptoms at a severity level consistent with a PTSD diagnosis average 100 to 105 (McDermott et al., 2009; Tull, Barrett, et al., 2007), and samples of outpatients with BPD average 125 (Gratz & Gunderson, 2006; Gratz, Rosenthal, et al., 2006).

Altogether, findings suggest that the DERS may be a useful measure for assessing changes in emotion regulation difficulties as a result of acceptance- and mindfulness-based treatments. Based on an acceptance-based conceptualization of emotion regulation, scores on the DERS have been found to be related in expected ways to the other processes of change examined in this book, evidencing significant positive associations with experiential avoidance and significant negative associations with mindfulness and self-compassion. Further, DERS scores have been found to be correlated with various forms of psychopathology and maladaptive behaviors thought either to stem from emotion dysregulation or to serve an emotion-regulating or emotionally avoidant function. Finally, findings that DERS scores are sensitive to change over time suggest that it may have utility in the assessment of mechanisms of change in treatment.

EVIDENCE FOR EMOTION REGULATION AS A MECHANISM OF CHANGE IN ACCEPTANCE- AND MINDFULNESS-BASED TREATMENTS

Given evidence that emotion regulation difficulties play a central role in numerous forms of psychopathology (Gratz, Rosenthal, et al., 2006; Roemer et al., 2009; Tull, Barrett, et al., 2007) and that adaptive emotion regulation is associated with greater emotional adjustment (Berking, Orth, Wupperman, Meier, & Caspar, 2008), treatments that promote adaptive emotion regulation may be expected to decrease psychopathology and increase well-being and adaptive functioning. Indeed, prospective studies have shown that the greater use of adaptive emotion regulation skills, such as emotional awareness, emotional acceptance, and the ability to engage in goal-directed behavior when distressed, predicts lower levels of negative affect and anxiety and higher levels of positive affect two weeks later (Berking et al., 2008). Although few studies to date have examined changes in emotion regulation processes as a result of acceptance- and mindfulness-based treatments, preliminary evidence suggests that these treatments may promote more adaptive emotion regulation across various patient populations.

Changes in Emotion Regulation Following Acceptance- and Mindfulness-Based Treatments

Improvements in emotion regulation have been reported following several brief acceptance- and mindfulness-based interventions. For example, Leahey and colleagues (2008) conducted a ten-week mindfulness-based cognitive behavioral group intervention for binge eating. The overarching goal of this intervention was to reduce the risk for negative health-related outcomes following bariatric surgery by increasing awareness of eating triggers and eating patterns (including the identification of internal experiences that precede binge eating), promoting mindful eating and mindfulness of emotions, and teaching adaptive emotion regulation skills. Findings of a small-scale trial among seven bariatric surgery patients indicated improvements in both binge eating and emotion regulation from pre- to post-treatment. Specifically, in addition to decreasing binge eating from clinical to non-clinical levels, this intervention resulted in meaningful improvements in all dimensions of emotion regulation difficulties assessed in the DERS, with the average overall DERS score decreasing from 99 to 85 over the course of treatment.

Tull, Schulzinger, Schmidt, Zvolensky, and Lejuez (2007) also found that participation in a brief acceptance- and mindfulness-based behavioral intervention was associated with reductions in emotion regulation difficulties. Specifically, these researchers examined the effects of a six-week adjunctive acceptance- and mindfulness-based behavioral intervention for heightened anxiety sensitivity among heroin-dependent patients in residential substance abuse treatment. This brief intervention combines two key components: psychoeducation about anxiety, anxiety sensitivity, and heroin use as a method of experiential avoidance, and interoceptive exposure exercises and skills training focused on heightening emotional acceptance, tolerance, and nonevaluative awareness (in order to facilitate willingness to experience anxiety and associated bodily sensations). In a preliminary case study of a long-term heroin user in residential substance abuse treatment, Tull, Schulzinger, and colleagues (2007) examined the impact of this treatment on anxiety sensitivity, heroin cravings, and emotion regulation difficulties. Their findings indicated reductions in all three areas from pre- to post-treatment. Of particular relevance to this chapter, the patient reported a decrease in emotion regulation difficulties as measured by the DERS, with scores decreasing from 88 (consistent with the average score reported among treatment-seeking substance users; Fox et al., 2007) to 70 (somewhat lower than the average score found among nonclinical samples; Gratz & Roemer, 2004).

Finally, providing further evidence for the utility of acceptance- and mindfulness-based treatments in promoting adaptive emotion regulation, research indicates clinically significant improvements in emotion regulation following completion of a fourteen-week acceptance-based emotion regulation group therapy for self-harming women with BPD. Developed specifically to treat self-harm by directly targeting the function of this behavior, this adjunctive group therapy teaches participants more adaptive ways of responding to their emotions (Gratz & Gunderson, 2006), systematically targeting each of the proposed dimensions of emotion regulation described above. In the preliminary trial of the efficacy of this treatment, female outpatients with BPD who engaged in recent, recurrent self-harm were randomly assigned to receive this group therapy in addition to their current outpatient therapy or to continue with their current outpatient therapy alone for fourteen weeks. These two conditions were then compared on outcome measures of emotion dysregulation, emotional avoidance, frequency of self-harm, severity of BPD symptoms, and severity of depression, anxiety, and stress symptoms (see Gratz & Gunderson, 2006). As expected, results indicated significant between-group differences (with large effect sizes) on all measures at post-treatment, with participants who received the group therapy in addition to their regular outpatient treatment evidencing significant improvements (with large effect sizes) on all measures. Further, the vast majority of participants who received the group therapy (83 percent) reached normative levels of functioning on the outcomes specifically targeted by the treatment: emotion dysregulation and experiential avoidance.

Evidence that adaptive emotion regulation increases following acceptance- and mindfulness-based treatments (Gratz & Gunderson, 2006; Leahey et al., 2008; Tull, Schulzinger, et al., 2007) suggests that problems stemming from emotion regulation difficulties may decrease as a result of these treatments and, conversely, aspects of functioning thought to be related to or facilitated by adaptive emotion regulation may increase. However, more direct support for emotion regulation as a mechanism of change in acceptance- and mindfulness-based treatments would be provided by findings that changes in emotion regulation mediate changes in psychiatric symptoms and adaptive functioning from pre- to post-treatment.

Emotion Regulation as a Mediator of Changes in Symptoms Following Acceptance- and Mindfulness-Based Treatments

Although little research has specifically examined the mediating role of changes in emotion regulation in symptom improvement following acceptance- and mindfulness-based treatments, preliminary data on the acceptance-based emotion regulation group therapy described above (see Gratz & Gunderson, 2006) provide suggestive support for this possibility. Specifically, we examined whether changes in emotion dysregulation and emotional avoidance mediated changes in self-harm frequency following completion of the group therapy. Mediation was examined using a cross product test, which directly tests the significance of the difference between the direct and indirect (mediated) effects. In particular, the mediational analyses used the nonparametric method of bootstrapping (which does not assume normal distribution of the cross product), with parameter estimates based on three thousand bootstrap samples specifically. Results of these mediational analyses indicate that changes in self-harm were mediated by changes in emotion dysregulation and emotional avoidance in total ($p < 0.05$). Further, individual mediators of changes in self-harm at post-treatment included emotional avoidance ($p < 0.05$) and two particular dimensions of emotion dysregulation: lack of access to effective emotion regulation strategies ($p < 0.05$) and difficulties controlling impulsive behaviors when distressed ($p < 0.07$).

Thus, although preliminary in nature and based on a small sample size, these findings provide initial support for the mediating role of changes in emotion regulation in symptom improvement following acceptance-based treatments.

CONCLUSIONS

Clinicians and researchers alike are increasingly acknowledging the potential benefits of incorporating acceptance- and mindfulness-based approaches into treatments for a variety of clinical disorders and maladaptive behaviors. As such, the past two decades have seen the development of innovative mindfulness- and acceptance-based treatments, including DBT, ACT, MBCT, MBSR, and ABBT for generalized anxiety disorder (GAD), among others. Further, research is beginning to provide convincing evidence for the utility of these interventions across a wide range of difficulties, including BPD (Lynch, Trost, Salsman, & Linehan, 2007), depression (Kenny & Williams, 2007; Teasdale et al., 2002), GAD (Roemer et al., 2008), panic disorder (Levitt & Karekla, 2005), PTSD (Orsillo & Batten, 2005), obsessive-compulsive disorder (Singh, Wahler, Winton, & Adkins, 2004), psychosis (Gaudiano & Herbert, 2006), substance use (Alterman, Koppenhaver, Mulholland, Ladden, & Baime, 2004; Witkiewitz, Marlatt, & Walker, 2005), generalized social anxiety disorder (Dalrymple & Herbert, 2007; Koszycki, Benger, Shlik, & Bradwejn, 2007), and bipolar disorder (Williams et al., 2008).

Although limited, the theoretical and empirical literature reviewed above suggests that one process through which acceptance- and mindfulness-based interventions may bring about behavioral change and symptom reduction is emotion regulation. Indeed, evidence suggests that a number of brief acceptance- and mindfulness-based treatments lead to improvements in emotion regulation difficulties, consistent with clinical literature on the central elements of these treatments and their theorized effects. Further, preliminary data on one acceptance-based treatment suggest that improvements in maladaptive behavior as a result of treatment were mediated by changes in emotion dysregulation and avoidance (Gratz & Gunderson, 2006). These findings build upon the rapidly growing body of literature demonstrating that emotion dysregulation is a clinically relevant construct that may play a central role in the development and maintenance of diverse forms of psychopathology, and highlight the importance of targeting emotion regulation difficulties within acceptance- and mindfulness-based interventions. Yet, despite the growing evidence for emotion regulation as a clinically relevant underlying etiological mechanism and treatment target, the research in this area is in its earliest stages and much remains to be explored.

In particular, although findings indicate that emotion dysregulation in general is associated with a variety of clinical difficulties, further research is needed to explore the specific dimensions of emotion regulation most relevant to various forms of psychopathology. Indeed, evidence for the unique role of different emotion regulation difficulties in specific clinical disorders and maladaptive behaviors would have important implications for the development of more targeted (and ultimately effective) interventions. Although research in this area is still in its infancy, preliminary findings provide evidence for the differential relevance of particular dimensions of emotion regulation difficulties to specific forms of psychopathology. For example, Salters-Pedneault and colleagues (2006) found that all dimensions of emotion regulation difficulties (with the exception of lack of emotional awareness) were significantly elevated among individuals with probable GAD (compared to those without GAD) when controlling for negative affect. On the other hand, only the specific dimensions of difficulties controlling impulsive behaviors when distressed, limited access to effective emotion regulation strategies, and lack of emotional clarity have been found to differ between trauma-exposed individuals with probable PTSD and those without PTSD when controlling for negative affect (Tull, Barrett, et al., 2007).

Further, research suggests that the relevance of specific dimensions of emotion dysregulation to deliberate self-harm may differ as a function of the individual's co-occurring psychiatric difficulties. Specifically, whereas emotional nonacceptance has been found to be associated with self-harm among inpatients with substance use disorders (Gratz & Tull, in press) and college students without BPD pathology (Gratz, Breetz, & Tull, in press), it is not associated with self-harm among individuals with clinically relevant levels of BPD pathology, for whom other dimensions of emotion dysregulation and the related factor of emotional inexpressivity emerge as most relevant (Gratz et al., in press). Likewise, findings suggest that difficulties engaging in goal-directed behaviors when distressed may be particularly relevant to self-harm among patients with substance use disorders (Gratz & Tull, in press). The specific dimension of lack of access to effective emotion regulation strategies, on the other hand, appears to be relevant to self-harm in general (regardless of the individual's BPD or substance use disorder diagnostic status; Gratz et al., in press; Gratz & Tull, in press). Further research examining the unique role of specific dimensions of emotion dysregulation in the development and maintenance of psychopathology has the potential to inform the development of targeted interventions for a variety of clinical difficulties.

Finally, it will be important for research to continue to examine the extent to which conceptualizations of emotion regulation overlap with the related constructs of mindfulness, acceptance, willingness, and experiential avoidance. Only by elucidating the distinct and overlapping dimensions of these constructs will we be able to establish the unique role each plays in the pathogenesis of psychopathology and promotion of emotional health. In support of this line of inquiry, Roemer and colleagues (2009) found that despite a strong association between emotion regulation and mindfulness, each explained a substantial amount of unique variance in the severity of symptoms of GAD. Continued clarification of the conceptualization of these related constructs may aid in the refinement of existing measures, as well as the development of new methods for assessing emotion regulation, willingness, acceptance, and mindfulness in both clinical and basic research. Further, an improved understanding of the conceptualization and assessment of these various constructs may facilitate the refinement of existing treatment protocols by increasing our ability to dismantle acceptance- and mindfulness-based treatments and identify their active components.

REFERENCES

Alterman, A. I., Koppenhaver, J. M., Mulholland, E., Ladden, L. J., & Baime, M. J. (2004). Pilot trial of effectiveness of mindfulness meditation for substance abuse patients. *Journal of Substance Use, 9*, 259-268.

Baer, R. A., Smith, G. T., Hopkins, J., Krietemeyer, J., & Toney, L. (2006). Using self-report assessment methods to explore facets of mindfulness. *Assessment, 13*, 27-45.

Berking, M., Orth, U., Wupperman, P., Meier, L. L., & Caspar, F. (2008). Prospective effects of emotion regulation skills on emotional adjustment. *Journal of Counseling Psychology, 55*, 485-494.

Chapman, A. L., Gratz, K. L., & Brown, M. Z. (2006). Solving the puzzle of deliberate self-harm: The experiential avoidance model. *Behaviour Research and Therapy, 44*, 371-394.

Cisler, J. M., Olatunji, B. O., & Lohr, J. M. (2009). Disgust sensitivity and emotion regulation potentiate the effect of disgust propensity on spider fear, blood-injection-injury fear, and contamination fear. *Journal of Behavior Therapy and Experimental Psychiatry, 40*, 219-229.

Cole, P. M., Michel, M. K., & Teti, L. O. (1994). The development of emotion regulation and dysregulation: A clinical perspective. In N. A. Fox (Ed.), *The development of emotion regulation: Biological and behavioral considerations. Monographs of the Society for Research in Child Development, 59* (Serial No. 240).

Dalrymple, K. L., & Herbert, J. D. (2007). Acceptance and commitment therapy for generalized social anxiety disorder: A pilot study. *Behavior Modification, 31*, 543-568.

Flett, G. L., Blankstein, K. R., & Obertynski, M. (1996). Affect intensity, coping styles, mood regulation expectancies, and depressive symptoms. *Personality and Individual Differences, 20*, 221-228.

Fox, H. C., Axelrod, S. R., Paliwal, P., Sleeper, J., & Sinha, R. (2007). Difficulties in emotion regulation and impulse control during cocaine abstinence. *Drug and Alcohol Dependence, 89*, 298-301.

Fox, H. C., Hong, K. A., & Sinha, R. (2008). Difficulties in emotion regulation and impulse control in recently abstinent alcoholics compared with social drinkers. *Addictive Behaviors, 33*, 388-394.

Gaudiano, B. A., & Herbert, J. D. (2006). Acute treatment of inpatients with psychotic symptoms using acceptance and commitment therapy: Pilot results. *Behaviour Research and Therapy, 44*, 415-437.

Gratz, K. L. (2006). Risk factors for deliberate self-harm among female college students: The role and interaction of childhood maltreatment, emotional inexpressivity, and affect intensity/reactivity. *American Journal of Orthopsychiatry, 76*, 238-250.

Gratz, K. L., Breetz, A., & Tull, M. T. (in press). The moderating role of borderline personality in the relationships between deliberate self-harm and emotion-related factors. *Personality and Mental Health.*

Gratz, K. L., Bornovalova, M. A., Delany-Brumsey, A., Nick, B., & Lejuez, C. W. (2007). A laboratory-based study of the relationship between childhood abuse and experiential avoidance among inner-city substance users: The role of emotional nonacceptance. *Behavior Therapy, 38*, 256-268.

Gratz, K. L., & Chapman, A. L. (2007). The role of emotional responding and childhood maltreatment in the development and maintenance of deliberate self-harm among male undergraduates. *Psychology of Men and Masculinity, 8*, 1-14.

Gratz, K. L., & Gunderson, J. G. (2006). Preliminary data on an acceptance-based emotion regulation group intervention for deliberate self-harm among women with borderline personality disorder. *Behavior Therapy, 37*, 25-35.

Gratz, K. L., Lacroce, D. M., & Gunderson, J. G. (2006). Measuring changes in symptoms relevant to borderline personality disorder following short-term treatment across partial hospital and intensive outpatient levels of care. *Journal of Psychiatric Practice, 12*, 153-159.

Gratz, K. L., Paulson, A., Jakupcak, M., & Tull, M. T. (2009). Exploring the relationship between childhood maltreatment and intimate partner abuse: Gender differences in the mediating role of emotion dysregulation. *Violence and Victims, 24*, 68-82.

Gratz, K. L., & Roemer, L. (2004). Multidimensional assessment of emotion regulation and dysregulation: Development, factor structure, and initial validation of the Difficulties in Emotion Regulation Scale. *Journal of Psychopathology and Behavioral Assessment, 26*, 41-54.

Gratz, K. L., & Roemer, L. (2008). The relationship between emotion dysregulation and deliberate self-harm among female undergraduate students at an urban commuter university. *Cognitive Behaviour Therapy, 37*, 14-25.

Gratz, K. L., Rosenthal, M. Z., Tull, M. T., Lejuez, C. W., & Gunderson, J. G. (2006). An experimental investigation of emotion dysregulation in borderline personality disorder. *Journal of Abnormal Psychology, 115*, 850-855.

Gratz, K. L., & Tull, M. T. (in press). The relationship between emotion dysregulation and deliberate self-harm among inpatient substance users. *Cognitive Therapy and Research.*

Gratz, K. L., Tull, M. T., Baruch, D. E., Bornovalova, M. A., & Lejuez, C. W. (2008). Factors associated with co-occurring borderline personality disorder among inner-city substance users: The roles of childhood maltreatment, negative affect intensity/reactivity, and emotion dysregulation. *Comprehensive Psychiatry, 49*, 603-615.

Greenberg, L. S., & Safran, J. D. (1987). *Emotions in psychotherapy.* New York: Guilford.

Hayes, S. C., Luoma, J. B., Bond, F. W., Masuda, A., & Lillis, J. (2006). Acceptance and commitment therapy: Model, processes, and outcomes. *Behaviour Research and Therapy, 44*, 1-25.

Hayes, S. C., Strosahl, K. D., & Wilson, K. G. (1999). *Acceptance and commitment therapy: An experiential approach to behavior change.* New York: Guilford.

Johnson, K. A., Zvolensky, M. J., Marshall, E. C., Gonzalez, A., Abrams, K., & Vujanovic, A. A. (2008). Linkages between cigarette smoking outcome expectancies and negative emotional vulnerability. *Addictive Behaviors, 33*, 1416-1424.

Kabat-Zinn, J. (2005). *Full catastrophe living: Using the wisdom of your body and mind to face stress, pain, and illness.* New York: Delta Trade Paperback/Bantam Dell.

Kenny, M. A., & Williams, J. M. G. (2007). Treatment-resistant depressed patients show a good response to mindfulness-based cognitive therapy. *Behaviour Research and Therapy, 45*, 617-625.

Kopp, C. B. (1989). Regulation of distress and negative emotions: A developmental view. *Developmental Psychology, 25*, 343-354.

Koszycki, D., Benger, M., Shlik, J., & Bradwejn, J. (2007). Randomized trial of a meditation-based stress reduction program and cognitive behavior therapy in generalized social anxiety disorder. *Behaviour Research and Therapy, 45*, 2518-2526.

Larsen, R. J., & Diener, E. (1987). Affect intensity as an individual difference characteristic: A review. *Journal of Research in Personality, 21*, 1-39.

Larsen, R. J., Diener, E., & Emmons, R. A. (1986). Affect intensity and reactions to daily life events. *Journal of Personality and Social Psychology, 51*, 803-814.

Leahey, T. M., Crowther, J. H., & Irwin, S. R. (2008). A cognitive-behavioral mindfulness group therapy intervention for the treatment of binge eating in bariatric surgery patients. *Cognitive and Behavioral Practice, 15*, 364-375.

Levitt, J. T., & Karekla, M. (2005). Integrating acceptance and mindfulness with cognitive behavioral treatment for panic disorder. In S. M. Orsillo & L. Roemer (Eds.), *Acceptance- and mindfulness-based approaches to anxiety: Conceptualization and treatment*. New York: Springer.

Li, C. R., Huang, C., Yan, P., Bhagwagar, Z., Milivojevic, V., & Sinha, R. (2008). Neural correlates of impulse control during stop signal inhibition in cocaine-dependent men. *Neuropsychopharmacology, 33*, 1798-1806.

Linehan, M. M. (1993). *Cognitive-behavioral treatment of borderline personality disorder*. New York: Guilford.

Livesley, W. J., Jang, K. L., & Vernon, P. A. (1998). Phenotypic and genetic structure of traits delineating personality disorder. *Archives of General Psychiatry, 55*, 941-948.

Lynch, T. R., Trost, W. T., Salsman, N., & Linehan, M. M. (2007). Dialectical behavior therapy for borderline personality disorder. *Annual Review of Clinical Psychology, 3*, 181-205.

McDermott, M. J., Tull, M. T., Gratz, K. L., Daughters, S. B., & Lejuez, C. W. (2009). The role of anxiety sensitivity and difficulties in emotion regulation in posttraumatic stress disorder among crack/cocaine-dependent patients in residential substance abuse treatment. *Journal of Anxiety Disorders, 23*, 591-599.

Melnick, S. M., & Hinshaw, S. P. (2000). Emotion regulation and parenting in AD/HD and comparison boys: Linkages with social behaviors and peer preference. *Journal of Abnormal Child Psychology, 28*, 73-86.

Mennin, D. S. (2006). Emotion regulation therapy: An integrative approach to treatment-resistant anxiety disorders. *Journal of Contemporary Psychotherapy, 36*, 95-105.

Mennin, D. S., Heimberg, R. G., Turk, C. L., & Fresco, D. M. (2005). Preliminary evidence for an emotion dysregulation model of generalized anxiety disorder. *Behaviour Research and Therapy, 43*, 1281-1310.

Orsillo, S. M., & Batten, S. V. (2005). Acceptance and commitment therapy in the treatment of posttraumatic stress disorder. *Behavior Modification, 29*, 95-129.

Putnam, K. A., & Silk, K. R. (2005). Emotion dysregulation and the development of borderline personality disorder. *Development and Psychopathology, 17*, 899-925.

Roemer, L., Lee, J. K., Salters-Pedneault, K., Erisman, S. M., Orsillo, S. M., & Mennin, D. S. (2009). Mindfulness and emotion regulation difficulties in generalized anxiety disorder: Preliminary evidence for independent and overlapping contributions. *Behavior Therapy, 40*, 142-154.

Roemer, L., & Orsillo, S. M. (2005). An acceptance-based behavior therapy for generalized anxiety disorder. In S. M. Orsillo & L. Roemer (Eds.), *Acceptance- and mindfulness-based approaches to anxiety: Conceptualization and treatment.* New York: Springer.

Roemer, L., & Orsillo, S. M. (2007). An open trial of an acceptance-based behavior therapy for generalized anxiety disorder. *Behavior Therapy, 38*, 72-85.

Roemer, L., Orsillo, S. M., & Salters-Pedneault, K. (2008). Efficacy of an acceptance-based behavioral therapy for generalized anxiety disorder: Evaluation in a randomized controlled trial. *Journal of Consulting and Clinical Psychology, 76*, 1083-1089.

Salters-Pedneault, K., Roemer, L., Tull, M. T., Rucker, L., & Mennin, D. S. (2006). Evidence of broad deficits in emotion regulation associated with chronic worry and generalized anxiety disorder. *Cognitive Therapy and Research, 30*, 469-480.

Salters-Pedneault, K., Tull, M. T, & Roemer, L. (2004). The role of avoidance of emotional material in the anxiety disorders. *Applied and Preventive Psychology, 11*, 95-114.

Segal, Z. V., Williams, J. M. G., & Teasdale, J. D. (2002). *Mindfulness-based cognitive therapy for depression: A new approach to preventing relapse.* New York: Guilford.

Singh, N. N., Wahler, R. G., Winton, A. S. W., & Adkins, A. D. (2004). A mindfulness-based treatment of obsessive-compulsive disorder. *Clinical Case Studies, 3*, 275-287.

Teasdale, J. D., Moore, R. G., Hayhurst, H., Pope, M., Williams, S., & Segal, Z. V. (2002). Metacognitive awareness and prevention of relapse in depression: Empirical evidence. *Journal of Consulting and Clinical Psychology, 70*, 275-287.

Thompson, R. A. (1994). Emotion regulation: A theme in search of definition. In N. A. Fox (Ed.), *The development of emotion regulation: Biological and behavioral considerations. Monographs of the Society for Research in Child Development, 59* (Serial No. 240).

Thompson, R. A., & Calkins, S. D. (1996). The double-edged sword: Emotional regulation *for* children at risk. *Development and Psychopathology, 8*, 163-182.

Tull, M. T. (2006). Extending an anxiety sensitivity model of uncued panic attack frequency and symptom severity: The role of emotion dysregulation. *Cognitive Therapy and Research, 30*, 177-184.

Tull, M. T., Barrett, H. M., McMillan, E. S., & Roemer, L. (2007). A preliminary investigation of the relationship between emotion regulation difficulties and posttraumatic stress symptoms. *Behavior Therapy, 38*, 303-313.

Tull, M. T., & Gratz, K. L. (2008). Further examination of the relationship between anxiety sensitivity and depression: The mediating role of experiential avoidance and difficulties engaging in goal-directed behavior when distressed. *Journal of Anxiety Disorders, 22*, 199-210.

Tull, M. T., & Roemer, L. (2007). Emotion regulation difficulties associated with the experience of uncued panic attacks: Evidence of experiential avoidance, emotional nonacceptance, and decreased emotional clarity. *Behavior Therapy, 38*, 378-391.

Tull, M. T., Schulzinger, D., Schmidt, N. B., Zvolensky, M. J., & Lejuez, C. W. (2007). Development and initial examination of a brief intervention for heightened anxiety sensitivity among heroin users. *Behavior Modification, 31*, 220-242.

Tull, M. T., Stipelman, B. A., Salters-Pedneault, K., & Gratz, K. L. (2009). An examination of recent non-clinical panic attacks, panic disorder, anxiety sensitivity, and emotion regulation difficulties in the prediction of generalized anxiety disorder in an analogue sample. *Journal of Anxiety Disorders, 23*, 275-282.

Vujanovic, A. A., Zvolensky, M. J., & Bernstein, A. (2008). The interactive effects of anxiety sensitivity and emotion dysregulation in predicting anxiety-related cognitive and affective symptoms. *Cognitive Therapy and Research, 32*, 803-817.

Wegner, D. M. (1994). Ironic processes of mental control. *Psychological Review, 101*, 34-52.

Wegner, D. M., Schneider, D. J., Carter, S. R., & White, T. L. (1987). Paradoxical effects of thought suppression. *Journal of Personality and Social Psychology, 53*, 5-13.

Whiteside, U., Chen, E., Neighbors, C., Hunter, D., Lo, T., & Larimer, M. (2007). Difficulties regulating emotions: Do binge eaters have fewer strategies to modulate and tolerate negative affect? *Eating Behaviors, 8*, 162-169.

Williams, J. M. G., Alatiq, Y., Crane, C., Barnhofer, T., Fennell, M. J. V., Duggan, D. S., et al. (2008). Mindfulness-based cognitive therapy (MBCT) in bipolar disorder: Preliminary evaluation of immediate effects on between-episode functioning. *Journal of Affective Disorders, 107*, 275-279.

Witkiewitz, K., Marlatt, G. A., & Walker, D. (2005). Mindfulness-based relapse prevention for alcohol and substance use disorders. *Journal of Cognitive Psychotherapy, 19*, 211-228.

Zanarini, M. C., Frankenburg, F. R., Hennen, J., & Silk, K. R. (2003). The longitudinal course of borderline psychopathology: 6-year prospective follow-up of the phenomenology of borderline personality disorder. *American Journal of Psychiatry, 160*, 274-283.

Zeman, J., & Garber, J. (1996). Display rules for anger, sadness, and pain: It depends on who is watching. *Child Development, 67*, 957-973.

APPENDIX: DIFFICULTIES IN EMOTION REGULATION SCALE

Below are some statements about emotions and how you cope with emotional situations. Read each statement and choose a response that indicates how much each one applies to you.

1	2	3	4	5
Almost Never	Sometimes	About half the time	Most of the time	Almost always

_______ 1. I am clear about my feelings.

_______ 2. I pay attention to how I feel.

_______ 3. I experience my emotions as overwhelming and out of control.

_______ 4. I have no idea how I am feeling.

_______ 5. I have difficulty making sense out of my feelings.

_______ 6. I am attentive to my feelings.

_______ 7. I know exactly how I am feeling.

_______ 8. I care about what I am feeling.

_______ 9. I am confused about how I feel.

_______ 10. When I'm upset, I acknowledge my emotions.

_______ 11. When I'm upset, I become angry with myself for feeling that way.

_______ 12. When I'm upset, I become embarrassed for feeling that way.

_______ 13. When I'm upset, I have difficulty getting work done.

_______ 14. When I'm upset, I become out of control.

_______ 15. When I'm upset, I believe that I will remain that way for a long time.

_______ 16. When I'm upset, I believe that I'll end up feeling very depressed.

_______ 17. When I'm upset, I believe that my feelings are valid and important.

_______ 18. When I'm upset, I have difficulty focusing on other things.

_______ 19. When I'm upset, I feel out of control.

_______ 20. When I'm upset, I can still get things done.

_______ 21. When I'm upset, I feel ashamed with myself for feeling that way.

_______ 22. When I'm upset, I know that I can find a way to eventually feel better.

_______ 23. When I'm upset, I feel like I am weak.

_______ 24. When I'm upset, I feel like I can remain in control of my behaviors.

_______ 25. When I'm upset, I feel guilty for feeling that way.

_______ 26. When I'm upset, I have difficulty concentrating.

_______ 27. When I'm upset, I have difficulty controlling my behaviors.

_______ 28. When I'm upset, I believe that there is nothing I can do to make myself feel better.

_______ 29. When I'm upset, I become irritated with myself for feeling that way.

________ 30. When I'm upset, I start to feel very bad about myself.

________ 31. When I'm upset, I believe that wallowing in it is all I can do.

________ 32. When I'm upset, I lose control over my behaviors.

________ 33. When I'm upset, I have difficulty thinking about anything else.

________ 34. When I'm upset, I take time to figure out what I'm really feeling.

________ 35. When I'm upset, it takes me a long time to feel better.

________ 36. When I'm upset, my emotions feel overwhelming.

SCORING

(Note: R = reverse-scored item)

Lack of emotional awareness: Sum 2R, 6R, 8R, 10R, 17R, and 34R.

Lack of emotional clarity: Sum 1R, 4, 5, 7R, and 9.

Nonacceptance of emotional responses: Sum 11, 12, 21, 23, 25, and 29.

Difficulties engaging in goal-directed behavior: Sum 13, 18, 20R, 26, and 33.

Impulse control difficulties: Sum 3, 14, 19, 24R, 27, and 32.

Limited access to emotion regulation strategies: Sum 15, 16, 22R, 28, 30, 31, 35, and 36.

CHAPTER 5

Self-Compassion as a Mechanism of Change in Mindfulness- and Acceptance-Based Treatments

Ruth A. Baer, University of Kentucky

Self-compassion is closely related to mindfulness. Both are important concepts in Buddhist writings about human suffering and how to relieve it (Kornfield, 1993), and both have recently become topics of great interest in Western psychology. Westerners tend to think of compassion as a feeling of caring, concern, or sympathy extended to others who are suffering (Neff, 2004). We admire people who are compassionate toward others and believe that kindness is an important character strength (Peterson & Seligman, 2004). On the other hand, we also seem to think that too much compassion toward the self is inadvisable because it will lead to "letting yourself get away with anything" (Neff, 2003b, p. 226). Accordingly, people are often harsh and unkind to themselves during difficult times, blaming and criticizing themselves in ways that would seem cruel if directed toward others (Germer, 2009; Neff, 2003a). Buddhist psychology regards the self and others as interdependent and maintains that without compassion for the self it isn't possible to extend compassion to others. A growing evidence base suggests that self-compassion is associated with numerous aspects of healthy psychological functioning and that it can be cultivated through skills and practices that are helpful in a variety of populations.

DEFINING SELF-COMPASSION

Buddhist-based descriptions of compassion (toward self or others) are largely consistent with contemporary definitions. In the Buddhist tradition, compassion involves awareness and understanding of the suffering or distress of others and a desire to alleviate it. It includes the recognition that failings and inadequacies are universal human experiences and an openhearted willingness to face the suffering of others rather than denying or turning away from it (Goldstein & Kornfield, 2001). In Western psychology, the definition of self-compassion that is most consistent with Buddhist thought has been articulated by Neff (2003a), who describes self-compassion as a multifaceted construct with three essential elements: treating oneself kindly and without harsh judgment; recognizing that mistakes, failures, and hardships are part of the common human experience; and maintaining a balanced awareness of painful thoughts and feelings rather than avoiding, suppressing, or overidentifying with them.

Another definition is offered by McKay and Fanning (2000), who suggest that compassion in general, and self-compassion in particular, is a set of three skills: understanding, acceptance, and forgiveness. As applied to the self, understanding refers to insights about how experiences, thoughts, feelings, and behaviors all influence each other in ways that make sense, even if the results at any given moment are undesirable. Acceptance refers to full acknowledgment of the facts of a situation without judgment or evaluation. Self-forgiveness, which arises out of understanding and acceptance, includes recognition of personal wrongdoing, learning from one's mistakes, letting go of self-blame, and moving forward with strong intentions to do better in the future.

Another way of defining self-compassion comes from the work of Gilbert and colleagues (Gilbert, 2000; Gilbert & Irons, 2004, 2005; Gilbert & Procter, 2006), who developed compassionate mind training, a form of psychotherapy that emphasizes the development of self-compassion. Their conceptualization of self-compassion is rooted in biologically based capacities for caring for others, believed to have evolved because they contribute to survival. These capacities include a desire to care for others, sensitivity to distress (ability to recognize it in others), sympathy (being emotionally moved by others' distress), tolerance of distress (willingness to be aware of others' distress rather than trying to avoid or escape it), empathy (understanding the source of others' distress and what is required to alleviate it), nonjudgment (not being critical of the situation or the behavior of those who are distressed), and an emotional tone of warmth. Self-compassion is the application of these capacities to one's own experience. That is, self-compassionate people have genuine concern for their own well-being, are sensitive and sympathetic to their own distress, can tolerate their distress without self-criticism or judgment, understand the causes of their distress, and treat themselves with warmth. Gilbert and Procter (2006) also note that people can learn to recognize self-compassion as a desirable quality and work to cultivate their self-compassion skills as a way of improving their mental health.

Because self-compassion has received little attention in Western psychological literature until very recently, it's helpful to consider how it differs from better-known characteristics. Neff (2003a) provides a useful discussion of several processes that are distinct from self-compassion. For example, self-compassion is not self-centeredness. Because self-compassion includes acknowledging that suffering and inadequacies are part of the universal human experience, it is believed to encourage feelings of compassion for others rather than a self-centered focus on one's own concerns. Self-compassion also can be distinguished from self-pity, which often includes a self-absorbed quality and a tendency to forget that many others have suffered in similar ways. Self-pity can also involve overidentification, in which the individual becomes excessively immersed in negative emotion and unable to adopt an objective perspective. Self-compassion also doesn't imply a self-indulgent, lazy, or passive approach to personal flaws or weaknesses. True self-compassion includes the desire to heal oneself kindly, and therefore encourages patient and gentle efforts to change behavior to correct mistakes or weaknesses that cause harm or distress to oneself or others. Although many people seem to believe that harshness toward the self is necessary to motivate these efforts, self-condemnation can be so unpleasant that it may lead to avoidance of self-observation and self-awareness, which will interfere with the adaptive behaviors required for growth and change.

A critically important distinction can be made between self-compassion and self-esteem (Neff & Vonk, 2008). Self-esteem results from an evaluative process in which personal abilities, performance, or characteristics are compared to standards. These comparisons lead to judgments about personal value or worth in domains that are believed to be important (work, school, relationships, appearance, and so on). Self-esteem often involves social comparisons in which personal competencies or attributes are compared to those of others, and it sometimes relies on the opinions of others, so that self-esteem is increased if the respect or approval of others is apparent. A large body of literature shows that low self-esteem is related to numerous psychological difficulties (Harter, 1999). Accordingly, many efforts to improve self-esteem have been described in the research literature and the popular press (e.g., McKay & Fanning, 2000), and it is clear that challenging distorted negative evaluations of the self can be beneficial (Fennell, 2004). Healthy forms of self-esteem have been identified. Deci and Ryan (1995) describe a form of true self-esteem that is self-determined and autonomous and doesn't depend on social approval or the outcomes of situations. Similarly, Kernis (2003) suggests that optimal self-esteem is founded on stable and noncontingent self-evaluations. However, it is also clear that high self-esteem can be maladaptive. It may be related to narcissism, self-absorption, and a lack of concern for others (Seligman, 1995). In attempts to preserve their self-esteem, people may engage in maladaptive behaviors, such as ignoring, dismissing, or reacting aggressively to constructive feedback or viewpoints that differ from their own (Baumeister, Smart, & Boden, 1996). They also may engage in downward social comparisons in a way that leads to increased prejudice against others (Neff & Vonk, 2008).

Self-compassion, therefore, is a way of relating to oneself that isn't based on evaluation, performance standards, or the approval of others. It motivates constructive behavior out of a sense of caring for oneself and others rather than from a need for higher achievements, greater recognition, or better performance than others. It avoids the problematic outcomes of negative self-judgment, discourages self-centeredness, and promotes connection to others by recognizing that hardships and failures are universal human experiences.

ASSESSING SELF-COMPASSION

Neff (2003b) developed the Self-Compassion Scale (SCS) to measure three distinct but closely related components of self-compassion. *Self-kindness* refers to extending kindness and understanding to oneself, rather than harsh self-criticism. *Common humanity* is the recognition that suffering is part of the universal human experience and need not lead to isolation or disconnection from others. *Mindfulness* refers to holding negative thoughts and emotions in balanced awareness rather than overidentifying with them. Scale items were written to reflect these three components. Factor analyses revealed that positively and negatively worded items formed separate factors, so the scale includes six intercorrelated subscales. The self-kindness subscale assesses the tendency to be kind, patient, and understanding toward oneself when feeling emotional pain or experiencing failure. Negatively worded items that describe the opposite of self-kindness comprise the self-judgment scale, which assesses the tendency to be self-critical, disapproving, and intolerant toward one's flaws and difficult experiences. The common humanity subscale measures the recognition that feelings of failure, inadequacy, and emotional pain are shared by most others, whereas the isolation subscale measures feelings of separation, aloneness, and disconnection from others at times of failure or distress. The mindfulness subscale assesses the tendency to take a balanced view, keep things in perspective, and be open and accepting toward difficult feelings and situations, whereas the overidentification subscale assesses the tendency to get carried away with or consumed by negative feelings. Negatively worded items are reverse scored so that higher scores represent higher levels of self-compassion.

In a large sample of students (Neff, 2003b), each subscale had adequate to good internal consistency. Factor analyses suggested that the six subscales all represent elements of the overarching construct of self-compassion. The SCS total score wasn't correlated with a measure of social desirability, suggesting that responses weren't influenced by an intention to create a positive impression. Consistent with predictions, total score on the SCS was negatively correlated with measures of self-criticism, anxiety, depression, and neurotic perfectionism and positively correlated with measures of social connectedness, emotional intelligence, and life satisfaction. Self-compassion wasn't significantly correlated with a tendency to set high personal standards, suggesting that self-compassion doesn't encourage people to set either lower or higher standards for themselves; rather it encourages them to treat themselves with kindness and understanding when they fall short of their standards. In this study, women had significantly lower self-compassion scores than men. In particular, women had higher scores on the subscales measuring self-judgment, isolation, and overidentification, and lower scores on the mindfulness subscale. These differences are consistent with the well-established tendency for women to be more self-critical and ruminative than men.

In a second sample of students, Neff (2003b) found good test-retest reliability for the SCS over a three-week interval, suggesting that responses are reasonably consistent over time. As predicted, self-compassion was moderately correlated with self-esteem. However, whereas the self-esteem measures were also correlated with a measure of narcissism, self-compassion wasn't correlated with narcissism. These findings suggest that self-compassion is distinct from self-esteem and doesn't include feeling superior to others. Self-compassion was a significant predictor of mental health after controlling for self-esteem and was negatively correlated with rumination and suppression of thoughts, suggesting that self-compassionate individuals neither avoid nor become excessively entangled with their negative thoughts and emotions.

Overall, these results suggest that the SCS is sufficiently reliable and valid to justify its use in additional studies of self-compassion, and that self-compassion is an adaptive attitude toward the self that facilitates psychological health. The SCS is available at www.self-compassion.org.

SELF-COMPASSION AND OTHER ASPECTS OF PSYCHOLOGICAL FUNCTIONING

Subsequent studies using the SCS have shown interesting relationships between self-compassion and other aspects of psychological functioning. For example, Neff, Kirkpatrick, and Rude (2007) asked students to participate in a mock job interview in which they wrote for several minutes about their greatest weakness. Students with higher self-compassion scores reported less anxiety immediately after this task, even after controlling for baseline levels of general negative affect. Thus, the results suggested that high self-compassion is an effective buffer against situational anxiety elicited by this task. This pattern wasn't found for self-esteem scores. Analyses of the writing samples showed that students with higher self-compassion scores also used fewer first-person singular pronouns (I, me, my) and more first-person plural pronouns (we). They also used more words referring to friends, family, and communications with others, suggesting a less isolated and more interconnected view of themselves. Self-esteem scores, in contrast, were not significantly related to these aspects of the writing samples. Finally, self-compassion scores weren't correlated with the use of negative emotion words (nervous, sad, angry) in the writing sample, suggesting that self-compassion doesn't necessarily reflect low levels or avoidance of negative affect during the task. Rather, it appears that self-compassionate individuals recognized the negative affect elicited by the task but responded with greater awareness of the commonality of such experiences and thus felt less anxious afterward.

In another interesting study, Adams and Leary (2007) investigated the effects of self-compassion on restrained eaters who had just eaten a forbidden food. Restrained eaters are consistently trying to limit their food intake, are often on diets, and have many rules about what foods to eat and to avoid. Research indicates that restrained eaters show a paradoxical reaction to violating their diet rules. When they eat a forbidden food, they often show a disinhibition effect in which they eat even more afterward, perhaps to distract themselves from the self-criticism and negative emotion occasioned by the diet violation, which they perceive as a stressful experience. This effect has been seen in numerous studies in which both restrained and unrestrained eaters are asked to consume a high-calorie food, such as a milkshake, and then asked to do taste ratings of another food, such as candy. Unrestrained eaters tend to eat less candy during the taste test if they've just had a milkshake, probably because they feel satiated. In contrast, restrained eaters typically eat more candy during the taste test if they've just had a milkshake, perhaps because they feel distressed about consuming the milkshake and their resolve to avoid forbidden foods is temporarily weakened.

Adams and Leary (2007) asked female college students to eat a doughnut while viewing a video, ostensibly to learn more about eating while watching TV. Afterward, the experimenter spoke to half of them in a way designed to induce a feeling of self-compassion, stating that although people sometimes feel guilty about eating a doughnut, everyone eats unhealthfully at times and a single doughnut makes little difference, so there's no need to feel bad about it. The other participants didn't hear this message. Next, all participants were provided with bowls of small candies and asked to complete a taste-rating form. They were told that they could eat as much of the candy as they liked. The candies remained available while participants completed a final questionnaire. The restrained eaters who didn't hear the self-compassion induction showed the typical disinhibition effect. That is, they felt more distress about eating the doughnut and ate more candy during the taste test and while completing the final questionnaire. However, restrained eaters who had heard the self-compassion message showed the opposite pattern. They reported less distress about eating the doughnut and ate less candy during the rest of the experiment. These results suggest that even a very brief self-compassion induction can counteract the usual self-criticism and harsh judgments that typically lead restrained eaters to overeat following a diet violation.

Other studies have shown many correlations between high levels of self-compassion and healthy psychological functioning. For example, high levels of self-compassion are related to feelings of autonomy, competence, optimism, wisdom, curiosity, personal initiative, and positive affect. People with high self-compassion scores show higher levels of motivation to learn and grow for intrinsic reasons rather than for the approval of others or to avoid failure (Neff, Hsieh, & Dejitterat, 2005). They show greater relationship satisfaction and attachment security. Overall, this body of literature provides convincing evidence that self-compassion is related to psychological health and well-being (see Neff, 2009, for an overview).

RELATIONSHIPS BETWEEN SELF-COMPASSION AND MINDFULNESS

Mindfulness is generally defined as a type of nonjudgmental and accepting attention that is brought to bear on experiences occurring in the present moment, including internal phenomena such as sensations, cognitions, and emotions, and external stimuli such as sights, sounds, and smells (see chapter 1 in this volume for more detail). The relationship between mindfulness and self-compassion has been described in several ways. Some authors suggest that adopting a mindful stance toward experiences of the present moment includes an attitude of self-compassion or self-kindness. For example, Kabat-Zinn (2003) notes that the words for mind and heart are the same in Asian languages and that mindful attention to present-moment experience "includes an affectionate, compassionate quality within the attending, a sense of openhearted friendly presence and interest" (p. 145). Similarly, Marlatt and Kristeller (1999) suggest that mindfulness involves paying attention to one's immediate experience with an attitude of acceptance and loving-kindness.

Others, however, have cautioned against confusing the central elements of mindfulness with common outcomes of practicing mindfulness, or with skills or attitudes that may be helpful in cultivating mindful states. For example, Bishop and colleagues (2004) suggest that self-compassion may be a result of practicing mindfulness over time, rather than a component of mindfulness. Brown, Ryan, and Creswell (2007) make a similar point, suggesting that compassion may be an outcome associated with mindfulness or an attitude that aids in cultivating mindfulness.

In Neff's conceptualization (2003a), mindfulness is one of three components of self-compassion. All three components are essential, and all are described as reciprocally facilitating and enhancing each other. A mindful stance toward ongoing experience is necessary for feelings of self-kindness and common humanity to arise. That is, in order to respond to painful thoughts and emotions in a compassionate way, it is necessary to observe and acknowledge them as they occur, without either suppressing them or becoming excessively caught up in them. In addition, the nonjudgmental stance that is inherent to mindfulness reduces self-criticism, which allows feelings of kindness and common humanity to grow. Thus, mindfulness is required for the other two components to be present. At the same time, however, the other two components are believed to facilitate mindfulness. Self-kindness and the recognition that suffering is universal are likely to reduce the perceived severity or impact of negative thoughts and emotions, which will lessen the temptation to avoid, suppress, or deny them and make it easier to maintain mindful awareness of them without ruminating about them.

EFFECTS OF MINDFULNESS TRAINING ON SELF-COMPASSION

It seems clear that self-compassion is an adaptive way of relating to oneself and that mindfulness and self-compassion are closely related. Therefore, it is important to consider whether the types of mindfulness training that are offered in current mindfulness- and acceptance-based interventions lead to increases in self-compassion. Three studies have examined this question.

Shapiro, Astin, Bishop, and Cordova (2005) provided mindfulness-based stress reduction (MBSR; Kabat-Zinn, 1982, 1990), an eight-week group intervention based on the intensive practice of mindfulness meditation exercises, to a group of health care professionals. Participants were physicians, nurses, social workers, physical therapists, and psychologists who were interested in reducing stress and professional burnout and increasing overall well-being. They were randomly assigned to MBSR or to a wait-list control group. The MBSR group showed a significant increase in self-compassion over the eight-week period, whereas the control group didn't. The MBSR group also showed greater reductions in perceived stress. Results suggest that increased self-compassion may be a mechanism through which the intervention led to reductions in perceived stress. However, only ten participants completed the MBSR course. The small sample size makes it impossible to draw firm conclusions about the mechanisms of change.

Shapiro, Brown, and Biegel (2007) studied the effects of MBSR in a group of therapists in training in a master's program in counseling psychology. Participants weren't randomized but were compared to a group of students in the same graduate program who didn't complete the MBSR program. Participants in the MBSR program showed significant decreases in perceived stress, negative affect, anxiety, and rumination, and increases in positive affect, mindfulness, and self-compassion. Degree of change in mindfulness was correlated with degree of change in self-compassion, rumination, anxiety, and perceived stress, suggesting that increased mindfulness may be at least partially responsible for the other positive outcomes. However, a full mediational analysis was not conducted, and therefore firm conclusions about mediation cannot be drawn.

Moore (2008) examined the effects of brief mindfulness exercises on self-compassion in a group of first-year trainees in clinical psychology. The goal of this study was to develop a mindfulness course that was less time-consuming than traditional MBSR, which typically requires weekly two-hour sessions for eight weeks. In this case, participants met for fourteen short sessions during their lunch hour over a one-month period. Participants completed the self-compassion scale before and after this short course, as well as measures of mindfulness and perceived stress. A significant increase on the self-kindness subscale of the SCS was noted, but no change was seen for the other subscales or for the total score. Mindfulness increased slightly, but perceived stress did not change. Again, however, only ten participants completed the course, and means and standard deviations were not provided in the paper. Furthermore, the mindfulness training wasn't provided by an experienced teacher. Instead, during each session a script for a mindfulness exercise was read by one of the participants, and it appears that no group discussion of experiences was conducted. It is therefore difficult to draw conclusions about the effects of the mindfulness training on self-compassion levels in this study. The lack of change in perceived stress, which is usually found in studies of MBSR, combined with the lack of an experienced teacher and group discussion, suggests that the mindfulness training may have been less effective than in MBSR.

If mindfulness meditation cultivates self-compassion, then long-term practitioners should show higher scores on the SCS than short-term practitioners or nonmeditators. A few studies have tested this idea. Neff (2003b) compared self-compassion scores from a sample of forty-three Buddhists with a long-term meditation practice to those from a nonmeditating student sample and found higher scores in the meditators for all SCS subscales and for the total score, even after controlling for self-esteem. The two samples differed only marginally on self-esteem, suggesting that Buddhist meditation practices cultivate self-compassion much more than self-esteem.

Lykins and Baer (2009) included the SCS and many other measures in a study of psychological functioning in a sample of 182 long-term practitioners of mindfulness meditation. This group had much higher levels of education than seen in the general population, and many worked in mental health or medical professions. Therefore, a comparison group with similar demographic characteristics, including level of education and professional training and experience, but with no history of regular meditation practice, completed the same measures. The experienced meditators scored significantly higher than the nonmeditators on the SCS. In addition, duration of meditation experience was significantly correlated with SCS scores, even after controlling for age, education, and experience in the mental health field. These findings are consistent with the idea that mindfulness meditation encourages the development of self-compassion.

Conflicting findings were reported by Ortner, Kilner, and Zelazo (2007), who found that self-compassion wasn't correlated with duration of meditation experience in a sample recruited from a Buddhist meditation center. However, this study had a much smaller sample size (only twenty-eight) and didn't include a nonmeditating comparison group.

Overall, this group of studies provides preliminary evidence that mindfulness training may enhance self-compassion. However, these findings must be interpreted cautiously, for several reasons. Because comparisons between long-term meditation practitioners and nonmeditating control groups have all been cross-sectional, these studies cannot rule out the possibility that people who are naturally higher in self-compassion are more likely to take up and maintain the practice of meditation. And even if mindfulness training does lead to increased self-compassion, it isn't entirely clear how this happens. Perhaps the cultivation of mindfulness skills leads naturally to the emergence of self-compassion. If so, the processes that account for this need clarification. However, it's also possible that increases in self-compassion are encouraged by meditation practices that are more explicitly intended to cultivate compassion toward self and others. These practices, particularly loving-kindness meditation, are closely related to mindfulness meditation and are often included in MBSR. Buddhist meditation centers also provide guidance and instruction in loving-kindness meditation. Therefore, it's likely that long-term practitioners of mindfulness meditation have had at least some exposure to loving-kindness practices.

LOVING-KINDNESS AND COMPASSION MEDITATION

As mentioned, loving-kindness meditation, an ancient Buddhist practice from the Theravadan tradition, is closely related to mindfulness meditation (Salzberg, 1995). Its purpose is to cultivate feelings of warmth and kindness toward oneself and others. Like other forms of meditation, it is typically practiced while sitting still, often with the eyes closed or gazing softly at a neutral point. Attention is first directed toward the flow of the breath. Participants then picture someone who loves or has loved them unconditionally and experience the associated feelings of warmth and caring. If they can't bring such a person to mind, they may imagine someone treating them that way or contemplate a person toward whom they feel unconditional love. They then extend these warm and loving feelings toward themselves, often repeating (silently and inwardly) a sequence of phrases, such as "May I be healthy," "May I be happy," "May I be safe," and "May I be peaceful." After extending loving-kindness to themselves for a few minutes, participants then shift their focus to someone they love and repeat the phrases for this person ("May she be happy" and so on) while radiating feelings of caring and goodwill toward this person. Over time, either within a session or across multiple sessions, attention is shifted to casual acquaintances or strangers, to people whom they dislike or have had difficult interactions with, and ultimately to all living beings. Unlike mindfulness meditation, which involves simply attending, in a nonjudgmental and accepting way, to the experiences that are present in each moment, loving-kindness meditation invites participants to do something in particular: to repeat specific phrases while imagining specific people or other living beings and cultivating feelings of warmth and caring.

Some MBSR teachers include loving-kindness meditation in the eight-week course, while others do not. If it is included, it's most commonly introduced during the all-day weekend session that some programs offer during week six. A recent review of thirty studies of MBSR (Carmody & Baer, 2009) found that thirteen of them (43 percent) included the all-day session. In some cases, this was a half-day session, and many didn't report whether loving-kindness meditation was practiced during the session. Thus, it isn't clear how often loving-kindness meditation is included in MBSR, and the empirical literature hasn't examined the effects on psychological outcomes of including loving-kindness meditation in MBSR.

A few studies, however, have examined the effects of loving-kindness meditation as an intervention in its own right. Carson and colleagues (2005) developed and tested an eight-week loving-kindness meditation program for adults with chronic lower back pain. The intervention included eight weekly ninety-minute group sessions. Loving-kindness exercises were practiced each week and assigned for homework practice. Sessions also included presentation of didactic information about pain, anger, and other topics and group discussion about practicing the meditations and applying loving-kindness in daily life. Patients were randomly assigned to this intervention or to the routine care provided by their medical outpatient programs. Those in the loving-kindness program showed significant improvements in pain and psychological distress, whereas those who received the usual care didn't. Daily reports on practice and symptoms showed that greater loving-kindness practice on a given day was associated with lower pain that day and lower anger ratings the following day. Overall, the results suggested that the practice of loving-kindness meditation may reduce pain, anger, and psychological distress in chronic pain patients.

Fredrickson, Cohn, Coffey, Pek, and Finkel (2008) studied the effects of a seven-week loving-kindness meditation intervention in a nonclinical sample of employees at an information technology services company. Participants were randomly assigned to the intervention or to a waitlist control group who received the intervention after the study ended. The meditation training included six sixty-minute group sessions with twenty to thirty members per group. Each session included a guided meditation, discussion, and presentation of didactic information about applying loving-kindness in daily life. Participants were asked to practice at home, with recordings for guidance, at least five days per week. Results showed that loving-kindness meditation produced steady increases over time in the daily experience of positive emotions, which in turn led to increases in numerous aspects of adaptive functioning, including mindfulness, purpose in life, and social support, among others. These changes predicted increased life satisfaction and reduced depressive symptoms. Findings are consistent with Fredrickson's broaden-and-build theory of positive emotions (2001), which suggests that positive emotions temporarily broaden people's attention and thinking, allowing them to take on new ideas and perspectives that help them build personal resources and abilities that in turn contribute to increased happiness and well-being. This study also provides strong support for an increase in positive emotions as a result of daily practice of loving-kindness meditation.

Several other studies have examined the effects of loving-kindness meditation or compassion meditation. Hutcherson, Seppala, and Gross (2008) found that a seven-minute loving-kindness meditation in a laboratory setting led to an increase in positive mood and increased ratings of connectedness with a neutral stranger. Johnson and colleagues (2009) reported three clinical case studies suggesting that loving-kindness meditation may be useful to patients with schizophrenia. However, they noted that two of the patients had difficulty with concentration during the loving-kindness meditations and opted to practice mindfulness meditation instead. They suggested that previous experience with mindfulness meditation may be necessary for this population to engage in loving-kindness meditation. Finally, Pace and colleagues (2009) studied a form of compassion meditation based on Tibetan Buddhist practices that differ somewhat from the loving-kindness practices described earlier. This approach uses cognitive, analytic methods to challenge unexamined thoughts and feelings about other people, such as the commonly held view that people can be categorized as friends, enemies, or strangers. Practices designed to cultivate spontaneous feelings of empathy and love for oneself and others also are incorporated. In the study by Pace and colleagues (2009), undergraduate students participated in these practices twice a week over six weeks, and home practice was encouraged. Participants who engaged in more home practice showed less negative emotion and healthier immune function following a stressful laboratory task in which they gave a short speech and performed mental arithmetic before an audience.

Unfortunately none of the studies of loving-kindness or compassion meditation have included measures of self-compassion. It is therefore impossible to conclude whether participants' levels of self-compassion increased or whether an increase in self-compassion was responsible for the other positive outcomes.

OTHER WAYS OF TEACHING SELF-COMPASSION

McKay and Fanning (2000) describe a cognitive behavioral approach to increasing self-esteem that includes methods designed to cultivate self-compassion. When faced with situations that normally elicit judgmental, self-critical thoughts (e.g., "I'm incompetent"), they suggest that participants think through a series of questions and statements designed to promote understanding, acceptance, and forgiveness of themselves. In this way, judgmental thoughts are replaced with statements such as "I'm sorry this happened, but it was merely an attempt to meet my needs" and "It's over, I can let go of it" (McKay & Fanning, 2000, p. 93). They also describe a form of compassion meditation that involves sitting quietly with eyes closed, practicing relaxation, visualizing oneself clearly, and directing compassionate messages toward oneself.

Compassionate mind training (Gilbert & Procter, 2006), described earlier, is a form of psychotherapy for adults with high levels of shame and self-criticism. Its overriding goal is to help participants develop self-compassion so that they can feel safe enough to engage in therapeutic work without being overwhelmed by feelings of shame and threat. It seeks to change an internalized dominating and attacking style in which internal self-criticism functions like external social stimuli, eliciting stress, anxiety, and depressive symptoms along with shame and its associated desire to hide or conceal oneself. Compassionate mind training attempts to replace this entire pattern with a caring and compassionate way of relating to oneself when distressed. Its methods include teaching clients to generate caring, reassuring, and soothing thoughts and images, along with feelings of warmth, sympathy, and acceptance toward oneself. It includes many methods that are consistent with cognitive behavioral therapy, including psychoeducation, self-monitoring of thoughts and feelings, testing ideas, and behavioral practice. It also includes elements of mindfulness- and acceptance-based treatments, such as decentering and acceptance. Preliminary findings have shown significant reductions in psychological symptoms, including shame and self-criticism, and increased ability to self-soothe in the presence of self-critical thoughts (Gilbert & Procter, 2006). Although self-compassion per se wasn't measured in this study, the observed changes in self-criticism, self-soothing, and self-reassurance are consistent with improvements in self-compassion.

CONCLUSIONS

Self-compassion is closely related to mindfulness, and like mindfulness, it can be cultivated through meditation practices that originate in the Buddhist tradition and have been adapted for secular use in Western settings. Methods of teaching self-compassion that aren't based on Buddhist meditation have also been developed. Self-compassion is clearly an adaptive way of relating to the self and is associated with many aspects of psychological well-being. The evidence that self-compassion is a mediator of change in mindfulness- and acceptance-based treatments isn't as strong as for other potential mechanisms, such as mindfulness or psychological flexibility. Full mediation analyses haven't been conducted. However, the research shows that mindfulness training can lead to increases in self-compassion and that increased self-compassion is associated with improved well-being and healthy psychological functioning. Future research must conduct more rigorous mediation analyses. It is also important to clarify the extent to which self-compassion overlaps with mindfulness, and whether mindfulness and self-compassion make independent contributions to healthy psychological functioning.

REFERENCES

Adams, C. E., & Leary, M. R. (2007). Promoting self-compassionate attitudes toward eating among restrictive and guilty eaters. *Journal of Social and Clinical Psychology, 26*, 1120-1144.

Baumeister, R. F., Smart, L., & Boden, J. M. (1996). Relation of threatened egotism to violence and aggression: The dark side of high self-esteem. *Psychological Review, 103*, 5-33.

Bishop, S. R., Lau, M., Shapiro, S., Carlson, L., Anderson, N. C., Carmody, J., et al. (2004). Mindfulness: A proposed operational definition. *Clinical Psychology: Science and Practice, 11*, 230-241.

Brown, K. W., Ryan, R. M., & Creswell, D. J. (2007). Mindfulness: Theoretical foundations and evidence for its salutary effects. *Psychological Inquiry, 18*, 211-237.

Carmody, J., & Baer, R. A. (2009). How long does a mindfulness-based stress reduction program need to be? A brief review of class contact hours and effect sizes for psychological distress. *Journal of Clinical Psychology, 65*, 627-638.

Carson, J. W., Keefe, F. J., Lynch, T. R., Carson, K. M., Goli, V., Fras, A. M., et al. (2005). Loving-kindness meditation for chronic low back pain. *Journal of Holistic Nursing, 23*, 287-304.

Deci, E. L., & Ryan, R. M. (1995). Human autonomy: The basis for true self-esteem. In M. H. Kernis (Ed.), *Efficacy, agency, and self-esteem*. New York: Plenum.

Fennell, M. J. V. (2004). Depression, low self-esteem, and mindfulness. *Behaviour Research and Therapy, 42*, 1053-1067.

Fredrickson, B. L. (2001). The role of positive emotions in positive psychology: The broaden-and-build theory of positive emotions. *American Psychologist, 56*, 218-226.

Fredrickson, B. L., Cohn, M. A., Coffey, K. A., Pek, J., & Finkel, S. M. (2008). Open hearts build lives: Positive emotions, induced through loving-kindness meditation, build consequential personal resources. *Journal of Personality and Social Psychology, 95*, 1045-1062.

Germer, C. K. (2009). *The mindful path to self-compassion: Freeing yourself from destructive thoughts and emotions*. New York: Guilford.

Gilbert, P. (2000). Social mentalities: Internal "social" conflicts and the role of inner warmth and compassion in cognitive therapy. In P. Gilbert & K. G. Bailey (Eds.), *Genes on the couch: Explorations in evolutionary psychotherapy*. Hove, UK: Brunner-Routledge.

Gilbert, P., & Irons, C. (2004). A pilot exploration of the use of compassionate images in a group of self-critical people. *Memory, 12*, 507-516.

Gilbert, P., & Irons, C. (2005). Focused therapies and compassionate mind training for shame and self-attacking. In P. Gilbert (Ed.), *Compassion: Conceptualizations, research, and use in psychotherapy*. London: Routledge.

Gilbert, P., & Procter, S. (2006). Compassionate mind training for people with high shame and self-criticism: Overview and pilot study of a group therapy approach. *Clinical Psychology and Psychotherapy, 13*, 353-379.

Goldstein, J., & Kornfield, J. (2001). *Seeking the heart of wisdom: The path of insight meditation*. Boston: Shambhala.

Harter, S. (1999). *The construction of the self: A developmental perspective*. New York: Guilford.

Hutcherson, C. A., Seppala, E. M., & Gross, J. J. (2008). Loving-kindness meditation increases social connectedness. *Emotion, 8*, 720-724.

Johnson, D. P., Penn, D. L., Fredrickson, B. L., Meyer, P. S., Kring, A. M., & Brantley, M. (2009). Loving-kindness meditation to enhance recovery from negative symptoms of schizophrenia. *Journal of Clinical Psychology, 65*, 499-509.

Kabat-Zinn, J. (1982). An outpatient program in behavioral medicine for chronic pain patients based on the practice of mindfulness meditation. *General Hospital Psychiatry, 4*, 33-47.

Kabat-Zinn, J. (1990). *Full catastrophe living: Using the wisdom of your body and mind to face stress, pain, and illness.* New York: Delacorte.

Kabat-Zinn, J. (2003). Mindfulness-based interventions in context: Past, present, and future. *Clinical Psychology: Science and Practice, 10*, 144-156.

Kernis, M. H. (2003). Optimal self-esteem and authenticity: Separating fantasy from reality. *Psychological Inquiry, 14*, 83-89.

Kornfield, J. (1993). *A path with heart.* New York: Bantam Books.

Lykins, E. L., & Baer, R. A. (2009). Psychological functioning in a sample of long-term practitioners of mindfulness meditation. *Journal of Cognitive Psychotherapy, 23*, 226-241.

Marlatt, G. A., & Kristeller, J. L. (1999). Mindfulness and meditation. In W. R. Miller (Ed.), *Integrating spirituality into treatment.* Washington, DC: American Psychological Association.

McKay, M., & Fanning, P. (2000). *Self-esteem* (3rd ed.). Oakland, CA: New Harbinger.

Moore, P. (2008). Introducing mindfulness to clinical psychologists in training: An experiential course of brief exercises. *Journal of Clinical Psychology in Medical Settings, 15*, 331-337.

Neff, K. D. (2003a). Self-compassion: An alternative conceptualization of a healthy attitude toward oneself. *Self and Identity, 2*, 85-101.

Neff, K. D. (2003b). The development and validation of a scale to measure self-compassion. *Self and Identify, 2*, 223-250.

Neff, K. D. (2004). Self-compassion and psychological well-being. *Constructivism in the Human Sciences, 9*, 27-37.

Neff, K. D. (2009). Self-compassion. In M. R. Leary & R. H. Hoyle (Eds.). *Handbook of individual differences in social behavior*. New York: Guilford.

Neff, K. D., Hsieh, Y., & Dejitterat, K. (2005). Self-compassion, achievement goals, and coping with academic failure. *Self and Identity, 4*, 263-287.

Neff, K. D., Kirkpatrick, K. L., & Rude, S. S. (2007). Self-compassion and adaptive psychological functioning. *Journal of Research in Personality, 41*, 139-154.

Neff, K. D., & Vonk, R. (2008). Self-compassion versus global self-esteem: Two different ways of relating to oneself. *Journal of Personality, 77*, 23-50.

Ortner, C. N. M., Kilner, S., & Zelazo, P. D. (2007). Mindfulness meditation and reduced emotional interference on a cognitive task. *Motivation and Emotion, 31*, 271-283.

Pace, T. W. W., Negi, L. T., Adame, D. D., Cole, S. P., Sivilli, T. I., Brown, T. D. et al. (2009). Effect of compassion meditation on neuroendocrine, innate immune and behavioral responses to psychosocial stress. *Psychoneuroendocrinology, 34*, 87-98.

Peterson, C., & Seligman, M. E. P. (2004). *Character strengths and virtues: A handbook and classification*. New York: Oxford University Press.

Salzberg, S. (1995). *Loving-kindness: The revolutionary art of happiness*. Boston: Shambhala.

Seligman, M. E. (1995). *The optimistic child*. Boston: Houghton Mifflin.

Shapiro, S. L., Astin, J. A., Bishop, S. R., & Cordova, M. (2005). Mindfulness-based stress reduction for health care professionals: Results from a randomized trial. *International Journal of Stress Management, 12*, 164-176.

Shapiro, S. L., Brown, K. W., & Biegel, G. M. (2007). Teaching self-care to caregivers: Effects of mindfulness-based stress reduction on the mental health of therapists in training. *Training and Education in Professional Psychology, 1*, 105-115.

Chapter 6

Spiritual Engagement as a Mechanism of Change in Mindfulness- and Acceptance-Based Therapies

Jean L. Kristeller, Indiana State University

As spiritual growth is becoming increasingly accepted as a valid therapeutic goal, an increasing range of therapeutic approaches are directing attention to explicitly engaging the spiritual dimension and measuring spirituality as an outcome variable (Miller, 1999; Miller & Thoreson, 2003). It is only in the contemporary context that wholly secular meditation practices have developed. Therefore, it is impossible to consider the full value of meditation or mindfulness practice without considering the role and the psychology of spiritual experience, even if spiritual and religious goals are no longer viewed as essential to meditative practice (Bond et al., 2009; Seeman, Dubin, & Seeman, 2003). Not only do all current meditative practices derive from religious traditions, but the purported effects of meditative practice, such as emotional equanimity, heightened compassion for others, and engaging in "right action," overlap substantially with what is generally considered religious or spiritual experience.

At the same time, much of the writing about meditation and spirituality or religion draws explicitly on Buddhist formulations regarding human nature (Rosch, 2002). Many of the most prominent writers in the mindfulness meditation tradition, including Jack Kornfield (1993), Joseph Goldstein (2002), Thich Nhat Hanh (1975), and Sylvia Boorstein (2003), repeatedly address the relationship between formal meditative practice, spiritual engagement, and ways to bring mindfulness into all aspects of life. Spiritual effects of meditation may exist separately and yet interact with or contribute to effects of meditation in other domains, such as physical health, emotional or behavioral regulation, or relationship to self or others. The empirical literature that links the development of spiritual engagement to meditation and other mindfulness practices is limited but growing. It is indeed somewhat ironic that while innumerable traditional sources address meditation as a spiritual practice, there is still less empirical research on this aspect of meditation than virtually any of the other well-recognized domains of effects (Bond et al., 2009; Kristeller, 2003). There are several reasons for this: First, over the last forty years efforts to introduce meditation practices as therapeutic approaches, such as Jon Kabat-Zinn's mindfulness-based stress reduction (MBSR) program (1990), have generally, and understandably, been directed at secularizing meditation as much as possible, separating various approaches from their religious roots, primarily in Buddhism and Hinduism. At the same time, much of the empirical work in the psychology of religion has been generated from a Christian perspective and rarely addresses the effects of meditative or contemplative practice. And while the potential role of spirituality as a mediator in acceptance-based therapies has been noted (Dimidjian & Linehan, 2003; Hayes, 1984), spirituality generally hasn't been examined empirically within either acceptance and commitment therapy (ACT; Hayes, Strosahl, & Wilson, 1999) or dialectical behavior therapy (DBT; Linehan, 1993). Yet exploring this aspect of mindfulness and related practices may contribute profoundly to a fuller understanding of the potential benefits of cultivating mindfulness, both within the therapeutic context and as an aspect of basic psychological processes (Rosch, 2002).

Furthermore, as interest grows in considering spirituality within the context of psychotherapy (Miller, 1999) and looking at universal elements of spiritual experience, it is increasingly apparent that exploring the spiritual aspects of meditation is important to a full understanding of meditation as a psychological process (Rubin, 1996; Welwood, 2000). As will be discussed below, a core aspect of the how we address this question depends on how spirituality is defined—an issue of considerable debate. This chapter will take the perspective that spiritual experience is a universal human capacity, although varying from individual to individual in the degree to which it exists and might be cultivated, whether through meditation or by other means. This chapter will also consider how understanding the spiritual aspects of meditation might enhance therapeutic applications of meditation and, in doing so, further illuminate some of the underlying psychological processes in both mindfulness- and acceptance-based therapies.

DEFINITIONS OF SPIRITUALITY

The first challenge is to consider what is meant by the term "spirituality." Efforts to define spiritual or religious experience from a psychological perspective have a long history. Perspectives that William James first expressed in 1902 in *The Varieties of Religious Experience*, which were influenced by his interest in Eastern practices, have garnered renewed interest and respect after being largely supplanted in the mid-twentieth century by a focus on religious attitudes, beliefs, and activities. The value of examining spirituality as a psychological process entirely distinct from religious content has been gaining ground, particularly in light of the developing neuroscience of spiritual experience (Newberg & Waldman, 2009; Vaillant, 2008) that suggests this may be a universal human capacity which, while expressed in religious frameworks, can exist separately from them.

Efforts to define the distinctions between religion and spirituality as viable and measurable constructs have been challenging. Although a growing number of individuals identify themselves as spiritual but not religious, the majority of Americans identify themselves as both religious and spiritual, challenging the measurement of each as a distinct process. Nevertheless, the two concepts, although overlapping for many, have come to be viewed as psychologically distinct. Individuals participating in meditation or mindfulness-based therapies are likely to represent the full range of self-identity in regard to seeing themselves as being spiritual, religious, both, or neither. This must be considered in regard to both measuring spirituality and understanding the role of spirituality and the impact of meditation practice.

The distinction between spirituality and religion may be relatively narrow, as in the widely used framework developed by Hill and Pargament (2003). They characterize spirituality as a search for or engagement with the sacred via experience of a divine being or object, "ultimate reality," or "ultimate truth." Their definition of religion is similar, but with the addition of rituals, beliefs, and community. Other definitions of spirituality, as will be reviewed below, focus more on the emotional tone of the experience or on a shift in experience of self, largely independent of religious experience or a sense of the transcendent.

A diverse range of experience is encompassed within the scope of spirituality, from the readily accessible to the dramatic. In considering how meditative practice or mindfulness might affect spirituality, it is obviously very important to distinguish among such experiences, as they may relate quite differently to shifts in other types of response, whether cognitive, emotional, or physical, and to different types or levels of practice (Seeman et al., 2003). Relatively accessible experiences involve feelings of awe, feelings of inner peace, perceiving higher levels of meaning, experiencing a sense of unity, engaging the sacred, or the spontaneous flowing of compassion and altruistic love (Post, 2003). Somewhat more unusual effects fall within the sphere of peak experience, originally expounded by Maslow (1962). More dramatic, and generally associated with intense meditative practice, are mystical experiences characterized by altered states of consciousness and a sense of profound inner transformation and enlightenment. From a different perspective, spirituality has been associated with the loosening of sense of self; this definition is particularly compatible with Buddhist psychology.

Clearly, spirituality is conceptualized in many distinct and sometimes divergent ways. For the purposes of this chapter, key definitions include the following:

- A sense of inner peace
- Love, compassion, and connectedness
- Peak experience
- No-self
- A connection to a higher meaning
- A sense of the sacred
- Mystical experience
- A sense of transcendent awareness of a higher being or of linking to a higher being

Among these definitions, the first five might be applied entirely outside the realm of religious belief and could be subsumed under other types of functioning (emotional regulation, a caring relationship with others, basic cognitive processes). The final three definitions remain more closely linked to religious experience. Overall, the range of these definitions is striking, especially given that each may point to distinct underlying processes, and therefore different conclusions regarding the interface of meditation and spirituality.

APPROACHES TO MEASURING SPIRITUALITY AND RELIGIOUSNESS

Efforts to empirically measure distinct aspects of spirituality and religiousness date back a number of decades. Allport first proposed his influential model of intrinsic versus extrinsic religiousness in 1950. In 1984 Gorsuch raised the concern that the plethora of measures published at that point largely overlapped, positing that most of these measures tapped into subfactors of a single superordinate general religion/spirituality factor. However, measures of religion/spirituality have continued to multiply, with Hill and Hood (1999) reviewing 120 in their handbook of measures of religiousness (they reserved review of measures of spirituality for a forthcoming second volume). More recently, Pargament's positive and negative religious coping framework has contributed substantively to the literature (Pargament, Koenig, & Perez, 2000), and spirituality has been identified as a key variable to assess in adjustment to illness with the development of the Functional Assessment for Chronic Illness Therapy—Spiritual (FACIT-Sp), based on extensive interviews with cancer patients (Brady, Peterman, Fitchett, Mo, & Cella, 1999). Also noteworthy, the Fetzer Institute/National Institute on Aging 1999 think tank conference focused on developing a multidimensional model for religiousness and spirituality that continues to influence the field; it is operationalized in the Multidimensional Measure of Religiousness/Spirituality, with both a full version (MMRS; Fetzer Institute, 1999) and a briefer version (BMMRS; Idler et al., 2003).

More recent work has utilized factor analysis to explore distinct underlying processes in religious and spiritual engagement. Research with undergraduates (Johnson, Sheets, & Kristeller, 2008), replicated in the general public, identified six or seven stable factors across a wide range of scales. The first and most robust is a general factor including both religiousness and spiritual engagement, consistent with Gorsuch's model. Numerous scales seem to tap into this factor, and other investigators (e.g., Idler et al., 2003) have also identified such a general factor as most prominent. Most measures of this general factor also presume a belief in a higher being (a transcendent God), and by containing items using such language, have limited usefulness for atheist or Buddhist populations who, while not believing in a transcendent God, may nevertheless report spiritual experiences. Another factor is consistently defined by the inner meaning and peace factor of the FACIT-Sp (Brady et al., 1999), an eight-item scale that intentionally avoids references to God, allowing it to be more widely used for both clinical and research purposes. A third factor, predicated on belief in a judging, critical God, is measured by Pargament's negative religious coping scale and captures what is best referred to as spiritual distress in response to a crisis, reflecting anger at God or self-blame. Another important factor, defined by Hood's mysticism scale, relates to intense experiences often associated with advanced or transformative meditative practice (Hood, 1975; Wulff, 2000) and overlaps with Maslow's concept of peak experience (1962).

A recent factor analysis of the BMMRS (Masters et al., 2009) identified several overlapping factors, including connecting with God as a comforting force, personal spirituality or inner peace, and spiritual distress, in addition to several factors related to religious practice or religious community. An additional dimension consistently referenced in the traditional literature on both spirituality and meditation is a heightened sense of compassionate love or connectedness (Post, 2003; Underwood, 2008). A measure of this, the Compassionate Love Scale, has recently been developed by Sprecher and Fehr (2005).

The multitude of ways of defining spirituality indicates the need to recognize spirituality as a higher-order construct—one that points to a wide range of experiences and processes, but one which also may require that an explicit definition and related measurement approach be used for a particular application of the term. A parallel is the complexity of the term "depression"; decades of research have led to a substantial understanding of the viable and diverse meanings of the word "depression" (as a mood, as an aspect of bipolar disorder, as deep and reactive sadness, and so on). While the term "depression" continues to be used both professionally and colloquially to refer to a range of experiences, in any given research or clinical application care is taken to limit the focus to the goal or measurement approach appropriate to the specific definition of "depression" under consideration. Comparable research in the area of spirituality is relatively new, and far more work is needed before the broad field of experience that this term points to is fully delineated.

SPIRITUAL EXPERIENCE AND MEDITATION

Before considering the limited empirical literature on the relationship between meditation practice and spiritual experience, it may be helpful to review the meditative process from a theoretical and functional perspective. Although the focus in this volume is on mindfulness-based meditation and related mindfulness-based therapies, demarcations between meditative approaches are inherently blurred and may be even more so when considering spiritual effects. Furthermore, almost all religious traditions have incorporated elements of meditative or contemplative practice, and it is not apparent at this point in what ways the quality of spiritual experience differs by type of practice. Although most of the contemporary focus on the psychology of meditative practice has been on Eastern Buddhist and Hindu traditions, there is increasing recognition of underlying similarities in process and experience with other traditions, such as Jewish Hasidic prayers, Sufi mystical traditions, and Christian contemplative prayer (Goleman, 1988; Shafii, 1988). (In Christianity, the term "contemplation" is parallel to the term "meditation" as it has entered contemporary usage from the Asian traditions, whereas the term "meditation" generally refers to more active, reflective prayer, in which the mind is analytically engaged with sacred content.) Because individuals from a wide range of faith traditions may become involved in mindfulness-based therapeutic practices, it is useful to understand some of the conceptual similarities and differences among meditation practices drawn from different faith traditions, particularly when considering spiritually related elements or goals.

Despite the wide variations in meditative practices, there are common elements. These include a particular way of focusing attention, the engagement of a nonjudgmental rather than analytic thought process, and, often, the use of repetition (Bond et al., 2009). The most common distinction is between concentrative and mindfulness meditation (Goleman, 1988). However, from both a therapeutic and a spiritual perspective, it is useful to expand this categorization to include guided meditation, in which attention is directed to a particular focus that is intended to convey meaning, as in cultivating compassion. The guiding may come from without, as in a led practice, or from within, as in focusing on a particular type of physical or psychological experience.

In the concentrative traditions, such as Hinduism, the focus of attention is on a particular object, frequently a word, phrase, prayer, or mantra;

the word "mantra" refers to a sound or word that manifests certain meanings and is repeated to invoke the power of those meanings for the individual. In Catholicism, the rosary or repetition of the Jesus Prayer (drawn from Eastern Orthodox practice), plays a similar role. The breath is also often used as an object of awareness, and counting the breath may be used as a focus. In true concentrative practices, the goal is to maintain focus as much as possible on the particular object of attention. A primary purpose of these practices, both traditionally and in contemporary use, is to cultivate a greater capacity for stability of attention (Lutz et al., 2007).

In mindfulness practices, attention is purposefully kept open, either attending to a general focus, such as the breath or body experiences rather than a word or phrase, or, in open awareness practices, attending to whatever enters the field of awareness without typical analytic engagement or thinking about the object of awareness. In contrast to cultivating stability of attention, mindfulness practice is directed toward cultivating clarity of awareness (Lutz et al., 2007). However, it can be argued that both types of practice are directed at cultivating a capacity to disengage from reactivity to whatever is coming into awareness, by shifting attention either to another object of thought or experience (for example, the mantra) or to a different relationship to the thought as in mindful awareness. Traditional meditation literature associates both types of practice with cultivation of spiritual experience.

The third type of meditation, involving guided or directed meditation, is particularly pertinent to spiritual engagement. This type of practice is intended to engage a particular focus, but in a mindful rather than analytic or judgmental way. The focus in guided meditation is broader than in concentrative meditation, generally with a spiritual connotation in traditional practices (a particular chant, the symbolic mandala of Tibetan tantric practices, a Zen koan, and the like) or involving complex universal experiences such as images of death or suffering or feelings of compassion, as in loving-kindness meditations. In contemporary therapeutic practice, various focal points have been utilized, including pain; other physical sensations, such as hunger (Kristeller, Baer, & Wolever, 2006) or stress (Kabat-Zinn et al., 1992); depressive thoughts (Teasdale, 1999; Teasdale, Segal, & Williams, 1995; Teasdale et al., 2000); or interpersonal connectedness (Carson, Carson, Gil, & Baucom, 2004). One contemporary form of meditation that has been systematically investigated (Oman, Hedberg, & Thoresen, 2006) is passage meditation, one of eight parts of a multifaceted group treatment program explicitly intended to cultivate spirituality (the

Eight-Point Program; Easwaran, 1991). In passage meditation, the focus is on repetition of religious and spiritual passages. Incorporating spiritual content almost certainly heightens the likelihood of a spiritual experience as a function of meditation practice, but it is unclear to what extent it is necessary to having a spiritual experience.

Meditation traditions may primarily utilize one or another type of practice (concentrative, mindfulness, or guided), but elements of all three generally exist, either explicitly or implicitly. For example, within Tibetan meditative traditions, each variant occurs: focused attention or one-pointed concentration (samatha), open presence (vipassana, or insight), and cultivation of particular mind states, such as compassion (Lutz et al., 2007; Thrangu & Johnson, 2004). However, the demarcations among these elements are not necessarily sharp. For example, mindfulness techniques often use the breath as a way of training and stabilizing attention. Conversely, the concentrative traditions generally include instructions to relate mindfully to extraneous material that enters awareness by observing it nonjudgmentally and effortlessly, rather than engaging with it. For example, Transcendental Meditation is a mantra meditation in which a word is repeated continuously in coordination with the breath, but the Transcendental Meditation literature discounts the "concentrative" label, emphasizing a more relaxed engagement of the mantra to still the mind and engage an awareness of inner quiet, and de-emphasizing the sustained effortful concentration that accompanies some of the other concentrative traditions. Furthermore, although Transcendental Meditation is often presented as a stress management tool, the primary intent, consistent with Hindu tradition, is to promote general self-growth, transformation, and transcendent spiritual experience (Maharishi Mahesh Yogi, 1968). Easwaran's integrative approach (Bormann et al., 2006; Easwaran, 1991) also draws on Hindu mantra meditation and emphasizes the process of engaging inner peace and spirituality. Within clinical practice, use of mantra meditation can be powerful both for disengaging the "chattering" mind and for deepening a sense of spiritual engagement.

The extent and manner in which distinctions among different types of meditative practice are meaningful from a psychological perspective remain to be investigated, whether in regard to spiritual goals or a range of other goals. Theoretically, different meditative approaches may cultivate different processes and types of spiritual engagement, but there are virtually no intervention studies that directly compare different meditation techniques. The mantra-based or prayer-based practices have been associated with trancelike experiences or altered states, at least for some individuals. Use of a mantra may more effectively shut off usual thought processes while opening the individual to atypical cognitive processes. Mindfulness practices, particularly as they relate to ACT therapies, are intended to keep the individual in the present moment, possibly limiting the likelihood of mystical or transcendent experiences, particularly in novices. At the same time, mindfulness practice may facilitate suspension of identification with the self, also noted as a path to spiritual experience. Walsh, in a compelling account of his own experiences contrasting mindfulness practice with a more spiritually engaging practice, addresses the underlying distinctions that may be mediated by neurological processes (Walsh, Victor, & Bitner, 2006). Guided practice may facilitate yet another distinct process: the active cultivation of the spiritual self. How each of these spirituality-related processes might mediate change in other areas, such as physical or emotional well-being, deserves further exploration.

The striking similarities between some aspects of Christian contemplative prayer and Eastern practices broaden the possibilities for developing interventions. Therapeutically, clients may be more comfortable working within their own traditions, making it useful to understand the parallel elements. And as of yet, there is little empirical literature on the physiological or psychological effects of Christian prayer that is parallel to the systematic investigation of mindfulness meditation. Among the many recognized types of Christian prayer, such as contemplative prayer, meditative prayer, or petitionary prayer, akin to asking God for a favor (Foster, 1992), contemplative prayer is most similar to elements of Buddhist and Hindu meditative practice.

Contemplative prayer, sometimes referred to centering prayer (Keating, 2002) has been identified as the type of Christian prayer designed to "free us from our addiction to words" (Foster, 1992, p. 155), a goal familiar within Buddhist practice. Foster instructs, "Begin by seating yourself comfortably and then slowly and deliberately let all tension and anxiety drop away. Become aware of God's presence in the room... If frustrations or distractions arise, simply lift them up into the arms of the Father and let him care for them...not suppressing our inner turmoil but letting go of it... It is even more than a neutral psychological relaxing. It is an active surrendering, a 'self-abandonment to divine providence'... Because the Lord is present with us, we can relax and let go of everything... We allow his great silence to still our noisy hearts" (1992, pp. 161-162). If God is interpreted as existing within, the parallels to the processes of mindfulness are apparent, in particular the disengaging from analytic or ruminative thinking and opening up to whatever inner experience occurs in a nonjudgmental way. The stages of progress are also comparable: Foster describes the first step as simply realization of our inner distractions and lack of inner unity; then comes contact with the "listening silence"; next is a sense of being more alive, accompanied by feelings of love and adoration; and finally comes attainment of spiritual ecstasy or mystical experience, which may emerge but which cannot be willfully engaged.

As in Buddhism, some Christian practices, include use of prayer and practice not only at specific times, but constantly throughout the day in the background of awareness. Thich Nhat Hanh (1975) speaks repeatedly of silently using the breath, and perhaps a word of prayer, to refocus and remain mindful. Foster (1992) recommends a practice referred to as unceasing prayer, using specific activities or events as reminders until practicing prayer in the back of one's mind becomes habitual. In the process, engaging one's spiritual—or mindful—self becomes more habitual and petty frustrations and irritated reactions to minor events, such as being stuck in traffic, will decrease. With ongoing practice, the person may experience an opening of awareness of others, a decrease in preoccupation with self, and a natural growing of compassion. Again, the common elements are clear: use of the breath and repetition of a brief, spiritually meaningful word to disengage from disturbing thoughts and emotions and to connect with a source of spiritual experience or understanding, however that is conceptualized. Whether such mindful pauses are experienced as spiritual may be a function of the context in which they are learned or practiced.

Parallels also exist in Jewish and Muslim practices. As is the case within many Western religious traditions, meditation practice in Judaism is associated with the more mystical streams of religious development. Verman and Shapiro (1996) identify five Jewish meditation practices: meditation on oneness or on the holy name of God, meditation on the breath, chanting holy letters in combination with the breath, meditations on light imagery as reflecting the divine, and meditations on opening the heart. The breath plays an important role as a focus of spiritual understanding, both in terms of the symbolic nature of breath and as specific breath techniques. This symbolism of breathing as taking in Divine life energy is parallel to Hindu perspectives and to the Chinese concept of qi.

The primary meditative tradition within Islam is Sufism. The most common form for Sufi meditation is chanting a sacred phrase, such as *La ilaha illa 'llah* ("There is no god but God") together with deep and rhythmic breathing, practiced in the service of *zikr*, awareness or "rememberance" (the literal translation) of the Divine in all. This is first practiced out loud and then, after a certain level of accomplishment, silently to oneself (Goleman, 1988). The breath is seen as a primary path to realization of the Divine within, which is then expanded to allow integration of the spiritual into every moment of life, proceeding along well-defined stages in development of spiritual awareness, again comparable to those identified in other traditions, with the optimal practice being an interplay between absorptive practice that cultivates the mystical, and mindful practice that cultivates integration of the spiritual into daily life.

Integrated contemporary models of meditation, framed explicitly within religious/spiritual contexts, have been developed, including Sri Eknath Easwaran's aforementioned Eight-Point Program to spiritual growth, which incorporates regular meditative practice and prayer from many religious traditions, and which has been empirically explored (Bormann et al., 2006). The practice is characterized by repetition of lengthier sacred passages, which are memorized and then repeated to oneself for a period of time, much as in Christian contemplative prayer, and also includes silent repetition of short mantras in the background of one's mind throughout the day. Other components include slowing down, cultivating one-pointed attention, putting others first, and seeking spiritual companionship. A more recently developed integrative approach, Spiritual Self-Schema (3-S+) therapy, developed for the treatment of addiction, blends Buddhist teachings, mindfulness and concentrative meditation practice, and cognitive behavioral therapy in a twelve-session program (Avants & Margolin, 2004; Margolin, et al., 2007). While explicitly drawing on Buddhist principles, it is also tailored to each participant's own spiritual and religious beliefs. These approaches are clearly multifaceted and therefore present the challenge of separating out spiritual effects from the effects of other components. This is also true of other similarly complex programs, including MBSR.

MEDITATION, MINDFULNESS, AND SPIRITUALITY: MEDIATING GROWTH

As noted earlier, there are surprisingly few studies of the direct effects of meditation practice on spirituality, and even fewer that address the possible mediating role of spirituality on other aspects of functioning as the result of such practice. Nevertheless, a body of research literature is beginning to develop exploring the impact of meditation of different aspects of spiritual experience. How we can illuminate, assess, and understand these processes is the core question of this chapter. Therefore, within this formative period of investigation, rather than first considering the possible mediating mechanisms of spirituality as a unified construct, it is important to begin by looking at aspects of spirituality separately, at least from the perspective of developing theoretically valid and testable models. The following sections provide an overview of the research to date on the interface between meditation and spirituality organized by key concepts of spirituality listed earlier in this chapter, while also highlighting the value (and limitations) of particular measurement approaches. In this context, I'll briefly review both conceptual issues and the current empirical evidence as it begins to illuminate the processes involved.

Spirituality as a Sense of Inner Peace

A sense of inner peace appears to be one of the more accessible elements of heightened spiritual engagement, and the FACIT-Sp meaning and peace factor is proving to be a particularly robust measure of this aspect of spiritual well-being. Participants in the MBSR program (Kabat-Zinn, 1990), which has little or no explicit focus on spiritual experience, reported an increased sense of inner peace and a suspension of mundane concerns on the FACIT-Sp (as adapted for a general population). The degree to which this occurred was directly related to self-reported improvement in health symptoms and psychological well-being (Carmody, Reed, Kristeller, & Merriam, 2008). Improvement in mindfulness in this population, measured both by the Mindful Attention Awareness Scale (MAAS; Brown & Ryan, 2003) and the Toronto Mindfulness Scale (TMS; Lau et al., 2006), was related to improvement on the FACIT-Sp, with the strongest relationships between the TMS and the meaning and peace subscale of the FACIT-Sp. Exploring how a sense of meaning and peace can be cultivated in individuals struggling with a tremendous life challenge, such as cancer, also speaks to the value of mindfulness practice (Carlson, Labelle, Garland, Hutchins, & Birnie, 2009). A study of the MBSR program in cancer patients (Garland, Carlson, Cook, Lansdell, & Speca, 2007) found significant improvements on the FACIT-Sp, in contrast to changes in a comparison group enrolled in a healing arts program.

Bormann and her associates (2006) randomized ninety-three HIV+ men and women to a program in which some participants were taught spiritually oriented mantra-based meditation drawing on Easwaran's program (1991) or to an education intervention with a comparable structure. Participants met for five weekly ninety-minute group sessions. During treatment, the group first chose a mantra that was personally resonant for them, drawn from world faith traditions. Other sessions supported their practice and taught one-pointed attention and the value of slowing down and maintaining a practice. Sitting meditation was limited to five-minute group practice periods. The emphasis was on frequent repetition of the chosen mantra in the back of the mind throughout the day, both when faced with stressful situations that led to intrusive thoughts, and also during low-stress periods to increase the association between the mantra and relaxation. Participants were also encouraged to intentionally slow down mentally and behaviorally while using the mantra, which could be considered an aspect of mindfulness. In addition to showing improvements relative to the control group related to quality of life and emotional regulation, the first group also had significantly greater improvement in spiritual faith but not on spiritual well-being as measured by the FACIT-Sp. Furthermore, at ten weeks greater use of the mantra strongly predicted spiritual faith, meaning and peace, and overall quality of life. While no mediator analyses were presented, the results suggest that the intervention allowed a disengagement from typical reactions to stress, along with cultivation of multiple aspects of spiritual engagement, including religiousness and a sense of meaning and inner peace. These results further suggest that inner sense of meaning and peace may take somewhat longer to develop than does enhancing one's connection to religious faith.

Margolin and Avants (Avants & Margolin, 2004; Margolin, et al., 2007) found that their Spiritual Self-Schema therapy program for HIV+ drug addicts, briefly described above, increased a sense of inner peace, spiritual faith, and a feeling of God's presence. In a randomized trial, impulsivity and addictive behaviors markedly decreased, and individuals tended to ascribe their improvement to both their mindfulness practice and a deepening of their spirituality.

Spirituality as Love and Compassion

Cultivating love and compassion for others is widely considered a beneficial aspect of meditation practice, and also a virtually universal aspect of spirituality. Cultivating the capacity to suspend critical judgment, of either oneself or others, is a core element of teaching in the mindfulness traditions and in ACT. Again, one of the challenges of conceptualizing the role of spirituality as a mediator in meditation practice is whether suspension of critical judgment is, in itself, an expression of spirituality or a process that can be understood separately from spirituality. For example, individuals might consider themselves compassionate without being spiritual. It may be that lifting one's attention away from everyday worries, preoccupations, or anger at others is a necessary, although not sufficient, element in cultivating a sense of altruistic love and compassion for others (Kristeller & Johnson, 2005).

Within the context of meditation and prayer, cultivation of love, compassion, and acceptance and a lifting of critical judgment appear to be aspects of spirituality that are particularly well suited to guided meditation, and are being shown to be effective within mindfulness-based treatments for couples and families (Carson et al., 2004; Gale & Walsh, 2009). Powerful practices within vipassana traditions are various loving-kindness meditations, often associated with Thich Nhat Hanh's teachings (2006). These meditations guide participants to direct loving-kindness first toward the self, then outward to others, and ultimately to those with whom they have had difficult interactions. Cultivating compassion has also been creatively explored using Easwaran's passage meditation approach in an eight-week Eight-Point Program group enrolling health care practitioners (Oman, Thoresen, & Hedberg, 2009). Participants chose a personally relevant passage from a range of spiritual wisdom traditions to memorize and then gently focus on during a daily thirty-minute meditation period. Compared to a wait list control group, compassion markedly increased and was sustained through several months of follow-up; effects were related to amount of adherence reported and were stronger for individuals who identified themselves at baseline as less spiritually engaged.

The mirror opposite of compassion for oneself or others is anger or negative self-judgment. Substantial evidence is accruing that spiritual distress or negative religious coping is a distinct aspect of religious belief and experience (Johnson et al., 2008; Masters et al., 2009) that is particularly toxic in terms of both physical health and psychological adjustment. Particularly within Christianity, such negative religious coping is associated with belief in the judgment of God, and the concepts of sin, guilt, and retribution.

Spirituality as No-Self

A cornerstone of Buddhism is the transcendence of self. Overidentification with the self is viewed as a core contributor to *dukkha*, or distress, and to limits in one's ability to engage with "right action" or "right thought." Connecting to what is considered the spirit, whether that of a transcendent other or the representation of the nonself within the self, is viewed as a core element of spirituality. Hayes (1984) made the argument that spirituality is the sense of no-self, pointing to something that is inherently outside the realm of usual senses (i.e., the "spirit") but within the capacity of the human mind, without the need to point to a transcendent presence. While Hayes had not yet framed this theoretical perspective within the context of mindfulness or ACT, he was identifying an important distinction between the usual course of self-observation—the self-talk of cognitive behavioral analysis—and a different type of awareness that is dispassionate and concerned with context, rather than content. Such a disengagement of identify of "self" from one's thoughts can also be powerful within a more limited application of this concept. In the Mindfulness-Based Eating Awareness Treatment (MB-EAT) program (Kristeller et al., 2006), we determined that compulsive overeaters found it very powerful to recognize this principle of no-self in regard to habits, feelings, or, in particular, thoughts. For some participants, the conceptual understanding "I am not my thoughts" is the path that leads away from compulsive and reactive behavior while also helping them open to the experience of no-self.

How this sense of no-self can be measured, identified as a neurophysiological process (Austin, 1998; Newberg & Waldman, 2009), systematically cultivated, or captured as a mediator of other changes while engaged within therapeutic dialogue (Mathers, Miller, & Ando, 2009) remains on the edge of our empirical understanding. Therefore, one of the challenges in defining spirituality as this state of no-self is understanding the construct itself: Is no-self readily accessible, in which case it may be a primary mediator of other changes, even for beginning practitioners of mindfulness? Or is it relatively difficult to engage, representing a profound, qualitative shift in inner experience, such as that referred to as *kensho* or satori in Zen practice (Austin, 1998)? Another challenge, yet unfulfilled, is measurement of no-self, both as a momentary state and as a more enduring capacity. Meeting this challenge is necessary to exploring no-self as a mediator, regardless of how it is construed.

Spirituality as a Sense of the Sacred

Hill and Pargament (2003) identify a sense of the sacred as distinguishing the everyday or mundane from the spiritual. For example, walking in nature can be experienced as spiritual by one person and as ordinary by another person or at another time. Another way of considering this is in terms of imbuing aspects of life with higher meaning. On the FACIT-Sp, inner meaning and inner peace may be two separable factors, as shown in a recent study of cancer patients (Canada, Murphy, Fitchett, Schover, & Peterman, 2008). Certainly, ACT is structured to help people develop a sense of positive meaning in their lives in regard to engaging motivation to move in a different direction, and engaging "inner wisdom" may be a powerful way to construe the emergence of healthier choices as reactivity drops away. Within mindfulness practice, the concept of linking into a sense of inner wisdom that is nonreactive, more integrative, and carries more meaning can readily be reframed as linking into "higher" wisdom. In the MB-EAT program (Kristeller et al., 2006), we find that using the wording "inner wisdom" or "higher wisdom" helps make explicit a spiritual aspect of engaging "wiser" or healthier (in the broadest sense) eating patterns. One of the challenges related to this definition is distinguishing what might be conceived as sacred meaning from other types of meaning, in that many aspects of life might be framed as meaningful without necessarily being construed as sacred or spiritual.

Spirituality as a Sense of Transcendence or Linking to a Higher Being

Closely linked to a sense of the sacred is an experience of connecting with a transcendent God. Numerous measures are available for individuals with a religious belief in a transcendent God (Hill & Hood, 1999), and these are widely used in exploring emotional adjustment. Furthermore, within contemplative practices that are explicitly spiritual, guided practice that makes reference to connecting to a higher being may be very powerful when congruent with such beliefs (Griffith & Griffith, 2002). Wachholz and Pargament (2005, 2008) compared participants who either meditated on a mantra-type God-image spiritual phrase (such as "God is good") to those using a purely secular focus or who were instructed to simply relax for the designated twenty minutes. Both undergraduates and those who suffered from migraines showed significantly more response to the spiritual practice, in regard to both emotional adjustment and tolerance of physical pain.

The Index of Core Spiritual Experiences (INSPIRIT; Kass, Friedman, Leserman, & Zuttermeister, 1991) is a measure that taps primarily into a sense of engagement and closeness with some form of higher power or God, whether externally or internally present. In a study of the impact of the MBSR program on general well-being in undergraduates (Astin, 1997), there was a modest but significant increase on the INSPIRIT, independent of change in psychological well-being. Shapiro and her associates (Shapiro, Schwartz, & Bonner, 1998) also found improvements on INSPIRIT scores among medical and pre-med students in an MBSR program. These results suggest that while mindfulness practice may cultivate a sense of engagement with a higher power, this aspect of spiritual engagement doesn't necessarily relate to improvement in other elements of well-being. Another study (Jain et al., 2007) of a briefer version of the MBSR program (four 1.5-hour sessions), also with undergraduates, did find positive effects on measures of well-being but didn't show any significant changes on the INSPIRIT, suggesting a possible dose effect.

Another way to conceptualize a more universal application of the definition of spirituality as a connection to a transcendent God is to link it back into the definition of spirituality as no-self. From that perspective, the experience of linking to a higher being may be understood as a suspension of the usual sense of self, in combination with culturally transmitted beliefs in the existence of particular manifestations of God.

Cultivating Peak or Mystical Experience

Mystical experiences, although relatively unusual, are virtually synonymous with spirituality. There is an unquestionable association of traditional meditative practice with seeking and experiencing mystical experiences. However, as a therapeutic process, mindfulness meditation is not intended to function in this way, nor is this generally an aspect of practice that is evaluated. However, certain measures may be applicable within this context, notably Hood's Mysticism Scale (1975) and two tools designed to measure peak experience: the Experience Questionnaire (EQ; Privette & Bundrick, 1987, 1991) and the Peak Scale (PS; Mathes, Zevon, Roter, & Joerger, 1982). The term "peak experience" was introduced by Maslow (1962) to separate mystical-type experiences from their religious context and to emphasize the universality and psychological validity of the phenomena. Based on extensive interviews, the qualities of peak experiences pertinent to this discussion include focused, nondifferentiating, nonjudgmental absorption and awe; an ability to detach the self from the world; a loss, even if transient, of anxiety, defensiveness, and need for control; a heightened sense of all-embracing love; and a sense of a sacred "unitive consciousness" existing throughout all aspects of the world. Although this list is partial, it virtually encompasses descriptions of spiritual-type experiences in numerous texts on higher levels of meditative practice.

OTHER FACTORS IN SPIRITUAL DEVELOPMENT: INDIVIDUAL DIFFERENCES AND STAGE OF PRACTICE

In addition to various ways of construing spirituality, other factors need to be considered in developing an understanding of the link between spirituality and meditation in therapeutic growth. These include wide individual variation in the degree to which spirituality forms a core element of personal identity, and perhaps even in the degree to which a capacity for such experiences exists. Another important aspect to consider, particularly in regard to the research evidence, is the extent and depth of meditation practice.

Individual Differences in Capacity for and Interest in Spiritual Engagement

Regardless of how spiritual engagement may inform or facilitate growth in other aspects of a person's life, this capacity is presumed to be present in all or most individuals. Yet some individuals, regardless of other benefits associated with meditation practice, may resonate more with the spiritual value of such practice than do others, seeking out retreat environments or being drawn toward traditional forms of meditation that are more religiously linked. Therefore, the concept of spiritual intelligence, derived from Gardner's model of multiple intelligences (2004), may be useful in considering the impact of meditative practice on personal experience, either within the therapeutic arena or more generally. Emmons and others (Emmons, 2000; Vaughan, 2002; Zohar & Marshall, 2000) make the argument that spirituality fits Gardner's criteria for defining an intelligence; namely, evidence of an underlying neurological basis, the existence of exceptional individuals, identifiable core operations, and a developmental process marked by increasing competency. Emmons identifies five key characteristics of spiritual intelligence: capacity for transcendence, ability to enter into heightened spiritual states of consciousness, ability to invest everyday events and relationships with a sense of the sacred, ability to utilize spiritual resources for problems in living, and capacity to be virtuous. Empirically supported approaches to the measurement of spiritual intelligence are being developed (e.g., the Spiritual Sensitivity Scale; Tirri, Nokelainen, & Ubani, 2006).

Both the traditional and contemporary literature on meditation support the relevance of meditation practice to cultivating these core aspects of spiritual intelligence. Related to Gardner's criteria, there are universal elements of meditation practice encoded within religious traditions, a developmental process related to level of practice, growing evidence of a neurological basis for these experiences (D'Aquili & Newburg, 1998; Hyde, 2004; Rosch, 2002), and the existence of exceptional practitioners. Furthermore, in regard to Emmons's characteristics of spiritual intelligence, meditation has traditionally been identified as a means for cultivating a capacity for transcendence, entering into heightened spiritual states, investing experience with a sense of the sacred, and cultivating mindfulness and adaptability.

Therefore, meditation and related approaches toward cultivating spiritual capacities can be argued to be meaningful across a wide range of individuals, although to different degrees, for the purpose not of only spiritual experience, but also emotional, behavioral, and relationship balance. This is not to say that such practices are the only effective tools for cultivating spiritual intelligence or growth, but they can arguably be considered among the major tools.

Stage of Experience in Meditation

Stages of development of meditative practice and experience are well recognized in the traditional literature and play a role in contemporary understanding of meditative effects. Stages of response can be considered to occur within all domains of meditative experience (Kristeller, 2003), whether in regard to increasing emotional awareness and equanimity, physiological regulation, or spiritual growth. Wallace (2006), in describing stages within Buddhist practice, emphasizes shifts in attentional processes that slowly develop with hundreds, if not thousands, of hours of practice. Some researchers (Lutz et al., 2007) have defined a minimum of ten thousand hours of practice as indicative of an advanced practitioner; in contrast, most of the research relevant to clinical applications inherently involves novices who are new to the practice of meditation and may or may not resonate with the spiritual aspects of the experience.

At the same time, the stages of spiritual experience that Foster outlines in regard to Christian contemplative practice are strikingly similar to those reported from other traditions and point to the universality of the process involved. Foster identifies an early state as awakening a teachable spirit, during which one becomes more open to the spiritual aspect of oneself, followed by bringing a state of awareness, of listening prayer, to all activities during the day, whether mundane or more substantive. More intensive practice is associated with the mystical traditions and attaining states of spiritual ecstasy. In considering the applicability, therefore, of research on more advanced practitioners (e.g., Lutz et al., 2007; Newberg & Waldman, 2009) to processes of change in novices, it is important to keep level of practice in mind.

CONCLUSIONS

How can—or should—meditation be considered as a spiritual practice within the therapeutic context? The evidence to date, even if limited, suggests that meditative practice that explicitly engages spiritual themes will have positive effects on this aspect of people's experience, enriching their sense of meaning, helping to cultivate well-being, and contributing a sense of connectedness to others and to a wider field of being. For those who identify themselves as neither religious nor spiritual, introducing spirituality in terms of such universal themes may be helpful, separate from religious belief. In addition, therapists may want to familiarize themselves with the spiritual and religious traditions of different meditation practices. One purpose of doing so is to understand the perspectives of clients who are already engaged in meditation practices. Another reason is to be comfortable in encouraging clients to seek deeper personal practice within retreat environments, which are usually identified with specific spiritual or religious perspectives. In contrast, when first introduced to mindfulness meditation, given its association with Buddhism, some individuals may believe that engaging in even basic, secular-oriented practice somehow betrays their faith and values.

In the MB-EAT program, we anticipate this response in three ways: first, by reframing mindfulness meditation as an approach that grew out of Buddhist psychology as much as Buddhism as a religion; second, by pointing out that most religious traditions, including Christianity, contain elements of meditative and contemplative practice; and third, by explaining that these practices are used to help people cultivate "inner" or "higher levels" of wisdom and awareness. Considering these perspectives appears to help most people, regardless of personal religious beliefs, become more comfortable with exploring meditation practice for their own therapeutic purposes, whether that involves spiritual goals or not.

A related but distinct concern lies within the belief system of certain fundamentalist Christian denominations that explicitly label meditation practice, regardless of the type, as an "evil" or pagan practice through which the devil may enter the mind, introducing evil thoughts or experience (e.g., Groothuis, 2004). While the source of this teaching is somewhat obscure, perhaps related to earlier spiritualist or parapsychological claims regarding meditation, from a psychological perspective such fears may possibly be tied to the phenomena of emotional flooding or other distress that may arise for some individuals during practice (Walsh & Shapiro, 2006). Regardless of the source of such beliefs, they may be strongly held either by potential clients or by their family members, who may raise objections. Again, if such beliefs can be anticipated, they may be sensitively explored, but for some individuals, their religious background leads to concerns that will be resistant to discussion.

As spirituality comes to be understood as a universal psychological capacity, it is becoming more viable to consider how this aspect of meditation and related mindfulness practices may be cultivated to assist clients who are in spiritual distress or whose issues appear to involve spiritual growth or transformation. Whether the transformative potential of spiritual engagement requires either intensity of practice or duration of experience is a key question. Evidence currently points to a continuum in which cultivation of the spiritual empowers other processes. However, documenting spiritual effects of practicing meditation presents particular challenges, as the empirical side of this research area is still less developed than is comparable work in physiological, emotional, or behavioral domains. Only recently have measures of spiritual and religious experience that follow adequate methodological guidelines been developed, and as noted above, the use of some measures is limited for some individuals due to their presumption of a belief in a transcendent God. Functional brain imaging to examine neurological correlates of meditative experience holds considerable promise, although to date most of this research has used highly experienced meditators as their own controls, limiting the translation to therapeutic contexts.

Much of the richness of the spiritual aspects of meditation is evident within traditionally intact meditation practices, which presents distinct challenges to carrying out methodologically viable research. Not only does this limit the range of participants, it also, and importantly, introduces confounds related to the complexity of ritualized practices that extend beyond the meditative experience itself. So while the literature of those traditions may be able to inform hypotheses or provide evidence that is suggestive, it is imperative that the experiences of those individuals not be presumed to be on a continuum applicable to novice practitioners.

Nevertheless, evidence is growing that meditation practices carry the potential for cultivating a richer spiritual life for participants, an impact that is deepened when this aspect of the practice is explicitly engaged. Whether mindfulness approaches without a meditative component will create similar shifts is not yet known. The traditional literature certainly suggests that cultivating this aspect of self is powerful for bringing better balance to many aspects of experience, including emotional and physical well-being, relationships with others, and "right action." Whether engaging the spiritual self, either implicitly or explicitly, contributes to these effects within mindfulness-based programs is an exciting and challenging question to continue to explore.

REFERENCES

Allport, G. W. (1950). *The individual and his religion.* New York: Macmillan.

Astin, J. A. (1997). Stress reduction through mindfulness meditation: Effects on psychological symptomatology, sense of control, and spiritual experiences. *Psychotherapy and Psychosomatics, 66*, 97-106.

Austin, J. H. (1998). *Zen and the brain.* Cambridge, MA: MIT Press.

Avants, S. K., & Margolin, A. (2004). Development of spiritual self-schema therapy for the treatment of addictive and HIV risk behavior: A convergence of cognitive and Buddhist psychology. *Journal of Psychotherapy Integration, 14*, 253-289.

Bond, K., Ospina, M. B., Hooton, N., Dryden, D. M., Shannahoff-Khalsa, D., Carlson, L. E., et al. (2009). Defining a complex intervention: The development of demarcation criteria for "meditation." *Psychology of Religion and Spirituality, 1*, 129-137.

Boorstein, S. (2003). *Pay attention, for goodness sake: The Buddhist path to happiness.* New York: Ballantine.

Bormann, J. E., Gifford, A. L., Shively, M., Smith, T. L., Redwine, L., Kelly, A., et al. (2006). Effects of spiritual mantram repetition on HIV outcomes: A randomized controlled trial. *Journal of Behavioral Medicine, 29*, 359-376.

Brady, M. J., Peterman, A. H., Fitchett, G., Mo, M., & Cella, D. (1999). A case for including spirituality in quality of life measurement in oncology. *Psycho-Oncology, 8*, 417-428.

Brown, K. W., & Ryan, R. M. (2003). The benefits of being in the present: Mindfulness and its role in psychological well-being. *Journal of Personality and Social Psychology, 84*, 822-848.

Canada, A. L., Murphy, P. E., Fitchett, G., Schover, L. R., & Peterman, A. H. (2008). A 3-factor model for the FACIT-Sp. *Psycho-Oncology, 17*, 908-916.

Carlson, L. E., Labelle, L. E., Garland, S. N., Hutchins, M. L., & Birnie, K. (2009). Mindfulness-based interventions in oncology. In F. Didonna (Ed.), *Clinical handbook of mindfulness.* New York: Springer.

Carmody, J., Reed, G., Kristeller, J., & Merriam, P. (2008). Mindfulness, spirituality, and health-related symptoms. *Journal of Psychosomatic Research, 64*, 939-403.

Carson, J. W., Carson, K. M., Gil, K. M., & Baucom, D. H. (2004). Mindfulness-based relationship enhancement. *Behavior Therapy, 35*, 471-494.

D'Aquili, E. G., & Newburg, A. B. (1998). The neuropsychological basis of religions, or why God won't go away. *Zygon: Journal of Religion and Science, 33*, 187-201.

Dimidjian, S., & Linehan, M. M. (2003). Defining an agenda for future research on the clinical applications of mindfulness practice. *Clinical Psychology: Science and Practice, 10*, 166-171.

Easwaran, E. (1991). *Meditation: A simple 8-point path for translating spiritual ideals into daily life.* Tomales, CA: Nilgiri Press.

Emmons, R. A. (2000). Is spirituality an intelligence? Motivation, cognition, and the psychology of ultimate concern. *International Journal for the Psychology of Religion, 10*, 3-26.

Fetzer Institute. (1999). *Multidimensional measurement of religiousness/spirituality for use in health research.* Dearborn, MI: Fetzer Institute/National Institute on Aging Working Group.

Foster, R. J. (1992). *Prayer: Finding the heart's true home.* San Francisco: HarperSanFrancisco.

Gale, J., & Walsh, F. (2009). Meditation and relational connectedness: Practices for couples and families. In *Spiritual resources in family therapy* (2nd ed.). New York: Guilford.

Gardner, H. (2004). *Frames of mind: The theory of multiple intelligences.* New York: Basic Books.

Garland, S. N., Carlson, L. E., Cook, S., Lansdell, L., & Speca, M. (2007). A non-randomized comparison of mindfulness-based stress reduction and healing arts programs for facilitating post-traumatic growth and spirituality in cancer outpatients. *Supportive Care in Cancer, 15*, 949-961.

Goldstein, J. (2002). *One dharma: The emerging Western Buddhism.* San Francisco: Harper Collins.

Goleman, D. (1988). *The meditative mind: The varieties of meditative experience.* New York: G. P. Putnam & Sons.

Gorsuch, R. L. (1984). Measurement: The boon and bane of investigating religion. *American Psychologist, 39*, 228-236.

Griffith, J. L., & Griffith, M. E. (2002). *Encountering the sacred in psychotherapy: How to talk with people about their spiritual lives.* New York: Guilford.

Groothuis, D. (2004). Dangerous meditations. *Christianity Today, 48*, 78.

Hayes, S. C. (1984). Making sense of spirituality. *Behaviorism, 12*, 99-110.

Hayes, S. C., Strosahl, K., & Wilson, K. G. (1999). *Acceptance and commitment therapy.* New York: Guilford.

Hill, P. C., & Hood, R. W., Jr. (1999). *Measures of religiosity.* Birmingham, AL: Religious Education Press.

Hill, P. C., & Pargament, K. I. (2003). Advances in the conceptualization and measurement of religion and spirituality: Implications for physical and mental health research. *American Psychologist, 58*, 64-74.

Hood, R. W. (1975). The construction and preliminary validation of a measure of reported mystical experience. *Journal for the Scientific Study of Religion, 14*, 29-41.

Hyde, B. (2004). The plausibility of spiritual intelligence: Spiritual experience, problem solving and neural sites. *International Journal of Children's Spirituality, 9*, 39-52.

Idler, E. L., Musick, M. A., Ellison, C. G., George, L. K., Krause, N., Ory, M. G., et al. (2003). Measuring multiple dimensions of religion and spirituality for health research: Conceptual background and findings from the 1998 General Social Survey. *Research on Aging, 25*, 327-365.

Jain, S., Shapiro, S. L., Swanick, S., Roesch, S. C., Mills, P. J., Bell, I., et al. (2007). A randomized controlled trial of mindfulness meditation versus relaxation training: Effects on distress, positive states of mind, rumination, and distraction. *Annals of Behavioral Medicine, 33*, 11-21.

James, W. (1902). *The varieties of religious experience: A study in human nature.* New York: Longmans, Green and Co.

Johnson, T. J., Sheets, V. L., & Kristeller, J. L. (2008). Empirical identification of dimensions of religiousness and spirituality. *Mental health, religion, and culture, 11*, 745-767.

Kabat-Zinn, J. (1990). *Full catastrophe living: Using the wisdom of your body and mind to face stress, pain and illness.* New York: Delacorte.

Kabat-Zinn, J., Massion, A. O., Kristeller, J., Peterson, L. G., Fletcher, K. E., Pbert, L., et al. (1992). Effectiveness of a meditation-based stress reduction program in the treatment of anxiety disorders. *American Journal of Psychiatry, 149*, 936-943.

Kass, J. D., Friedman, R., Leserman, J., & Zuttermeister, P. C. (1991). Health outcomes and a new index of spiritual experience. *Journal for the Scientific Study of Religion, 30*, 203-211.

Keating, T. (2002). *Foundations for centering prayer and the Christian life.* New York: The Continuum International Publishing Group.

Kornfield, J. (1993). *A path with heart.* New York: Bantam Books.

Kristeller, J. L. (2003). Mindfulness meditation. In P. Lehrer, R. L. Woolfolk & W. E. Simes (Eds.), *Principles and practice of stress management.* New York: Guilford.

Kristeller, J. L., Baer, R. A., & Wolever, R. Q. (2006). Mindfulness-based approaches to eating disorders. In R. A. Baer (Ed.), *Mindfulness-based treatment approaches: Clinician's guide to evidence base and applications.* San Diego, CA: Elsevier.

Kristeller, J. L., & Johnson, T. (2005). Cultivating loving-kindness: A two-stage model of the effects of meditation on empathy, compassion, and altruism. *Zygon: Journal of Religion and Science, 40*, 391-407.

Lau, M. A., Bishop, S. R., Segal, Z. V., Buis, T., Anderson, N. D., Carlson, L., et al. (2006). The Toronto Mindfulness Scale: Development and validation. *Journal of Clinical Psychology, 62*, 1445-1467.

Linehan, M. M. (1993). *Cognitive-behavioral treatment of borderline personality disorder.* New York: Guilford.

Lutz, A., Dunne, J. D., Davidson, R. J., Zelazo, P. D., Moscovitch, M., & Thompson, E. (2007). Meditation and the neuroscience of consciousness: An introduction. In *The Cambridge handbook of consciousness.* New York: Cambridge University Press.

Maharishi Mahesh Yogi. (1968). *The science of being and art of living.* New York: Signet.

Margolin, A., Schuman-Olivier, Z., Beitel, M., Arnold, A., Fulwiler, C. E., & Avants, S. K. (2007). A preliminary study of Spiritual Self-Schema (3-S+) therapy for reducing impulsivity in HIV-positive drug users. *Journal of Clinical Psychology, 63*, 979-999.

Maslow, A. (1962). *Toward a psychology of being.* Princeton, NJ: Van Nostrand.

Masters, K. S., Carey, K. B., Maisto, S. A., Wolfe, T. V., France, C.R., Himawan, L., et al. (2009). Psychometric examination of the Brief Multidimensional Measure of Religiousness/Spirituality among college students. *International Journal for the Psychology of Religion, 19*, 106-120.

Mathers, D., Miller, M. E., & Ando, O. (Eds.). (2009). *Self and no-self: Continuing the dialogue between Buddhism and psychotherapy.* New York: Routledge/Taylor & Francis.

Mathes, E. W., Zevon, M. A., Roter, P. M., & Joerger, S. M. (1982). Peak experience tendencies: Scale development and theory testing. *Journal of Humanistic Psychology, 22*, 92-108.

Miller, W. R. (1999). *Integrating spirituality into treatment.* Washington, DC: American Psychological Association.

Miller, W. R., & Thoreson, C. E. (2003). Spirituality, religion, and health: An emerging research field. *American Psychologist, 58*, 24-35.

Newberg, A., & Waldman, M. R. (2009). *How God changes your brain.* New York: Ballantine.

Nhat Hanh, T. (1975). *The miracle of mindfulness.* Boston: Beacon Press.

Nhat Hanh, T. (2006). *True love: A practice for awakening the heart.* Boston: Shambhala.

Oman, D., Hedberg, J., & Thoresen, C. E. (2006). Passage meditation reduces perceived stress in health professionals: A randomized, controlled trial. *Journal of Consulting and Clinical Psychology, 74*, 714-719.

Oman, D., Thoresen, C. E., & Hedberg, J. (in press). Does passage meditation foster compassionate love among health professionals? A randomized trial. *Mental Health, Religion and Culture.*

Pargament, K. I., Koenig, H. G., & Perez, L. M. (2000). The many methods of religious coping: Development and initial validation of the RCOPE. *Journal of Clinical Psychology, 56*, 519-543.

Post, S. G. (2003). *Unlimited love: Altruism, compassion, and service.* Philadelphia: Templeton Foundation Press.

Privette, G., & Bundrick, C. M. (1987). Measurement of experience: Construct and content validity of the Experience Questionnaire. *Perceptual and Motor Skills, 65*, 315-332.

Privette, G., & Bundrick, C. M. (1991). Peak experience, peak performance, and flow: Correspondence of personal descriptions and theoretical constructs. *Journal of Social Behavior & Personality, 6*, 169-188.

Rosch, E. (2002). How to catch James's mystic germ: Religious experience, Buddhist meditation and psychology. *Journal of Consciousness Studies, 9*, 37-56.

Rubin, J. B. (1996). *Psychotherapy and Buddhism: Toward an integration.* New York: Plenum Press.

Seeman, T. E., Dubin, L. F., & Seeman, M. (2003). Religiosity/spirituality and physical health: A critical review of the evidence for biological pathways. *American Psychologist, 58*, 53-63.

Shafii, M. (1988). *Freedom from the self: Sufism, meditation and psychotherapy.* Human Sciences Press.

Shapiro, S. L., Schwartz, G. E., & Bonner, G. (1998). Effects of mindfulness-based stress reduction on medical and premedical students. *Journal of Behavioral Medicine, 21*, 581-599.

Sprecher, S., & Fehr, B. (2005). Compassionate love for close others and humanity. *Journal of Social and Personal Relationships, 22*, 629-651.

Teasdale, J. D. (1999). Emotional processing, three modes of mind and the prevention of relapse in depression. *Behaviour Research and Therapy, 37*, S53-S77.

Teasdale, J. D., Segal, Z., & Williams, J. M. (1995). How does cognitive therapy prevent depressive relapse and why should attentional control (mindfulness) training help? *Behaviour Research and Therapy, 33*, 25-39.

Teasdale, J. D., Segal, Z. V., Williams, J. M. G., Ridgeway, V. A., Soulsby, J. M., & Lau, M. A. (2000). Prevention of relapse/recurrence in major depression by mindfulness-based cognitive therapy. *Journal of Consulting and Clinical Psychology, 68*, 615-623.

Thrangu Rinpoche, K., & Johnson, C. (2004). *Essentials of mahamudra: Looking directly at the mind.* Boston: Wisdom Publications.

Tirri, K., Nokelainen, P., & Ubani, M. (2006). Conceptual definition and empirical validation of the Spiritual Sensitivity Scale. *Journal of Empirical Theology, 19*, 37-62.

Underwood, L. (2008). Measuring spirituality. *Journal of Nervous and Mental Disease, 196*, 715-716.

Vaillant, G. E. (2008). *Spiritual evolution: A scientific defense of faith.* New York: Broadway Books.

Vaughan, F. (2002). What is spiritual intelligence? *Journal of Humanistic Psychology, 42*, 16.

Verman, M., & Shapiro, D. H. (1996). Jewish meditation: Context and content, historical background, types, and purpose. In Y. Haruki, Y. Ishii, & M. Suzuki (Eds.), *Comparative and Psychological Study of Meditation*. Netherlands: Eburon Publishers.

Wachholtz, A. B., & Pargament, K. I. (2005). Is spirituality a critical ingredient of meditation? Comparing the effects of spiritual meditation, secular meditation, and relaxation on spiritual, psychological, cardiac, and pain outcomes. *Journal of Behavioral Medicine, 28*, 369-384.

Wachholtz, A. B., & Pargament, K. I. (2008). Migraines and meditation: Does spirituality matter? *Journal of Behavioral Medicine, 31*, 351-366.

Wallace, B. A. (2006). *The attention revolution.* Ithaca, NY: Snow Lion.

Walsh, R., & Shapiro, S. L. (2006). The meeting of meditative disciplines and Western psychology: A mutually enriching dialogue. *American Psychologist, 61*, 227-239.

Walsh, R., Victor, B., & Bitner, R. (2006). Emotional effects of sertraline: Novel findings revealed by meditation. *American Journal of Orthopsychiatry, 76*, 134-137.

Welwood, J. (2000). *Toward a psychology of awakening: Buddhism, psychotherapy, and the path of personal and spiritual transformation.* Boston: Shambhala.

Wulff, D. M. (2000). Mystical experience. In E. Cardena, S. J. Lynn & S. Krippner (Eds.), *Varieties of anomalous experience: Examining the scientific evidence.* Washington, DC: American Psychological Association.

Zohar, D., & Marshall, I. (2000). *SQ: Spiritual intelligence: The ultimate intelligence.* London: Bloomsbury.

CHAPTER 7

Meditation and Neuroplasticity: Using Mindfulness to Change the Brain

Michael T. Treadway, Vanderbilt University, and Sara W. Lazar, Massachusetts General Hospital

As Western culture has become more aware of Eastern spiritual traditions, scientists have been increasingly interested in verifying anecdotal claims from expert meditators regarding mindfulness practice. For almost fifty years, the practice of meditation and mindfulness has been studied by Western psychologists and neuroscientists looking to better understand its phenomenology, neurobiology, and clinical effects. Recently, these efforts have been bolstered by new imaging technologies that greatly enhance our capacity to explore the human brain in action.

One question that has received significant attention is whether meditation practices can induce *neuroplasticity*. This term refers to any form of lasting change that occurs in the structure or function of the brain. In this chapter, we focus on the question of meditation and neuroplasticity, providing an overview of the most recent studies exploring the impact of mindfulness and meditation practices on neuroplasticity, and discussing the clinical implications of these findings. In particular, we examine whether mindfulness-based or meditation-based changes in the brain are related to reduced suffering or improved well-being. It is not our intent to provide a complete review of this vast and diverse body of work; for extensive reviews of the older neurobiological literature, please see Cahn and Polich (2006), Austin (1998, 2006) or Murphy, Donovan, and Taylor (1997); for reviews of the clinical literature, see Lazar (2005) or Baer (2006). The goal of this chapter is to review the most recent literature and orient the reader to this developing research area and its implications for mindfulness-based interventions.

Although all forms of meditation are intended to increase one's capacity to be mindful, the Buddhist traditions place a particular emphasis on cultivating mindfulness. Therefore these traditions have served as the primary source for the mindfulness techniques now incorporated into Western psychotherapeutic practices such as dialectical behavior therapy (DBT), acceptance and commitment therapy (ACT), and mindfulness-based cognitive therapy (MBCT). As the focus of this chapter is mindfulness, in this chapter the term "meditation" will be used to denote the Buddhist meditation practices that cultivate mindfulness unless otherwise specified.

In the sections that follow, we review recent findings of neurobiological studies of mindfulness mediation. We begin by summarizing some of the neuroimaging techniques that have been used to explore mindfulness and some of the neural networks shown to be involved in the act of meditation. We then provide a review of studies showing evidence of neural plasticity resulting from long-term meditation practice. The final section addresses the possible ramifications of these findings for clinical interventions.

STUDYING MINDFULNESS AND THE BRAIN

The goal of the neuroscientific investigation of mindfulness meditation is to understand both the neural systems that are utilized to achieve meditative states and to determine the effects of regular mindfulness practice on brain function and structure. Meditation is associated with both state and trait-like effects. *State effects* refer to changes that occur in individuals while they actively meditate. In contrast, *trait-like effects* occur gradually over time as a consequence of sustained meditation practice and persist throughout the day. Trait-like effects are thought to result from stable, long-term transformations in brain activity and structure. Scientists can ask different questions when studying trait-like versus state effects, both of which may have clinical applications. Understanding state effects can help elucidate why mindfulness may be useful within a therapy session when dealing with painful memories or sudden bursts of emotion. Conversely, understanding long-term effects can help identify why mindfulness is useful for treating chronic conditions such as depression and anxiety disorders.

One primary challenge of studying the state effects of meditation is the complexity of meditation itself. When scientists want to investigate the neural systems that underlie a certain skill, they typically use tasks that are very simple, repetitive, and easy to monitor, such as reaction times to visual stimuli. Keeping tasks simple makes it easier to isolate specific areas of the brain involved in performing the task. In contrast, meditation is highly complex and variable from moment to moment. In one instance a person may be concentrating deeply on the breath, and in the next suddenly recall an errand to run. A few moments later the person may become mindful of having just been distracted and then return focus to the breath, but then a few moments later a childhood image suddenly pops up, and on and on. Focusing on the breath, remembering an errand, recognizing that you've become distracted, and seeing an image from the past all involve discrete brain systems. Should all of those systems be considered part of the meditative state? Or should the term "meditative state" only refer to brain regions that are active when the meditator actually focuses on the object of choice, such as the breath? How can scientists tease apart those moments of clear focus from moments of being distracted? Although our experimental technology is not yet capable of determining when the mind switches between these mental events, the application of new neuroscience techniques to the study of mindfulness is rapidly expanding our understanding.

Neuroimaging Methods

Technological innovations within the last twenty years have significantly improved our ability to assess human brain function. Collectively referred to as "neuroimaging," these techniques allow investigators to explore the function, structure, and neurochemical systems of the brain in vivo. We will begin by reviewing some of the most widely used neuroimaging methods. Those interested in learning more about these techniques are referred to Huettel, Song, and McCarthy (2008).

The most versatile technique is magnetic resonance imaging (MRI), which can be used to create 3-D images of the brain with extremely high clarity and spatial resolution. Because different types of neural tissue exert different effects on the magnetic field, it is possible to further segment these 3-D images into composite tissues classes of gray matter, white matter, and cerebrospinal fluid. These segmented images are extremely useful for neuroscientists, as they allow for the investigation of particular brain regions or tissue types. This work has led to many important findings in clinical populations, and to date, the majority of Axis I psychiatric disorders have been associated with region-specific changes in gray or white matter structure when compared to healthy control subjects. These findings suggest that alterations of brain structure may critically impact psychological health and mental well-being.

A special application of MRI widely used by cognitive scientists is functional magnetic resonance imaging (fMRI). This technique allows researchers to observe the brain in action while a study participant engages in a mental task, such as responding to visual stimuli or engaging in meditation. It is important to note that fMRI measures changes in blood flow to specific regions of the brain, and that these changes are only an indirect measure of neural activity (Sirotin & Das, 2009). This aside, fMRI has become a hugely popular technique, due to the fact that it is relatively low-cost and noninvasive yet provides excellent images of brain activity during complex tasks.

Two other neuroimaging techniques that allow researchers to observe brain activity are positron emission tomography (PET) and single photon emission computed tomography (SPECT). Developed more than a decade before fMRI, PET and SPECT also examine neuronal activity indirectly by measuring changes in blood flow and metabolism, but do so by recording the activity of a radioactive isotope injected into the study participant's blood. These techniques are less widely used than fMRI because of their greater expense, more invasive nature, and poorer spatial resolution.

Three other neuroimaging techniques frequently used include electroencephalography (EEG), electromyography (EMG), and magnetoencephalography (MEG). These techniques all share the strength of being direct measures of neuronal firing (as opposed to an indirect measure of blood flow) and can detect changes in neuronal activity at the millisecond level. While these techniques have been used to study meditation, they are outside the scope of this chapter. Interested readers are referred to Cahn and Polich (2006) for more information.

Neural Networks Engaged During Meditation

These neuroimaging techniques have offered unparalleled opportunities to explore complex mental activities such as meditation. From a cognitive neuroscience perspective, meditation is a highly heterogeneous and multifaceted task, involving both intense concentrative focus as well as an openness to sensory experiences, emotions, and thoughts. Furthermore, some meditation techniques, such as loving-kindness meditation (e.g., metta or tonglen), incorporate visualization or efforts to engender specific mind states. In seeking to divide meditation into its basic constituent elements, scientists have proposed a dichotomy between meditation processes involved in focused attention as compared to those involved in open awareness (Cahn & Polich, 2006; Lutz, Slagter, Dunne, & Davidson, 2008). Consistent with this notion, researchers have begun to identify specific neural networks believed to underlie the attentional control aspect of meditation as well as the open awareness aspect. A drawback to these studies is that they have often varied significantly in their design and the type of meditation studied, making it difficult to compare results in some cases. However, several consistent findings have emerged.

The first is the activation of the dorsolateral prefrontal cortex, an area that has been associated with executive decision making and attention. This area has been activated across a range of meditation styles, including mindfulness meditation (Baerentsen, Hartvig, Stødkilde-Jørgensen, & Mammen, 2001), Tibetan Buddhist imagery meditation (Newberg et al., 2001), Psalm recitation (Azari et al., 2001), Zen meditation (Ritskes, Ritskes-Hoitinga, Stodkilde-Jorgensen, Baerentsen, & Hartman, 2003), and kundalini yoga (Lazar et al., 2000).

Another frequent finding is that meditation leads to increased activation in the cingulate cortex, particularly the anterior subdivision. The anterior cingulate cortex (ACC) has been described as playing a primary role in the integration of attention, motivation, and motor control (Paus, 2001). A functional subdivision of the ACC into dorsal and rostral areas has also been proposed, in which the rostral portion is more activated by emotionally charged tasks, and the dorsal portion is more activated by cognitive tasks (Bush, Luu, & Posner, 2000). As the ACC is often associated with directing attention, it might be expected that more experienced meditators would show greater activation than novice meditators. Alternatively, as more experienced meditators often report that they can sustain periods of uninterrupted attention longer than novice meditators, it may result in less need for ACC activity. This was reported in a study by Brefczynski-Lewis, Lutz, Schaefer, Levinson, and Davidson in 2007. In this study, novice meditators showed more activity in the ACC as compared to Buddhist monks (Brefczynski-Lewis et al., 2007). However, when Hölzel and colleagues attempted to replicate these results using experienced insight (mindfulness) practitioners, they found that these participants showed more activity in the ACC compared to nonmeditators (Hölzel et al., 2007). This discrepancy may result from the fact that Brefczynski-Lewis and colleagues utilized highly trained monks, while Hölzel's group utilized experienced lay practitioners, whose ability to sustain attention was undoubtedly less developed than in the monks.

An additional region activated during meditation is the anterior insula (Lutz, Brefczynski-Lewis, Johnstone, & Davidson, 2008; Brefczynski-Lewis et al., 2007). The insula is associated with *interoception*, which is the perception of visceral feelings such as hunger and thirst, as well as balance and detection of heart rate and breathing rate. The insula has also been proposed as a key region involved in processing transient bodily sensations, thereby contributing to our experience of "selfness" (Craig, 2009). One hypothesis for increased activation of the insula during meditation is that it reflects the meditator's careful attention to the rising and falling of internal sensations. The insula has also been heavily implicated in studies of attention, with recent evidence suggesting that the insula may serve as a master switch for different attentional networks (Sridharan, Levitin, & Menon, 2008). This role is also consistent with the attentional demands required of meditation practice. Finally, the insula has also been associated with multiple psychiatric disorders, suggesting that normal insula function may be required for general well-being. For instance, altered activity of the insula has been found among depressed and healthy subjects during the induction of sad mood (Liotti, Mayberg, McGinnis, Brannan, & Jerabek, 2002), as well as during the experience of pain (Casey, Minoshima, Morrow, & Koeppe, 1996) or disgust (Wright, P., He, Shapira, Goodman, & Liu, 2004). Studies have also highlighted the role of the insula in internally generated emotions (Reiman et al., 1997) as well as during guilt (Shin et al., 2000).

EVIDENCE FOR MINDFULNESS-INDUCED NEUROPLASTICITY

One of the most pressing questions in the field of meditation research is whether mindfulness practice can produce long-lasting beneficial changes in the adult brain. Before this question can be answered, however, a more fundamental question must be addressed: Does the adult brain change? For most of the twentieth century, the answer to this question was believed to be no. The established wisdom in the field of neuroscience was that the composition of the adult mammalian brain remained relatively stable over the course of the animal's lifetime (age-dependent neuronal loss excepted).

Beginning in the early 1960s, challenges to this widely held belief began to surface (e.g., Altman, 1962). However, adult neuroplasticity wasn't widely recognized in animals for another two decades. Evidence has been even slower to accumulate regarding humans, but with the advent of noninvasive neuroimaging methods, numerous EEG and imaging studies have demonstrated the highly plastic and flexible nature of the human adult brain. For instance, MRI studies have shown changes in brain structure before and after having acquired expertise for a specific skill. In two such studies, one involving learning how to juggle and the other involving learning the routes required to become a licensed London taxi driver, researchers found increases in gray matter volume in specific regions associated with performing these tasks (Maguire et al., 2000; Draganski et al., 2004). Studies have also shown differences in the pattern of activation in various brain regions when learning a novel task as compared to a task that has been previously learned (Vogt et al., 2007; Sun, Miller, Rao, & D'Esposito, 2007). Finally, recent studies have demonstrated that relatively brief interventions aimed at improving cognitive performance on working memory tasks may result in an increase in expression of receptors for key neurotransmitters, such as dopamine (McNab et al., 2009).

Taken together, these studies suggest that the adult brain is in fact highly plastic and that experience-dependent changes at the structural, functional, and neurochemical level may occur over periods of time as brief as a few weeks. These data should be very encouraging to both neuroscience and clinical researchers, as they suggest that mindfulness practices have the potential to alter neural function, and that these effects may begin to accrue in a relatively short period of time. Researchers have also begun exploring the role of neuroplasticity in experienced meditators in order to elucidate the benefits of long-term practice. These studies have included examining changes in brain structure and activity, as well as changes in functional activity during a variety of tasks, such as attentional control and emotion regulation. These findings provide converging evidence supporting the hypothesis that regular mindfulness practice leads to long-lasting changes in the brain that have important implications for health and well-being.

Changes in Cortical Structure

In 2005, our group published a study examining the effects of long-term mindfulness practice on brain structure (Lazar et al., 2005). Twenty long-term mindfulness meditation practitioners and fifteen controls participated in a comparison of cortical thickness using high-resolution MRI images. Meditators and controls were matched for gender, age, race, and years of education. The long-term meditators had increased cortical thickness in the anterior insula and sensory cortex—regions involved in observing internal and external physical sensations, respectively. Interestingly, decreased volume in the anterior insula has been strongly implicated in several psychopathologies, including post-traumatic stress disorder (PTSD), social anxiety, specific phobias, and schizophrenia (Phillips, Drevets, Rauch, & Lane, 2003; Etkin & Wager, 2007; Crespo-Facorro et al., 2000; Wright, I. C., Rabe-Hesketh, Mellers, & Bullmore, 2000). Regions of the prefrontal cortex, an area devoted to decision making and cognitive processing, were also larger in meditators. Given the emphasis on observing sensory stimuli that occurs during meditation, thickening in these regions is consistent with reports of mindfulness practice.

Four additional studies have confirmed and extended the results from our group (Pagnoni & Cekic, 2007; Hölzel et al., 2008; Luders, Toga, Lepore, & Gaser, 2009; Vestergaard-Poulsen et al., 2009). Each study has used slightly different experimental methods and study populations, including practitioners of Zen and Tibetan Buddhist meditation. Despite these differences, three brain regions with altered gray matter structure have been identified in at least two studies, giving extra credence to the findings. These three regions are the right anterior insula, the hippocampus, and the left inferior temporal gyrus. The hippocampus plays a central role in memory, while the inferior temporal lobe is involved in creating the sense of agency. One important caveat to these finding is that these studies have all employed long-term meditation practitioners, so the observed differences could be due to other lifestyle differences between the groups, such as vegetarian diet or openness to new cultures. Recently, we completed a study examining the effects of mindfulness-based stress reduction (MBSR) on brain structure in healthy but stressed individuals new to meditation (Hölzel et al., in press). We were able to detect changes in the hippocampus and inferior temporal lobe after just eight weeks of practice (Hölzel et al., under review). Furthermore, the amygdala shrank in individuals who reported feeling less stressed, consistent with animal studies showing correlations between the size of the amygdala and stress behaviors (Hölzel et al., in press). These data indicate that meaningful changes in brain structure can happen in as little as two months of practice.

One interesting recent study focused on the brain stem, a region important for the control of basic functions such as breathing and heart rate. This study suggested that meditation may be associated with increased density of gray matter in the medulla oblongata in the brain stem (Vestergaard-Poulsen et al., 2009). Growth in this region was also identified in an ongoing MBSR study in our laboratory (Hölzel et al., under review). While these findings are preliminary, increased gray matter in these regions may suggest increased innervation from cortical centers, which might result in greater top-down control over largely automatic processes. If true, this would be consistent with self-reports of decreased arousal when reacting to aversive situations. Increased density in this region may also reflect enhanced projections from the brain stem to higher cortical regions involved in interoceptive awareness, such as the insula.

Related to these findings, several reports suggest that regular meditation practice may slow the gradual degeneration of neural tissue associated with normal aging. Both Lazar and colleagues and Pagnoni and colleagues reported that a subset of brain regions in experienced meditators failed to show the typical decline in gray matter volume with age, while individuals in control samples did show this decline (Lazar et al., 2005; Pagnoni & Cekic, 2007). These findings suggest that mindfulness practices may serve as a protective factor against decreases in gray matter and cognitive abilities associated with normal aging.

CHANGES IN ATTENTION AND COGNITIVE CONTROL

Drawing from the self-reported claims of meditation practitioners, changes in attentional resources have been the focus of several recent studies. In the cognitive psychology literature, "attention" is a blanket term that may be used to describe all or some of a set of discrete subprocesses that collectively underlie our ability to attend to different stimuli. Examples of these subprocesses include *alerting* (becoming aware of a sudden novel stimulus, such as a car horn honking), *sustained attention* to a single object, and *conflict monitoring* (remaining focused on a preferred stimulus despite the presence of a distracting or conflicting stimulus).

In an early study, Valentine and Sweet (1999) sought to directly compare the effects of mindfulness and concentration meditation on sustained attention in both novice and experienced practitioners of Zen meditation. In traditional Buddhist practice, beginning meditators are first instructed to concentrate on observing the breath. Over time, as meditators' ability to sustain attention on the breath increases, they're gradually instructed to broaden their attention to other external and internal stimuli. For this study, Valentine and Sweet classified all subjects as either mindfulness or concentration meditators depending on self-reports regarding their mental focus during meditation. Meditation subjects and a control group were compared on a task in which they had to count rapidly presented beeps, which is a measure of sustained attention. All meditators were significantly better than controls in their ability to detect all stimuli, suggesting that both groups had developed heightened attention as a result of their practice. However, the mindfulness meditators were significantly better in their ability to detect unexpected stimuli (tones with different repetition frequencies) compared to the concentration group, consistent with the intention of each practice. When the two meditation groups were subdivided based on total number of years they had practiced, there were striking and significant differences between novice and experienced subjects in the ability to detect the stimuli, with subjects having more than two years of practice able to detect approximately 5 percent more of the stimuli than the subjects with less than two years practice, regardless of meditation style. This last finding strongly suggests that the differences between the meditators and controls were due to practice effects and not to personality differences between groups.

In a more recent study, Jha and colleagues evaluated the effects of MBSR versus a one-month intensive meditation retreat as compared to a control group (Jha, Krompinger, & Baime, 2007). They reported that both the retreat and MBSR groups showed improvements in sustained attention relative to the control group. They did not, however, find differences in alerting or conflict monitoring. Another study found that individuals who received a week of training in a form of Chinese mindfulness meditation called integrative body-mind training showed improved performance during conflict monitoring as compared to a control group who received training in the relaxation response program (Tang et al., 2007). The discrepancy between these two studies may result from the different styles of meditation used, highlighting the importance of considering the heterogeneity of meditation style and practice when trying to compare results across studies. Finally, a third study exploring the effects of meditation training found that meditators improved on the Stroop task, a measure of cognitive control, following an eight-day Zen meditation retreat (Kozasa, Radvany, Barreiros, Leite, & Amaro, 2008). These studies of novices undergoing short meditation interventions again highlights the fact that one need not become a monk or practice for years in order to obtain important, demonstrable benefits of meditation practice.

Another longitudinal study sought to investigate whether intense meditation practice during a three-month silent retreat would increase an individual's attentional capacity. When two stimuli are presented in quick succession, people generally have trouble identifying the second stimulus, a phenomenon known as attentional blink. This reduced ability to process two stimuli in close temporal proximity is thought to be an index of stimuli competing for limited attentional resources (Shapiro, Arnell, & Raymond, 1997). Researchers found that meditators showed less of an attentional blink response after the three-month retreat. Consistent with these behavioral findings, simultaneously recorded EEG signals showed that individuals who performed best on the attentional blink task also exhibited the least amount of brain activity, suggesting that they were able to allocate their attentional resources more efficiently (Slagter et al., 2007; Slagter, Lutz, Greischar, Nieuwenhuis, & Davidson, 2009).

Functional Changes in Studies of Emotion Regulation and Stress

A commonly cited benefit of meditation practice is a decreased reactivity to one's own emotional experiences. In Western psychology, this process is typically referred to as emotion regulation (Gross & Thompson, 2007). In several seminal studies of healthy subjects, researchers have probed the neural circuitry involved in increasing or decreasing emotional responses to neutral, aversive, and positive photographs (Ochsner, Bunge, Gross, & Gabrieli, 2002; Ochsner et al., 2004). These studies have revealed that corticolimbic circuits play a critical role in successful emotional regulation. When trying to decrease their emotional response to aversive images, subjects exhibited increased activity in the ACC and dorsolateral prefrontal cortex, and this activity was associated with decreased activity in the amygdala, a region often associated with emotional arousal.

Several studies have sought to explore this emotion regulation network in adept meditators. One recent study examined differences in Tibetan monks and novice meditators in response to aversive sounds during meditation (Lutz, Brefczynski-Lewis, et al., 2008). These researchers reported that, in comparison to novice meditators, the monks showed increased activation in the anterior insula when hearing aversive as opposed to positive emotional sounds. The localization to the insula is consistent with known activation of this region by negative emotional stimuli (e.g.,

Phillips et al., 2003), as well as by prior reports suggesting that this region is altered through meditation experience (Lazar et al., 2005; Hölzel et al., 2008). These data imply that the structural changes associated with practice may underlie the improved emotion regulation demonstrated by the monks.

A second study, among a group of healthy college students who were nonmeditators, explored the relationship between self-reported trait mindfulness and identifying emotions expressed in facial stimuli (Creswell, Way, Eisenberger, & Lieberman, 2007). This study is unique in that it focused on mindfulness as an inherent skill outside of the context of meditation practice. The authors found that dispositional mindfulness, as measured by a validated self-report questionnaire, was correlated with increases in brain activity in the medial prefrontal cortex and inversely correlated with decreases in amygdala activity during an affect labeling task. It is well-known that the medial prefrontal cortex exerts top-down regulation on the amygdala, and a wide variety of pathological states, including depression, schizophrenia, PTSD, obsessive-compulsive disorder, and anorexia are associated with altered medial prefrontal cortex functioning. The authors propose that mindfulness may therefore be associated with improved prefrontal regulation of limbic responses, possibly helping explain part of why mindfulness is a useful component of therapy.

Finally, Farb and colleagues (2007) examined how MBSR training may impact neural networks involved in self-referential experience. Self-reference has historically been divided into two distinct forms: momentary self-awareness, focused on present experience, and extended self-reference, in terms of enduring characteristics, such as "I'm tall," "I'm generally upbeat," and so on. The authors hypothesized that mindfulness training may help individuals better discriminate between these two forms of self-reference. Using fMRI, they investigated the neural networks that became active during an experiential focus condition in which subjects focused on present-moment experiences, as compared to a narrative focus condition in which subjects considered their personality traits. The researchers found that while the control group showed significant overlap in brain regions activated during the experiential and narrative focus conditions, the group that had just completed an MBSR program did not. This suggests that one possible mechanism of action for mindfulness meditation is a decoupling of two self-referential neural networks that are normally integrated, along with a strengthening of the experiential network, which is consistent with the goals of MBSR training.

SUMMARY AND CLINICAL IMPLICATIONS

In this section we provide a brief summary of a few important clinical findings and explore how recent neurobiological studies of meditation and mindfulness may be relevant to clinical work. While still in its nascent stages, this research also highlights the possible role of meditation as an effective technique for *preventing* psychiatric illness, as studies suggest that MBSR promotes resilience, positive affect, and healthy aging.

Increased Time Living in the Moment

One of the hallmarks of long-term meditation practice is the ability to experience negative emotions without necessarily getting caught up in them. This skill has significant implications for the treatment of common forms of psychopathology, particularly mood and anxiety disorders. Both families of disorders involve excessive rumination on negative thoughts, and mindfulness training incorporates a set of techniques that helps individuals reduce their tendency to ruminate (Jain et al., 2007). If mindfulness can indeed help individuals decouple their present-moment experience from their long-term sense of narrative self, as suggested by Farb and colleagues (2007), this may explain how it helps individuals focus on their current experience rather than negative thoughts relating to past experiences or future worries.

Increased Positive Affect

Although many long-term practitioners have reported high levels of equanimity and contentment as a result of their meditation practice, objective measurement of the tantalizing link between mindfulness and happiness is difficult to quantify. However, a few studies have offered some hints that mindfulness practices may help foment positive affect, including among clinical populations.

A key to this increase in positive affect is enhanced emotion regulation. Successful emotion regulation has been shown to be a significant predictor of overall well-being (Gross & Thompson, 2007). Several of the studies discussed above have demonstrated that meditation experience results in alteration of key emotion regulation networks. Additionally, Richard Davidson and colleagues (2003) measured resting EEG patterns in healthy subjects before and after an eight-week MBSR intervention as compared to a control group. Davidson had previously shown that patients suffering from depression and anxiety have increased EEG power in the right half of the brain while resting quietly, while psychologically healthy subjects have greater activity on the left (Henriques & Davidson, 1991). Although the 2003 study was small, the results indicated that a leftward shift in resting EEG patterns could be detected after eight weeks of practice and that this shift persisted for three months after completion of the study. Importantly, the observed changes were also correlated with improved immune function.

Reduced Stress Reactivity

Cultivation of equanimity increases the practitioner's ability to experience negative events with less reactivity. Goleman and Schwartz (1976) hypothesized that meditators should demonstrate less physiological reactivity to unpleasant stimuli compared to controls. To test this hypothesis, they measured skin conductance responses from meditators and controls while the subjects viewed reenacted wood-shop accidents. Skin conductance response measures the amount of sweat produced as an indicator of autonomic arousal. Compared to controls, the meditation subjects experienced a slightly larger initial increase in skin conductance responses but then returned to baseline levels more quickly, indicating that they had heightened responses to the negative images but were able to quickly let go of the images and return to a state of mental calm and equilibrium. Presumably these subjects are less engaged in ruminative thoughts that would prolong their autonomic arousal.

More recent results from Tang and colleagues (2007) confirm this idea and suggest that meditation may reduce stress-related activity of the hypothalamic-pituitary-adrenal (HPA) axis, a major signaling pathway for stress. The HPA axis has been heavily implicated in mood and anxiety disorders, including depression and PTSD. Some theorists have argued that hyperactivity of the HPA axis may actually play a causal role in the development of these disorders (e.g., Holsboer, 2000). If mindfulness practices are indeed effective at reducing the activity of the HPA axis, then they may be able to function as a prevention technique for populations at risk of developing such disorders, including combat veterans and children exposed to stress early in life.

Enhanced Cognitive Vitality

Another potentially important benefit of long-term meditation is the protection against cortical thinning that normally occurs in old age. Two studies have independently demonstrated that in individuals who regularly practice meditation, certain parts of the brain appear to be protected from the normal patterns of reduced gray matter volume and cortical thinning associated with aging (Lazar et al., 2005; Pagnoni & Cekic, 2007). Given the growing increases in life expectancy, it is critical to identify practices that may improve cognitive longevity and therefore quality of life as we age. This is particularly true given that advanced age is a significant risk factor for other psychiatric disorders, such as major depression. Further study is needed to verify that meditation confers protection against age-related cognitive decline. If so, meditation could be a potentially powerful intervention for older adults.

CONCLUSIONS

The purpose of this chapter has been to provide an overview of the recent neurobiological literature on mindfulness meditation and the evidence for mindfulness-based neuroplasticity, as well as some of the clinical applications of this work. Given the heterogeneity of meditation techniques, future comparative studies are needed to elucidate both common mechanisms and differential effects associated with different styles of meditation practice. Particularly when working with clinical populations, studies are likely to find that different forms of meditation are more or less well-suited to help individuals with specific types of disorders. Learning how to select the right form of meditation practice to best match the needs of an individual patient is a critical next step in the clinical application of mindfulness-based treatment. Of crucial importance in this effort will be the use of longitudinal study designs, in which researchers can compare clinical and neurobiological changes in individuals at pre- and post-treatment time points.

Overall, clinicians should be encouraged by the results of the neurobiological research on meditation. This work strongly supports the hypothesis that meditation can change the structure and function of the brain, and that these changes are associated with cognitive and emotional benefits. While there is still much to understand, research findings generally support the use of meditation as a powerful technique in clinical practice.

REFERENCES

Altman, J. (1962). Are new neurons formed in the brains of adult mammals? *Science, 135*, 1127-1128.

Austin, J. H. (1998). *Zen and the brain: Toward an understanding of meditation and consciousness.* Cambridge, MA: MIT Press.

Austin, J. H. (2006). *Zen-brain reflections.* Cambridge, MA: MIT Press.

Azari, N. P., Nickel, J., Wunderlich, G., Niedeggen, M., Hefter, H., Tellmann, L., et al. (2001). Neural correlates of religious experience. *European Journal of Neuroscience, 13*, 1649-1652.

Baer, R. A. (2006). *Mindfulness-based treatment approaches: Clinician's guide to evidence base and applications.* San Diego, CA: Elsevier.

Baerentsen, K. B., Hartvig, N. V., Stødkilde-Jørgensen, H., & Mammen, J. (2001). Onset of meditation explored with fMRI. *NeuroImage, 13*, S297.

Brefczynski-Lewis, J. A., Lutz, A., Schaefer, H. S., Levinson, D. B., & Davidson, R. J. (2007). Neural correlates of attentional expertise in long-term meditation practitioners. *Proceedings of the National Academy of Sciences of the United States of America, 104*, 11483-11488.

Bush, G., Luu, P., & Posner, M. I. (2000). Cognitive and emotional influences in anterior cingulate cortex. *Trends in Cognitive Sciences, 4*, 215-222.

Cahn, B. R., & Polich, J. (2006). Meditation states and traits: EEG, ERP, and neuroimaging studies. *Psychological Bulletin, 132*, 180-211.

Casey, K. L., Minoshima, S., Morrow, T. J., & Koeppe, R. A. (1996). Comparison of human cerebral activation pattern during cutaneous warmth, heat pain, and deep cold pain. *Journal of Neurophysiology, 76*, 571-581.

Craig, A. D. (2009). How do you feel—now? The anterior insula and human awareness. *Nature Reviews. Neuroscience, 10*, 59-70.

Crespo-Facorro, B., Kim, J., Andreasen, N. C., O'Leary, D. S., Bockholt, H. J., & Magnotta, V. (2000). Insular cortex abnormalities in schizophrenia: A structural magnetic resonance imaging study of first-episode patients. *Schizophrenia Research, 46*, 35-43.

Creswell, J. D., Way, B. M., Eisenberger, N. I., & Lieberman, M. D. (2007). Neural correlates of dispositional mindfulness during affect labeling. *Psychosomatic Medicine, 69*, 560-565.

Davidson, R. J., Kabat-Zinn, J., Schumacher, J., Rosenkranz, M., Muller, D., Santorelli, S. F., et al. (2003). Alterations in brain and immune function produced by mindfulness meditation. *Psychosomatic Medicine, 65*, 564-570.

Draganski, B., Gaser, C., Busch, V., Schuierer, G., Bogdahn, U., & May, A. (2004). Neuroplasticity: Changes in grey matter induced by training. *Nature, 427*, 311-312.

Etkin, A., & Wager, T. D. (2007). Functional neuroimaging of anxiety: A meta-analysis of emotional processing in PTSD, social anxiety disorder, and specific phobia. *Journal of Psychiatry, 164*, 1476-1488.

Farb, N. A., Segal, Z. V., Mayberg, H., Bean, J., McKeon, D., Fatima, Z., et al. (2007). Attending to the present: Mindfulness meditation reveals distinct neural modes of self-reference. *Social Cognitive and Affective Neuroscience, 2*, 313-322.

Goleman, D. J., & Schwartz, G. E. (1976). Meditation as an intervention in stress reactivity. *Journal of Consulting and Clinical Psychology, 44*, 456-466.

Gross, J. J., & Thompson, R. A. (2007). Emotion regulation: Conceptual foundations. In J. J. Gross (Ed.), *Handbook of emotion regulation*. New York: Guilford.

Henriques, J. B., & Davidson, R. J. (1991). Left frontal hypoactivation in depression. *Journal of Abnormal Psychology, 100*, 535-545.

Holsboer, F. (2000). The corticosteroid receptor hypothesis of depression. *Neuropsychopharmacology, 23*, 477-501.

Hölzel, B. K., Carmody, J., Congleton, C., McCallister, A., Yerramsetti, S. M., & Lazar, S. W. (under review). *Meditation practice leads to increases in regional brain gray matter concentration.* Manuscript under review.

Hölzel, B. K., Carmody, J., Evans, K. C., Hoge, E. A., Dusek, J. A., Morgan, L., et al. (in press). Stress reduction correlates with structural changes in the amygdala. *Social Cognitive and Affective Neuroscience.*

Hölzel, B. K., Ott, U., Gard, T., Hempel, H., Weygandt, M., Morgen, K., et al. (2008). Investigation of mindfulness meditation practitioners with voxel-based morphometry. *Social Cognitive and Affective Neuroscience, 3*, 55-61.

Hölzel, B. K., Ott, U., Hempel, H., Hackl, A., Wolf, K., Stark, R., et al. (2007). Differential engagement of anterior cingulate and adjacent medial frontal cortex in adept meditators and non-meditators. *Neuroscience Letters, 421*, 16-21.

Huettel, S. A., Song, A. W., & McCarthy, G. (2008). *Functional magnetic resonance imaging* (2nd ed.). Sunderland, MA: Sinauer Associates.

Jain, S., Shapiro, S. L., Swanick, S., Roesch, S. C., Mills, P. J., Bell, I., et al. (2007). A randomized controlled trial of mindfulness meditation versus relaxation training: Effects on distress, positive states of mind, rumination, and distraction. *Annals of Behavioral Medicine, 33*, 11-21.

Jha, A. P., Krompinger, J., & Baime, M. J. (2007). Mindfulness training modifies subsystems of attention. *Cognitive, Affective and Behavioral Neuroscience, 7*, 109-119.

Kozasa, E. H., Radvany, J., Barreiros, M. A., Leite, J. R., & Amaro, E., Jr. (2008). Preliminary functional magnetic resonance imaging Stroop task results before and after a Zen meditation retreat. *Psychiatry and Clinical Neurosciences, 62*, 366.

Lazar, S. W. (2005). Mindfulness research. In R. D. Siegel & P. R. Fulton (Eds.), *Mindfulness and psychotherapy*. New York: Guilford.

Lazar, S. W., Bush, G., Gollub, R. L., Fricchione, G. L., Khalsa, G., & Benson, H. (2000). Functional brain mapping of the relaxation response and meditation. *Neuroreport, 11*, 1581-1585.

Lazar, S. W., Kerr, C. E., Wasserman, R. H., Gray, J. R., Greve, D. N., Treadway, M. T., et al. (2005). Meditation experience is associated with increased cortical thickness. *Neuroreport, 16*, 1893-1897.

Liotti, M., Mayberg, H. S., McGinnis, S., Brannan, S. L., & Jerabek, P. (2002). Unmasking disease-specific cerebral blood flow abnormalities: Mood challenge in patients with remitted unipolar depression. *American Journal of Psychiatry, 159*, 1830-1840.

Luders, E., Toga, A. W., Lepore, N., & Gaser, C. (2009). The underlying anatomical correlates of long-term meditation: Larger hippocampal and frontal volumes of gray matter. *NeuroImage, 45*, 672-678.

Lutz, A., Brefczynski-Lewis, J., Johnstone, T., & Davidson, R. J. (2008). Regulation of the neural circuitry of emotion by compassion meditation: Effects of meditative expertise. *PLoS One, 3*, e1897.

Lutz, A., Slagter, H. A., Dunne, J. D., & Davidson, R. J. (2008). Attention regulation and monitoring in meditation. *Trends in Cognitive Sciences, 12*, 163-169.

Maguire, E. A., Gadian, D. G., Johnsrude, I. S., Good, C. D., Ashburner, J., Frackowiak, R. S., et al. (2000). Navigation-related structural change in the hippocampi of taxi drivers. *Proceedings of the National Academy of Sciences of the United States of America, 97*, 4398-4403.

McNab, F., Varrone, A., Farde, L., Jucaite, A., Bystritsky, P., Forssberg, H., et al. (2009). Changes in cortical dopamine D1 receptor binding associated with cognitive training. *Science, 323*, 800-802.

Murphy, M., Donovan, S., & Taylor, E. (1997). *The physical and psychological effects of meditation: A review of contemporary research 1991-1996.* Petaluma, CA: Institute of Noetic Sciences.

Newberg, A., Alavi, A., Baime, M., Pourdehnad, M., Santanna, J., & d'Aquili, E. (2001). The measurement of regional cerebral blood flow during the complex cognitive task of meditation: A preliminary SPECT study. *Psychiatry Research, 106*, 113-122.

Ochsner, K. N., Bunge, S. A., Gross, J. J., & Gabrieli, J. D. (2002). Rethinking feelings: An fMRI study of the cognitive regulation of emotion. *Journal of Cognitive Neuroscience, 14*, 1215-1229.

Ochsner, K. N., Ray, R. D., Cooper, J. C., Robertson, E. R., Chopra, S., Gabrieli, J. D., et al. (2004). For better or for worse: Neural systems supporting the cognitive down- and up-regulation of negative emotion. *NeuroImage, 23*, 483-499.

Pagnoni, G., & Cekic, M. (2007). Age effects on gray matter volume and attentional performance in Zen meditation. *Neurobiology of Aging, 28*, 1623-1627.

Paus, T. (2001). Primate anterior cingulate cortex: Where motor control, drive and cognition interface. *Nature Reviews. Neuroscience, 2*, 417-424.

Phillips, M. L., Drevets, W. C., Rauch, S. L., & Lane, R. (2003). Neurobiology of emotion perception II: Implications for major psychiatric disorders. *Biological Psychiatry, 54*, 515-528.

Reiman, E. M., Lane, R. D., Ahern, G. L., Schwartz, G. E., Davidson, R. J., Friston, K. J., et al. (1997). Neuroanatomical correlates of externally and internally generated human emotion. *American Journal of Psychiatry, 154*, 918-925.

Ritskes, R., Ritskes-Hoitinga, M., Stodkilde-Jorgensen, H., Baerentsen, K., & Hartman, T. (2003). MRI scanning during Zen meditation: The picture of enlightenment? *Constructivism in the Human Sciences, 8*, 85-90.

Shapiro, K. L., Arnell, K. M., & Raymond, J. E. (1997). The attentional blink. *Trends in Cognitive Sciences, 1*, 204-211.

Shin, L. M., Dougherty, D. D., Orr, S. P., Pitman, R. K., Lasko, M., Macklin, M. L., et al. (2000). Activation of anterior paralimbic structures during guilt-related script-driven imagery. *Biological Psychiatry, 48*, 43-50.

Sirotin, Y. B., & Das, A. (2009). Anticipatory haemodynamic signals in sensory cortex not predicted by local neuronal activity. *Nature, 457*, 475-479.

Slagter, H. A., Lutz, A., Greischar, L. L., Francis, A. D., Nieuwenhuis, S., Davis, J. M., et al. (2007). Mental training affects distribution of limited brain resources. *PLoS Biology, 5*, e138.

Slagter, H. A., Lutz, A., Greischar, L. L., Nieuwenhuis, S., & Davidson, R. J. (2009). Theta phase synchrony and conscious target perception: Impact of intensive mental training. *Journal of Cognitive Neuroscience, 21*, 1536-1549.

Sridharan, D., Levitin, D. J., & Menon, V. (2008). A critical role for the right fronto-insular cortex in switching between central-executive and default-mode networks, *Proceedings of the National Academy of Sciences of the United States of America, 105*, 12569-12574.

Sun, F. T., Miller, L. M., Rao, A. A., & D'Esposito, M. (2007). Functional connectivity of cortical networks involved in bimanual motor sequence learning. *Cerebral Cortex, 17*, 1227-1234.

Tang, Y. Y., Ma, Y., Wang, J., Fan, Y., Feng, S., Lu, Q., et al. (2007). Short-term meditation training improves attention and self-regulation. *Proceedings of the National Academy of Sciences of the United States of America, 104*, 17152-17156.

Valentine, E. R., & Sweet, P. L. G. (1999). Meditation and attention: A comparison of the effects of concentrative and mindfulness meditation on sustained attention. *Mental Health, Religion and Culture, 2*, 59-70.

Vestergaard-Poulsen, P., van Beek, M., Skewes, J., Bjarkam, C. R., Stubberup, M., Bertelsen, J., et al. (2009). Long-term meditation is associated with increased gray matter density in the brain stem. *Neuroreport, 20*, 170-174.

Vogt, S., Buccino, G., Wohlschläger, A. M., Canessa, N., Shah, N. J., Zilles, K., et al. (2007). Prefrontal involvement in imitation learning of hand actions: Effects of practice and expertise. *NeuroImage, 37*, 1371-1383.

Wright, I. C., Rabe-Hesketh, S., Mellers, J., & Bullmore, E. T. (2000). Testing for laterality differences in regional brain volumes. *Archive of General Psychiatry, 57*, 511-512.

Wright, P., He, G., Shapira, N. A., Goodman, W. K., & Liu, Y. (2004). Disgust and the insula: FMRI responses to pictures of mutilation and contamination. *Neuroreport, 15*, 2347-2351.

Chapter 8

What Does Mindfulness Training Strengthen? Working Memory Capacity as a Functional Marker of Training Success

Amishi P. Jha, University of Pennsylvania; Elizabeth A. Stanley, Georgetown University; and Michael J. Baime, University of Pennsylvania

Over 1,500 years ago, the Indian Buddhist sage Master Asanga offered a useful description of mindfulness: "nonforgetfulness of the mind, having the function of nondistraction" (Wallace, 2005, p. 157). In this definition, seen repeatedly in other ancient texts, holding in mind and remembering the object of the mind were considered to be central features of *smriti*, the Sanskrit term for mindfulness. (In Pali, the language of the earliest Buddhist scriptures, it is known as *sati*). These ancient definitions emphasize the process of holding awareness from the *prior* moment into the present moment. They differ from current conceptualizations of mindfulness, which emphasize the ongoing process of attending to present-moment experience in a particular way, with no mention of holding onto any aspect of the prior moment (Kabat-Zinn, 1994). This distinction is subtle and may seem meaningless, since there is an apparent attentional interdependence between the prior moment and the present moment. Yet "holding" emphasizes the influence of a memory-related trace originating in the recent past as the entryway into our present-moment experience, while "attending to" emphasizes the contents of present-moment experience over the putative influence of recent memory.

An understanding of mindfulness offered by expert practitioners' first-person accounts detailed within ancient texts suggests that memory-related features of mindfulness are important (for review, see Wallace, 2005, pp. 58-60). It is striking that the historical framing of mindfulness, as the mental mode of remembering to attend to information most relevant to present-moment experience while remaining undistracted, is akin to the cognitive neuroscience construct of working memory. In this chapter, we provide an overview of theory and research on working memory and suggest that working memory capacity may be a useful functional marker of mindfulness. Further, we argue that advancing our understanding of the mechanisms of action by which mindfulness training produces salutary effects requires a richer account of its relationship to working memory.

WORKING MEMORY CAPACITY

Working memory capacity (WMC) is the capacity to selectively maintain and manipulate goal-relevant information without becoming distracted by irrelevant information over short intervals. As such, working memory capacity comprises attentional processes to select information and appropriate behavioral responses, and memory-related processes to maintain information in an active, easily accessible form. This capacity allows task-relevant information to be readily available in the service of current goals.

Working memory is used during many everyday activities, from holding in mind a list of beverage requests from guests while hosting a dinner party to remembering which clerk behind the bank counter is helping us with a complex multistep transaction. A variety of information can be maintained in working memory. Information can be verbal (beverage names), visual (facial features of bank clerks), spatial, conceptual, or phonetic. Importantly, errors in working memory performance are most likely when we encounter distraction and interference; for example, when a dinner guest bursts into celebratory song (verbal interference) or when all of the bank clerks are wearing similar uniforms and have short brown hair (visual interference). Working memory is beneficial when short-term but not long-term storage of information is most useful. In the real world, party guests are more likely to have a good time if they receive the beverages they requested this evening, as opposed to what they asked for at the last party.

LABORATORY EVALUATION OF WORKING MEMORY CAPACITY AND ATTENTION

Laboratory tasks for assessing working memory attempt to capture the critical components of storing information over very short intervals while resisting distraction. One widely used and well-validated task is the operation span task (Ospan). In this task, participants have to memorize unrelated words or, in some variants, letter sequences and also verify simple mathematical statements, such as "Is 10/2 – 2 = 1?" (Kane & Engle, 2002; Unsworth, Heitz, Schrock, & Engle, 2005). Words to be memorized alternate with equations to be verified, and after viewing a series of words and equations, the participants must report all of the words in the correct serial order. As the number of word-equation pairs increases, participants become progressively unable to report the words. The number of words that are consecutively reported without error is used to calculate an individual's operation span score. Performance measures on tasks indexing WMC, such as the Ospan, are highly correlated with performance on tasks measuring attentional processes. These include tasks of attentional orienting (Unsworth, Schrock, & Engle, 2004) and conflict monitoring (Redick & Engle, 2006).

As with working memory, attentional orienting and conflict monitoring systems are used frequently in everyday life. Orienting involves voluntarily directing attention to the most task-relevant subset of information and restricting information from all other less relevant inputs. In a clothing store, for example, we use our orienting system to selectively restrict our gaze toward the dressing room on the far left as we wait for our friend to exit so we can hurry to a movie that is about to start. We use our conflict monitoring system to prioritize between competing behaviors while overcoming habitual or automatic behavior. An example of successful conflict monitoring is when we walk past our own car in the mall parking lot and head toward our friend's car so that she can drive us to the movie theater. While habit might lead us straight to our car, our conflict monitoring system allows us to overcome this habitual behavior to guide us toward the appropriate destination for the task at hand. As is apparent from these examples, working memory, orienting, and conflict monitoring are all operating during most real-life scenarios. Even while orienting and conflict monitoring processes are guiding our present-moment behavior (gazing at the dressing room door or walking toward our friend's car), it is our working memory system that keeps active our plan to go to the matinee in our friend's car. Working memory also holds a representation of which one among the many dressing rooms is occupied by our friend. Thus, working memory is critical for guiding attentional processes in the service of current goals.

THE ROLE OF WORKING MEMORY IN DEALING WITH COGNITIVE AND AFFECTIVE CHALLENGES

Tasks in which mental content is emotionally neutral, such maintaining a list of our guests' beverage requests during a dinner party, are characterized as having "cold" cognitive demands. Complex analytical reasoning problems found on tests such as the LSAT and IQ tests are highly demanding of cold cognitive control. It is well established that higher WMC is tied to improved performance on cold cognitive tasks. For instance, performance on WMC tasks corresponds with general fluid intelligence scores and academic achievement (see Kane & Engle, 2002, for review). WMC also correlates with increased success on laboratory tests of orienting and conflict monitoring when stimuli are digits, numbers, letters, and symbols (Unsworth et al., 2004).

WMC is also sensitive to individual differences in the ability to manage mental content that is emotionally valenced, or "hot." Individuals with lower WMC suffer from more emotionally intrusive thoughts, have less success in suppressing positive and negative emotions, and have difficulty with emotion reappraisal tasks (Brewin & Smart, 2005; Schmeichel, Volokhov, & Demaree, 2008). Thus, WMC correlates with an individual's success at willfully guiding behavior while overcoming cognitive and affective (cold or hot) challenges, distractions, and conditioned response tendencies. At a dinner party, a host with high WMC is more likely to successfully fulfill drink requests, whether distractions come in the form of friends loudly singing Jimmy Buffett lyrics with various beverage names or an angry outburst from a guest who felt overlooked.

While individuals differ in their baseline level of WMC, and thus in their degree of success at cold and hot control, individuals at all levels of WMC suffer from degradation in their WMC after engaging in highly demanding tasks (Schmeichel, 2007). Importantly, reduced WMC is observed regardless of whether the task requires cold cognitive processing, such as performing a conflict monitoring task, or hot emotional processing, such as suppressing the experience of anxiety (Johns, Inzlicht, & Schmader, 2008) or inhibiting emotional expressions while watching an emotionally evocative video (Schmeichel, 2007). These lines of research reveal that WMC is a generalizable capacity, in that it can be used for both cognitive control and emotion regulation. They also reveal that WMC can be depleted, thus limiting the capacity to overcome cognitive or affective challenges.

Interestingly, although WMC fatigues after it is used intensively in demanding tasks, it can also be improved and strengthened through training. Many studies have demonstrated that working memory processes are bolstered with computer-based training methods that engage attention and working memory processes with affectively neutral stimuli (e.g., Olesen, Westerberg, & Klingberg, 2004; Persson & Reuter-Lorenz, 2008). The degree of improvement in working memory corresponds to practice duration (Jaeggi, Buschkuehl, Jonides, & Perrig, 2008) akin to a dose-response effect, wherein the more one practices the tasks, the more improvement in WMC is observed. Also, several recent studies of computer-based cognitive control training techniques report that in addition to improving attention and working memory, these training methods reduce affective symptoms in patients with anxiety (Siegle, Ghinassi, & Thase, 2007) and depression (Papageorgiou & Wells, 2000). In other words, these results suggest that it is possible to target improvements in cold cognitive operations and see benefits in affective symptoms. This directional effect mirrors the finding that individuals with higher WMC, as indexed on cold cognitive control tasks like the Ospan, are more successful at emotion reappraisal tasks than individuals with lower WMC (Schmeichel et al., 2008).

EFFECTS OF MINDFULNESS TRAINING ON ATTENTION TASKS

Very little is known about the impact of mindfulness training on WMC (Chambers, Lo, & Allen, 2008). Nonetheless, attention and working memory processes, when indexed in the context of tasks with affectively neutral content (such as symbols, neutral faces, digits, and letters), appear to be highly interdependent and interrelated (e.g., Jha, 2002). Several recent studies (discussed below) provide evidence that mindfulness training improves performance on attention tasks, leading to our prediction that this type of training is likely to improve WMC as well. Research studies examining the impact of mindfulness training on attention tasks have been conducted among both experienced long-term meditation practitioners and novices.

Attentional Improvements in Experienced Mindfulness Practitioners

Functional brain imaging has identified a set of neural structures that are activated during tasks that require the use of attention. These attention network regions include the dorsolateral prefrontal cortex, the superior parietal cortex, and the intraparietal sulcus. Using functional magnetic resonance imaging (fMRI) during performance of an attention task, Brefczynski-Lewis, Lutz, Schaefer, Levinson, and Davidson (2007) reported that systematic alterations in activity within these and other attention network regions varied as a function of the duration of long-term mindfulness practice. Neural and behavioral evidence also suggests that experienced mindfulness practitioners can further bolster attentional functioning by engaging in intensive periods of practice, such as during meditation retreats when participants engage in ten to twelve hours of contemplative practice daily. For example, participation in a three-month retreat by long-term practitioners resulted in performance improvements during the attentional blink task (Slagter et al., 2007). The attentional blink is an effect seen when participants are asked to notice two target stimuli (such as letters) presented in quick succession within a stream of rapidly presented stimuli of another type (such as numbers). The second target stimulus often is not reported; this is thought to be due to competition between the two targets for limited attentional resources. In the study by Slagter and colleagues, retreat participants but not control participants demonstrated a reduced attentional blink effect, suggesting that they had either learned to allocate their attentional resources more efficiently by the end of the retreat, or that those resources had increased.

Another aspect of attention that increases in efficiency with mindfulness practice is attentional alerting, which is the ability to achieve and sustain a vigilant or alert state of preparedness. One study has demonstrated increases in attentional alerting after a one-month retreat (Jha, Krompinger, & Baime, 2007), and other researchers have documented increases in sustained attention after a ten-day retreat (Chambers et al., 2008). Recently, Cahn and Polich (2009) investigated whether the degree of improvement in neural signatures of attention would track with self-reported time spent engaging in daily mindfulness practices among long-term practitioners. They found that attention-related brain wave signatures were largest in participants reporting more time engaging in mindfulness exercises each day. Thus, studies from long-term mindfulness practitioners provide strong support that mindfulness training improves attentional operations.

Attentional Improvements in Novice Mindfulness Practitioners

Attention may be improved with mindfulness training among novices as well. A recent study (Jha et al., 2007) examined how meditation training influences functioning of specific attentional subsystems. Since specific subsystems of attention are related to working memory (Jha, 2002), positive support that mindfulness training improves these aspects of attention would further support the hypothesis that mindfulness training improves WMC. In the study by Jha and colleagues (2007), novice participants receiving mindfulness training in the form of participation in an eight-week mindfulness training course akin to mindfulness-based stress reduction (MBSR; Kabat-Zinn, 1990) courses performed the Attention Network Test (ANT) before and after training.

The ANT has been devised to identify three functionally and neuroanatomically distinct cognitive networks—alerting, orienting, and conflict monitoring—during a single task (Fan, McCandliss, Sommer, Raz, & Posner, 2002). As described previously, alerting consists of achieving and sustaining a vigilant or alert state of preparedness, while orienting restricts processing to the subset of inputs relevant to current task goals, and conflict monitoring prioritizes among competing tasks and resolves conflict between goals and performance. The ANT combines methodology from two basic laboratory paradigms that have been used to investigate attentional subsystems: the attentional spatial cuing paradigm and the flanker paradigm (see Fan et al., 2002, for an overview).

Attentional spatial cuing paradigms provide a means to behaviorally index attentional alerting and orienting. In this paradigm, participants sit at a computer and perform a visual computer task similar to a simple video game. They are instructed to detect a target that is presented following either informative or neutral spatial cues. Informative cues provide spatial information regarding the target location with high probability. Neutral cues signal the imminent appearance of a target but provide no spatial information regarding its location. Neutral cues confer an attentional advantage when compared to no-cue trials. This advantage in performance is thought to be due to alerting. The neutral warning cue signifies that a target is forthcoming and thereby summons greater attentional resources to become available for their forthcoming deployment. Response times are slowest in identifying targets preceded by no cues, faster following neutral cues, and fastest following spatial cues. Comparisons of response times between no-cue and neutral trials assess alerting, and comparisons between neutral and informative cues assess orienting.

Flanker paradigms allow researchers to index conflict monitoring behavior by selectively manipulating the presence or absence of response competition while keeping other task demands constant. In this simple visual computer task, participants are instructed to identify a target by a two-alternative forced choice method; for example, determining if an arrow (<) is facing left or right. The target is surrounded by task-irrelevant "flankers" that are either of the same response category as the target (<<<) or of another response category (><>). Responses in trials in which the flanking stimuli indicate a different response than the central stimulus (incongruent condition) are significantly slower than those in trials in which all stimuli indicate the same response (congruent condition). Slower response times are attributed to the need for greater conflict resolution and monitoring during incongruent relative to congruent trials.

The ANT task incorporates both spatial cuing and flanker paradigms to manipulate both attentional cuing (informative, neutral, and no cues) and the type of target (congruent or incongruent flanker). The response time differences between pairs of conditions are used to assess the functioning of these three networks on this single task. Alerting is indexed by subtracting performance measures on neutral cue trials from no cue trials. Orienting is indexed by subtracting performance measures on spatial cue trials from neutral cue trials. Conflict monitoring is indexed by subtracting performance measures on congruent target from incongruent target trials.

In the 2007 study using the ANT (Jha et al., 2007), participants' training emphasized concentrative practices in which they were guided to selectively attend to some stimuli (their breath) while ignoring all other stimuli. The hypothesis was that mindfulness training emphasizing concentrative practice would be associated with greater efficiency in the functioning of voluntary attentional selection. Indeed, mindfulness training participants improved in their orienting performance relative to control participants.

In addition, other recent studies have found that conflict monitoring is improved in novices after a few days to several weeks of mindfulness training (Chan & Woollacott, 2007; Tang et al., 2007; Wenk-Sormaz, 2005). Since both orienting and conflict monitoring are forms of voluntary attentional selection, these results collectively suggest that mindfulness training in novices may indeed alter the functioning of voluntary input-level (orienting) and response-level (conflict-monitoring) selection processes.

EFFECTS OF MINDFULNESS TRAINING ON EMOTIONAL EXPERIENCE

The above studies review the benefits of mindfulness training on attentional functions in tasks using emotionally neutral stimuli. There is also considerable evidence that mindfulness training may alter information processing for emotional stimuli, may reduce affective symptoms, and may improve affective experience among patients with affective disorders, including generalized anxiety disorder and depression (Evans et al., 2008; Segal, Williams, & Teasdale, 2002; Williams, Russell, & Russell, 2008). Similar results have been found in healthy participants. For example, Jain and colleagues (2007) reported reductions in perceived stress and rumination after participation in a four-week MBSR program versus a relaxation training course. Consistent with this result, Broderick (2005) found that under induced negative mood, brief mindfulness instructions were more beneficial for reducing negative mood than a distraction strategy. Ortner, Kilner, and Zelazo (2007) similarly demonstrated the benefits of mindfulness training in dealing with negative affect. They reported that performance on a perceptual discrimination task requiring participants to remain undistracted after viewing negative disturbing images was improved after seven weeks of mindfulness training. Many other studies (e.g., Anderson, Lau, Segal, & Bishop, 2007; Davidson et al., 2003) also support the conclusion that participation in mindfulness training, whether over days (Broderick, 2005; Chambers et al., 2008), weeks (e.g., Anderson et al., 2007), or decades (e.g., Ortner et al., 2007), positively alters emotional experience by reducing negative mood and improving positive mood and well-being.

Carmody and Baer (2008) extended these findings by exploring the link between practice duration and mindfulness-related changes in emotional experience (see also Shapiro, Oman, Thoreson, Plante, & Flinders, 2008). They correlated the time that individuals spent engaging in formal mindfulness practices during an eight-week clinical MBSR course with changes in medical symptoms and mood following training. Importantly, they found a significant correspondence between practice time and self-reported improvements in well-being and other symptom measures.

WORKING MEMORY CAPACITY AS A MEDIATOR OF THE EMOTIONAL BENEFITS OF MINDFULNESS TRAINING

Clearly, the benefits of mindfulness training for emotional experience are well established. Yet it is unclear why mindfulness training improves emotional experience. One possibility is that the effects of mindfulness training are similar to computer-based cognitive control training (Siegle et al., 2007), in that mindfulness training produces primary improvements in cold cognitive control, which leads to improvements in emotional experience. According to this hypothesis, cold cognitive control mediates the effects of mindfulness training on emotion. Another possibility is that the effects of mindfulness training on emotional experience are a direct result of training and are not mediated by improvements in cold control processes. A third possibility is that mindfulness training has both direct and indirect effects on emotion regulation processes.

We recently explicitly investigated the interrelationships between mindfulness practice duration on cold and hot processes (Jha, Stanley, Kiyonaga, Wong, & Gelfand, in press; Stanley, Kiyonaga, Schaldach, & Jha, under review). We examined the influence of mindfulness training on WMC during the high-stress, resource-depleting period of predeployment military training in a group of Marine reservists. We recruited two predeployment military cohorts and provided mindfulness training to one group (N = 31) but not the other (N = 17). Four months prior to their deployment to Iraq, the mindfulness training group attended an eight-week course called Mindfulness-based Mind Fitness Training (MMFT), which is modeled after MBSR but modified for military contexts (Stanley et al., under review). This group also agreed to candidly log the amount of time they spent engaging in formal mindfulness exercises. Performance on the Ospan task was used to index WMC, and the Positive and Negative Affect Schedule (PANAS; Watson, Clark, & Tellegen, 1988) was used to index positive and negative affect at two time points, corresponding to the beginning (time 1) and end (time 2) of the mindfulness training course. We had three main questions: Do the intense demands of the predeployment period deplete WMC and degrade affective experience over time? Can mindfulness training bolster WMC and affective experiences during the predeployment period? And to the extent that there is a relationship between mindfulness training and affective experience, is it mediated by WMC?

While Ospan performance remained stable in a civilian control group (N = 12), it degraded over time in the military control group. Within the mindfulness training cohort, those who reported low practice time had performance degradation, while those who reported high practice time had improvements in performance over time. In addition, the predeployment interval impacted affective experience. Increases in negative affect and decreases in positive affect at time 2 versus time 1 were more pronounced in the mindfulness training participants who reported low vs. high practice time. In contrast, only minimal fluctuations in affective experience were observed in the group reporting high practice time. To determine if these affective changes were directly related to practice time as opposed to practice-related availability of WMC, we conducted a mediation analysis in the mindfulness training cohort. There was a direct relationship between positive affect and practice time. Yet the relationship between negative affect and practice time was indirect, and mediated by WMC. These preliminary findings suggest that negative and positive affect may be regulated through different mechanisms in the context of mindfulness training. That is, individuals who have engaged in sufficient mindfulness practice to bolster their WMC may use this capacity to control their negative affect, but not to boost their positive affect.

CONCLUSIONS

In sum, a review of the literature on WMC suggests many compelling links with mindfulness training. First, processes sensitive to WMC are also sensitive to mindfulness training, including attentional orienting (Unsworth et al., 2004; Jha et al., 2007), conflict monitoring (Redick & Engle, 2006; Chan & Woollacott, 2007), and the attentional blink (Colzato, Spape, Pannebakker, & Hommel, 2007; Slagter et al., 2007). Second, both WMC (Schmeichel, 2007) and mindfulness training (Carmody & Baer, 2008) correspond to the ability to bolster both cold cognitive performance on these attention tasks and hot emotion regulation processes. Finally, our recent results suggest that mindfulness training alters WMC and that improvements in WMC due to mindfulness training are related to changes in negative affect. Thus, as suggested by Asanga, nonforgetfulness and nondistraction, operationalized in the present-day construct of working memory capacity, may indeed be important components of mindfulness. Future studies investigating the clinical efficacy of mindfulness training should consider using WMC tasks, such as the Ospan, as proximal markers of training success, which may mediate other functional changes.

REFERENCES

Anderson, N. D., Lau, M. A., Segal, Z. V., & Bishop, S. R. (2007). Mindfulness-based stress reduction and attentional control. *Clinical Psychology and Psychotherapy, 14*, 449-463.

Brefczynski-Lewis, J. A., Lutz, A., Schaefer, H. S., Levinson, D. B., & Davidson, R. J. (2007). Neural correlates of attentional expertise in long-term meditation practitioners. *Proceedings of the National Academy of Sciences, 104*, 11483-11488.

Brewin, C. R., & Smart, L. (2005). Working memory capacity and suppression of intrusive thoughts. *Journal of Behavior Therapy and Experimental Psychiatry, 36*, 61-68.

Broderick, P. C. (2005). Mindfulness and coping with dysphoric mood: Contrasts with rumination and distraction. *Cognitive Therapy and Research, 29*, 501-510.

Cahn, B. R., & Polich, J. (2009). Meditation (vipassana) and the P3a event-related brain potential. *International Journal of Psychophysiology, 72*, 51-60.

Carmody, J., & Baer, R. A. (2008). Relationships between mindfulness practice and levels of mindfulness, medical and psychological symptoms and well-being in a mindfulness-based stress reduction program. *Journal of Behavioral Medicine, 31*, 23-33.

Chambers, R., Lo, B. C. Y., & Allen, N. B. (2008). The impact of intensive mindfulness training on attentional control, cognitive style, and affect. *Cognitive Therapy and Research, 32*, 303-322.

Chan, D., & Woollacott, M. (2007). Effects of level of meditation experience on attentional focus: Is the efficiency of executive or orientation networks improved? *Journal of Alternative and Complementary Medicine, 13*, 651-657.

Colzato, L. S., Spape, M. M. A., Pannebakker, M. M., & Hommel, B. (2007). Working memory and the attentional blink: Blink size is predicted by individual differences in operation span. *Psychonomic Bulletin and Review, 14*, 1051-1057.

Davidson, R. J., Kabat-Zinn, J., Shumacher, J., Rosenkrantz, M., Muller, D., Santorelli, S. F., et al. (2003). Alterations in brain and immune function produced by mindfulness meditation. *Psychosomatic Medicine, 65*, 564-570.

Evans, S., Ferrando, S., Findler, M., Stowell, C., Smart, C., & Haglin, D. (2008). Mindfulness-based cognitive therapy for generalized anxiety disorder. *Journal of Anxiety Disorders, 22*, 716-721.

Fan, J., McCandliss, B. D., Sommer, T., Raz, A., & Posner, M. I. (2002). Testing the efficiency and independence of attentional networks. *Journal of Cognitive Neuroscience, 14*, 340-347.

Jaeggi, S. M., Buschkuehl, M., Jonides, J., & Perrig, W. J. (2008). Improving fluid intelligence with training on working memory. *Proceedings of the National Academy of Sciences, 105*, 6829-6833.

Jain, S., Shapiro, S. L., Swanick, S., Roesch, S. C., Mills, P. J., Bell, I., et al. (2007). A randomized controlled trial of mindfulness meditation versus relaxation training: Effects on distress, positive states of mind, rumination, and distraction. *Annals of Behavioral Medicine, 33*, 11-21.

Jha, A. P. (2002). Tracking the time course of attentional involvement in spatial working memory: An event-related potential investigation. *Cognitive Brain Research, 15*, 61-69.

Jha, A. P., Krompinger, J., & Baime, M. J. (2007). Mindfulness training modifies subsystems of attention. *Cognitive, Affective, and Behavioral Neuroscience, 7*, 109-119.

Jha, A. P., Stanley, E. A, Kiyonaga, A., Wong, L., & Gelfand, L. (under review). *Examining the protective effects of mindfulness training on working memory capacity and affective experience.* Manuscript under review.

Johns, M., Inzlicht, M., & Schmader, T. (2008). Stereotype threat and executive resource depletion: Examining the influence of emotion regulation. *Journal of Experimental Psychology. General, 37*, 1-705.

Kabat-Zinn, J. (1990). *Full catastrophe living: Using the wisdom of your mind and body to face stress, pain, and illness.* New York: Delacorte.

Kabat-Zinn, J. (1994). *Mindfulness meditation for everyday life.* New York: Hyperion.

Kane, M. J., & Engle, R. W. (2002). The role of prefrontal cortex in working-memory capacity, executive attention, and general fluid intelligence: An individual-differences perspective. *Psychonomic Bulletin and Review, 9*, 637-671.

Olesen, P. J., Westerberg, H., & Klingberg, T. (2004). Increased prefrontal and parietal activity after training of working memory. *Nature Neuroscience, 7*, 75-79.

Ortner, C. N. M., Kilner, S. J., & Zelazo, P. D. (2007). Mindfulness meditation and reduced emotional interference on a cognitive task. *Motivation and Emotion, 31*, 271-283.

Papageorgiou, C., & Wells, A. (2000). Treatment of recurrent major depression with attention training. *Cognitive and Behavioral Practice, 7*, 407-413.

Persson, J., & Reuter-Lorenz, P. A. (2008). Gaining control training executive function and far transfer of the ability to resolve interference. *Psychological Science, 19*, 881-888.

Redick, T. S., & Engle, R. W. (2006). Working memory capacity and attention network test performance. *Applied Cognitive Psychology, 20*, 713-721.

Schmeichel, B. J. (2007). Attention control, memory updating, and emotion regulation temporarily reduce the capacity for executive control. *Journal of Experimental Psychology. General, 136*, 241-255.

Schmeichel, B. J., Volokhov, R. N., & Demaree, H. A. (2008). Working memory capacity and the self-regulation of emotional expression and experience. *Journal of Personality and Social Psychology, 95*, 1526-1540.

Segal, Z. V., Williams, J. M. G., & Teasdale, J. D. (2002). *Mindfulness-based cognitive therapy for depression: A new approach to preventing relapse.* New York: Guilford.

Shapiro, S. L., Oman, D., Thoresen, C. E., Plante, T. G., & Flinders, T. (2008). Cultivating mindfulness: Effects on well-being. *Journal of Clinical Psychology, 64*, 840-862.

Siegle, G. J., Ghinassi, F., & Thase, M. E. (2007). Neurobehavioral therapies in the 21st century: Summary of an emerging field and an extended example of cognitive control training for depression. *Cognitive Therapy and Research, 31*, 235-262.

Slagter, H. A., Lutz, A., Greischar, L. L., Francis, A. D., Nieuwenhuis, S., Davis, J. M., et al. (2007). Mental training affects distribution of limited brain resources. *PLoS Biology, 5*, e138.

Stanley, E. A., Kiyonaga, A., Schaldach, J. M., & Jha, A. P. (under review). *The effect of mindfulness training on mood disturbance and perceived stress levels in a pre-deployment military context.* Manuscript under review.

Tang, Y. Y., Ma, Y., Wang, J., Fan, Y., Feng, S., Lu, Q., et al. (2007). Short-term meditation training improves attention and self-regulation. *Proceedings of the National Academy of Sciences, 104*, 17152-17156.

Unsworth, N., Heitz, R. P., Schrock, J. C., & Engle, R. W. (2005). An automated version of the operation span task. *Behavior Research Methods, 37*, 498-505.

Unsworth, N., Schrock, J. C., & Engle, R. W. (2004). Working memory capacity and the antisaccade task: Individual differences in voluntary saccade control. *Journal of Experimental Psychology: Learning Memory and Cognition, 30*, 1302-1321.

Wallace, B. A. (2005). *Balancing the mind: A Tibetan Buddhist approach to refining attention.* New York: Snow Lion Press.

Watson, D., Clark, L. A., & Tellegen, A. (1988). Development and validation of brief measures of positive and negative affect: The PANAS scales. *Journal of Personality and Social Psychology, 54*, 1063-1070.

Wenk-Sormaz, H. (2005). Meditation can reduce habitual responding. *Alternative Therapies in Health and Medicine, 11*, 42-58.

Williams, J. M. G., Russell, I., & Russell, D. (2008). Mindfulness-based cognitive therapy: Further issues in current evidence and future research. *Journal of Consulting and Clinical Psychology, 76*, 524-529.

PART 2

Special Populations and Settings

CHAPTER 9

Acceptance and Mindfulness as Mechanisms of Change in Mindfulness-Based Interventions for Children and Adolescents

Michael P. Twohig, Clinton E. Field, Andrew B. Armstrong, and Angie L. Dahl, Utah State University

The focus of this chapter is to review the current state of the literature on acceptance and mindfulness processes in the treatment of children and adolescents. Although this work is less advanced than with adults, notable steps have been taken. In this chapter we clarify the processes that fall under the umbrella of acceptance and mindfulness and how they are used with children, review the measurement of these processes, review the effectiveness of these procedures with an emphasis on the mechanisms of action, and outline a variety of techniques and procedures that are useful in fostering these processes.

CURRENT PERSPECTIVES ON THE TREATMENT OF CHILDHOOD DISORDERS

Disorders seen in childhood and adolescence have been divided into externalizing, internalizing, and disorders involving behavioral deficits, such as learning disabilities, mental retardation, and developmental disabilities. Disorders such as elimination and tic disorders and childhood schizophrenia are more difficult to categorize. Behavior therapy is the most supported intervention for externalizing, tic, and elimination disorders, and cognitive behavioral therapy (CBT) is most supported for internalizing disorders, such as anxiety and mood disorders. Another area of emphasis that is developing within the broad umbrella of CBT is acceptance- and mindfulness-based interventions. These interventions have been presented as a notable deviation from behavior therapy and CBT assumptions and goals, although the accuracy of this statement is being discussed (e.g., Arch & Craske, 2008; Hayes, 2008; Hofmann & Asmundson, 2008). Here we briefly outline the purported differences in the research and philosophies they are based on, research objectives, focuses and goals of the treatments, and training in these therapies.

First, some acceptance- and mindfulness-based therapies are based on alternative lines of basic research, such as relational frame theory (Hayes, Barnes-Holmes, & Roche, 2001), or on technologies that originate in Eastern spiritual traditions, such as mindfulness practices (Kabat-Zinn, 1994). Second, acceptance- and mindfulness-based therapies generally are not defined topographically or by the procedures used; greater focus is placed on the psychological processes the interventions affect (Hayes, 2004). Third, traditional psychology has largely focused on first-order change processes, in which particular thoughts, feelings, sensations, or behaviors are targeted in order to regulate or decrease them. Traditionally, behavior therapy used first-order change to modify overt behavior, and cognitive therapy used the same procedures to modify inner experiences, such as anxiety and depression. Acceptance- and mindfulness-based therapies have a greater focus on changing the function of inner experiences over their form, frequency, or situational sensitivity (Segal, Williams, & Teasdale, 2002). First-order change procedures are still used to change overt behavior, but they are generally used less often to change inner experiences within acceptance- and mindfulness-based interventions. Fourth, these factors affect the treatment goals and desired outcomes in acceptance- and mindfulness-based interventions, where the targeted changes are the levels of impact that inner experiences (thoughts and feelings) have on behaviors. There is less concern for decreasing any particular inner experiences, including negative moods and thoughts. Finally, it is common for therapists who teach acceptance and mindfulness skills to personally practice the techniques. For example, the developers of mindfulness-based cognitive therapy (MBCT) suggest that therapists who use this intervention have their own mindfulness practice (Segal et al., 2002), and teachers of acceptance and commitment therapy (ACT) use experiential rather than didactic training methods (Hayes, Strosahl, & Wilson, 1999). This is consistent with the nature of the therapy sessions in these interventions, which are often more experiential than didactic.

CONCEPTUALIZING AND DEFINING ACCEPTANCE AND MINDFULNESS PROCESSES

Many processes fall under the umbrella of acceptance and mindfulness, and some of them have been reviewed in the previous chapters of this book. The research on acceptance and mindfulness processes in children and adolescents is limited but represented by work in ACT, MBCT, dialectical behavior therapy (DBT; Linehan, 1993), and mindfulness-based stress reduction (MBSR; Kabat-Zinn, 1990).

Acceptance and Commitment Therapy

ACT targets six processes in the hope of fostering the overarching process of *psychological flexibility*—the ability to act in any chosen direction at any moment regardless of the internal experience that is present. These six processes are *acceptance* (allowing one's inner experiences to occur without taking steps to regulate or control them), *defusion* (altering the literal or verbal context in which inner experiences occur so their effects on behavior are flexible), *being present* (consciously experiencing internal and external events as they are occurring, without attachment to evaluation or judgment), *self-as-context* (experiencing that there is an unchanging sense of self, where experiences occur, that cannot be harmed and is always present), *identifying and clarifying values* (qualities of living that are chosen moment by moment but can never be entirely achieved as a concrete goal or possessed as an object), and *committed action* (taking progressive steps in values-related directions). In ACT, committed action is the behavioral product of the other five processes.

Various activity-based exercises targeting ACT processes are appropriate for children and adolescents. For example, ACT therapists have often used the passengers on the bus metaphor (Hayes et al., 1999) to help children get a sense of self-as-context and how to behave in a manner consistent with one's values even in the presence of difficult internal experiences. In this metaphor, the bus has the ability to continue in a specified direction dictated by the driver (e.g., following one's values) despite the passengers on the bus, who represent internal experiences, including emotions and thoughts that may seem highly disruptive. Similarly, the child's toy often referred to as Chinese handcuffs or a Chinese finger trap has been used as a method for helping children understand the concepts of willingness and acceptance in the context of inconsistent or aversive internal experience. In this example, children are required to do the opposite of what "feels right." Most children are inclined to pull their fingers apart, which leads to further entrapment, but if they are willing, they can see how pushing their fingers together works better, despite the feeling that this is not the correct action to take (Hayes et al., 1999). This may help children understand that the most effective action might not show up as consistent with their internal experience.

Mindfulness-Based Cognitive Therapy and Mindfulness-Based Stress Reduction

MBCT for children (Semple & Lee, 2008) is a downward extension of the work that is implemented with adults. Special modifications are made to account for children's limited attentional abilities, the need for less didactic and more experiential teaching is addressed, and greater family involvement is incorporated. Therapy involves many varieties of mindfulness exercises done over ten sessions (Semple, Reid, & Miller, 2005). MBSR with children (Saltzman & Goldin, 2008) employs a similar approach in that it is also an adapted version of the work done with adults and is also done in a scheduled protocol (eight weeks). Treatment largely focuses on experientially based training in mindfulness skills and psychoeducation on the use of these skills. For example, to learn mindfulness children may be guided in mindful eating—taking time to notice the smell, texture, and color of the food prior to consumption. After taking one bite, children are instructed to take account of the experiences within their body, noticing the taste and the work of the tongue and teeth, all while maintaining curiosity about their eating experience (Saltzman & Goldin, 2008).

Dialectical Behavior Therapy

DBT for adolescents (e.g., Woodberry, Roy, & Indik, 2008) focuses on both acceptance and change procedures, which are applied as needed. Acceptance and mindfulness skills such as radical acceptance and specific mindfulness practices are taught as tools to promote distress tolerance, awareness of ongoing experience, and the ability to direct attention as desired. Distress tolerance is a skill that seems particularly pertinent to the work with children diagnosed with externalizing disorders; indeed, most of the work on DBT for children has focused on these types of problems (Katz, Cox, Gunasekara, & Miller, 2004; Rathus & Miller, 2002). In distress tolerance, adolescents are taught ways to experience negative thoughts, feelings, and emotions without engaging in problematic behaviors such as self-harm, substance use, or aggression. Concrete, readily available crisis skills are taught first (e.g., squeezing a stress ball, going for a bike ride, or playing the drums), followed by engagement with longer-lasting acceptance skills (Woodberry et al., 2008).

Training Parents in Acceptance and Mindfulness Processes

If the child is at a developmentally appropriate age, acceptance and mindfulness processes can be taught directly, but as with most therapies for children, caregiver support is necessary for optimal outcomes. There are two benefits to training caregivers in acceptance and mindfulness processes: caregivers can support the development of these processes in the child, and caregivers themselves may benefit from the use of these skills. Providing care for a child with a psychological disorder or administering a behavior management program can be stressful; research has shown that acceptance and mindfulness interventions can be useful for caregivers in these situations (e.g., Blackledge & Hayes, 2006).

MEASURING ACCEPTANCE AND MINDFULNESS PROCESSES IN CHILDREN, ADOLESCENTS, AND PARENTS

Few measurement tools specifically target acceptance and mindfulness processes in children, adolescents, and their parents, but more are being developed as interest in these interventions increases. The following is a review of currently available assessment tools that specifically target these processes in children, adolescents, and their caregivers.

The Avoidance and Fusion Questionnaire for Youth (AFQ-Y; Greco, Lambert, & Baer, 2008). Modeled after the Acceptance and Action Questionnaire (AAQ; Hayes et al., 2004), the AFQ-Y was designed to measure experiential avoidance and cognitive fusion in youth. Items such as "I must get rid of my worries and fears so I can have a good life" and "I push away thoughts and feelings I don't like" are rated on a five-point Likert scale. The AFQ-Y has seventeen items; an eight-item form (AFQ-Y8) can be used as a screening tool (Greco et al., 2008). In a large study with 1,369 fifth- through tenth-graders, internal consistency of the AFQ-Y and AFQ-Y8 were high (α = 0.90 and 0.83, respectively). Moderate correlations in expected directions were found between the AFQ-Y and AFQ-Y8 and measures of related constructs, such as acceptance and mindfulness, thought suppression, anxiety, problem behavior, and quality of life. Although change in AFQ-Y scores with treatment has not been assessed, available findings support the convergent and construct validity of the measure. The AFQ-Y is included as an appendix to this chapter.

Child Acceptance and Mindfulness Measure (CAMM; Greco & Baer, 2006). The CAMM, a ten-item measure of acceptance and mindfulness, is still under development but has been used with children and adolescents ages nine to eighteen. Items such as "I think about things that have happened in the past instead of thinking about things that are happening right now" and "I do things without thinking about what I'm doing" are rated on a five-point Likert scale. In a study of 606 middle school students, the CAMM had acceptable internal consistency (α = 0.84), a single-factor structure, and significant correlations in expected directions with measures of related constructs.

The Bull's-Eye Instrument About Valued Life–Primary Care Version (Lundgren, Dahl, & Hayes, 2008). This is a developmentally appropriate tool to measure youths' values and levels of consistency and persistence in living those values. Respondents place an X on a picture of a target, indicating how close they are to living according to their values in the domains of work, love, and play. The bull's-eye represents absolute consistency and persistence in behaving in valued ways, and the rings around the bull's-eye reflect varying degrees of consistency and persistence in values-oriented action. This tool has been used as a method of establishing treatment goals, as an outcome measure, and as a process measure with adults (Lundgren et al., 2008).

Observation Coding Manual–Child Version; Observation Coding Manual–Parent Version (OCM-C; Coyne & Burke, 2007a; OCM-P; Coyne & Burke, 2007b). The OCM measures child and parent acceptance and mindfulness processes during family treatment for children with obsessive-compulsive disorder (OCD). Observers score prompted and unprompted occurrences of parent and child experiential avoidance and acceptance during therapist-led exposure therapy. Overt behaviors (approach and escape) are coded, as are parent and child verbalizations. Initial data with twenty children (ages four to eight years) provided evidence for interrater reliability (0.77 to 0.96) of parental experiential avoidance.

Parental Acceptance and Action Questionnaire (PAAQ; Cheron, Ehrenreich, & Pincus, 2009). Modeled after the AAQ, the PAAQ is a fifteen-item questionnaire designed to measure parental experiential avoidance or the "level of experiential avoidance a caregiver had towards the experiences of the child in their care" (Cheron et al., 2009). PAAQ items deal with parents' experiences of their children's negative emotions (e.g., "It's okay for my child to feel depressed or anxious"). PAAQ items fall on one of two factors—inaction and unwillingness—and higher PAAQ scores indicate higher levels of parental experiential avoidance. Initial data from a sample of 154 children diagnosed with anxiety disorders, ranging in age from six to eighteen years old, and their parents showed internal consistency of $\alpha = 0.64$ for the inaction subscale and $\alpha = 0.65$ for the unwillingness subscale. To examine the relationship between parental experiential avoidance and parental psychopathology, PAAQ scores were compared to parents' scores on the Depression Anxiety Stress Scales (DASS; Lovibond & Lovibond, 1995), a self-report measure of general distress. PAAQ total scores and inaction scores correlated positively with DASS anxiety, depression, and total Scales, but not with the DASS stress scale. PAAQ unwillingness scores did not correlate significantly with any DASS scales. Therefore, it appears that the PAAQ inaction subscale may be related to parental psychopathology (Cheron et al., 2009).

Even though measures of acceptance and mindfulness processes in children, adolescents, and parents are available, additional research demonstrating their utility and psychometric adequacy is needed, as is a greater breadth of measurement devices and assessment tools suited to particular pathological processes. Because acceptance- and mindfulness-based interventions are generally new in psychotherapy, and even less developed for use with children, we can expect to see progress in this area in the coming years.

EMPIRICAL SUPPORT FOR ACCEPTANCE- AND MINDFULNESS-BASED TREATMENTS FOR CHILDREN AND ADOLESCENTS

Research using acceptance- and mindfulness-based treatments with children and adolescents is in the beginning stages and includes studies emerging from ACT, DBT for adolescents (DBT-A), MBCT for children (MBCT-C), and MBSR treatment approaches. Even though there is a breadth of research supporting acceptance- and mindfulness-based mechanisms of change in adults (Hayes, Luoma, Bond, Masuda, & Lillis, 2006), there are currently no published studies of particular components of these interventions among children or adolescents. As a result, the current review of the literature must focus on outcome studies. An important challenge for future research is to clarify whether changes in acceptance- and mindfulness-related processes are responsible for the beneficial outcomes observed with these treatments.

Studies of Acceptance and Commitment Therapy

Currently, there are six published studies utilizing ACT for children and adolescents with problems related to anorexia, chronic pain, or risky sexual activity. In a case study of a fifteen-year-old female diagnosed with anorexia nervosa, Heffner, Sperry, Eifert, and Detweiler (2002) used the finger trap metaphor to illustrate the futility of fighting against anorexia-related cognitions (e.g., "I'm a whale") and used present-moment awareness and defusion to encourage just noticing such thoughts without being controlled by them. A map identifying the client's valued directions (e.g., relationships with friends, good health, and involvement in sports and school) was developed, and the bus driver metaphor was used to help the client visualize herself driving the bus toward her valued directions despite the presence of pushy passengers on the bus (negative thoughts, feelings, and sensations) directing her elsewhere (e.g., "You shouldn't eat because you are too fat"). At the end of the intervention, the client's anorexic symptoms were substantially reduced and her weight had returned to a healthy level.

Several studies of ACT for chronic pain in children and adolescents have been reported (Greco, Blomquist, Acra, & Mouton, in press; Wicksell, Dahl, Magnusson, & Olson, 2005; Wicksell, Melin, & Olsson, 2006; Wicksell, Melin, Lekander, & Olson, 2009). All included identification of valued life directions (e.g., increased levels of independence, school attendance, and participation in activities) and specific behaviors required to move in those directions. Mindfulness, acceptance, and defusion exercises were used to encourage the ability and willingness to engage in valued behaviors even while feeling pain or discomfort. All of these studies showed increases in the ability to function (e.g., greater school attendance or participation in activities) and quality of life even in the absence of reductions in pain.

Finally, Metzler, Biglan, Noell, Ary, and Ochs (2000) described a behavioral intervention for risky sexual behavior in adolescents that included ACT-based strategies for increasing mindfulness and acceptance of negative thoughts and feelings while engaging in behavior consistent with the goal of safer sex. Participants reported fewer sexual interactions and fewer sexual partners.

While these studies report changes in the targeted outcomes, most did not measure acceptance, mindfulness, or related processes, making it impossible to determine whether changes in these processes are responsible for or play a role in the beneficial outcomes observed. The only exception is Metzler and colleagues (2000), who used an unvalidated measure of willingness (Hayes & Wilson, 1994) that assesses avoidance of unpleasant feelings and interference with valued behavior. That study did not note significant changes on the unwillingness scale.

Studies of Dialectical Behavior Therapy

Researchers have theorized that DBT, originally developed for treatment of adult women diagnosed with borderline personality disorder, may be effective with adolescents with similar difficulties with emotional control, relationships, and suicidality (e.g., Rathus & Miller, 2000; Miller, Rathus, & Linehan, 2007). DBT integrates mindfulness and acceptance skills with behavior change strategies (Linehan, 1993; Miller, Rathus, Linehan, Wetzler, & Leigh, 1997; Miller et al., 2007; Woodberry et al., 2008). Six published studies have utilized DBT-A with suicidal or oppositional defiant adolescents in inpatient or outpatient settings (Katz et al., 2004; Miller, Wyman, Huppert, Glassman, & Rathus, 2000; Nelson-Gray et al., 2006; Rathus & Miller, 2002; Sunseri, 2004; Woodberry & Popenoe, 2008). All have shown substantial decreases in suicidal and other psychological symptoms. Again, however, changes in mindfulness or acceptance were not measured, and therefore it is unclear whether development of these skills was related to therapeutic outcomes.

Studies of Mindfulness-Based Cognitive Therapy

MBCT is a combination of meditative mindfulness and cognitive therapy. The goal of treatment is to help clients mindfully and nonjudgmentally notice feelings, thoughts, and emotions and disengage from ruminative thought patterns. In MBCT-C, mindfulness techniques are used to enhance present-moment awareness and identify thoughts and feelings. The utility of MBCT-C was shown with five seven- and eight-year-olds with anxiety and related impairments (Semple et al., 2005). Each of the participants showed improvements in one or more areas of functioning (academic, internalizing problems, or externalizing problems). This initial investigation was furthered by Lee, Semple, Rosa, and Miller (2008) in a twelve-week open trial of MBCT-C in a nonclinical sample of children (ages nine to twelve) exhibiting academic difficulty. At post-treatment, parent reports suggested a reduction in internalizing and externalizing symptoms, although quantitative results were minimal. Child self-reports also indicated increased self-confidence, decreased stress, and better self-management of reactions. Additionally, treatment feasibility and acceptability were high in both interventions.

Studies of Mindfulness-Based Stress Reduction

MBSR combines meditation and mindfulness activities like yoga, mindful eating, and walking meditation in a short-term treatment plan. The goal of MBSR is for participants to live fully within the present and to experience a reduction of symptoms or learn to live with greater satisfaction while having symptoms. We located four studies utilizing MBSR with children, adolescents, and their parents.

Ott (2002) found that MBSR was effective in a nine-year-old girl struggling with nausea and epigastric pain. Bootzin and Stevens (2005) found that a group MBSR intervention was helpful for sleep deprivation in adolescents. Wall (2005) reported that an education program combining tai chi and MBSR led to increased peacefulness and self-awareness, improved sleep, and improved relationships and interconnectedness in eight hundred inner-city middle school students. Finally, Saltzman and Goldin (2008) evaluated an MBSR curriculum for fourth- through sixth-graders and their parents. Both children and parents noted increases in cognitive control of attention, less negative emotional reactivity, and more compassion.

Studies of Acceptance and Mindfulness Training for Parents

Much of the work in acceptance and mindfulness training for parents has been done in the realm of mindful parenting, though this work is still in its infancy. Although few empirical studies regarding mindfulness and parenting have been conducted, the numerous studies demonstrating the benefits of acceptance and mindfulness processes in adults (e.g., Arch & Craske, 2006; Eifert & Heffner, 2003) serve as preliminary support for combining these approaches with parenting interventions (Wahler, Rowinski, & Williams, 2008). We located three empirical studies of mindful parenting.

Altmaier and Maloney (2007) evaluated the use of the Mindful Parenting Program (MPP; Placone-Willey, 2002) with recently divorced parents of preschoolers. The goal of MPP is to train parents to use mindfulness skills to boost parent-child connectedness. The emphasis was on identifying interactions that promote disconnectedness (e.g., criticizing, projecting anger, or withdrawing emotionally) and replacing them with intentional interactions focused on connectedness and practiced in session (e.g., listening, displaying affection, or responding calmly). Participants completed the Toronto Mindfulness Scale (TMS; Lau et al., 2006), an adult measure not specific to parenting variables, to assess their levels of mindfulness, as well as practice logs to document self-observations and time spent in out-of-session practice of meditation and homework. Parents' TMS scores improved during the study but did not significantly correlate with practice data; thus, greater time engaged in mindfulness practice during the study did not necessarily translate into higher mindfulness scores. Further, increased mindfulness did not translate into reductions in self-reported parental stress or improved parent-child connectedness (Altmaier & Maloney, 2007).

Two empirical mindful parenting studies (Singh et al., 2006, 2007) have yielded more favorable results. Singh and colleagues (2006) taught mindfulness skills to three mothers of children diagnosed with autism (ages four to six years). All three children exhibited clinical levels of aggression, two also displayed substantial noncompliance, and the other engaged in frequent self-injurious behaviors. Treatment consisted solely of training in meditation-based mindfulness (e.g., observing the mind, present-moment awareness, and nonjudgmental acceptance). Interestingly, all three children showed rapid and sustained reductions in problem behaviors when their mothers began using the mindfulness skills. Mothers' subjective reports of parenting satisfaction and interaction satisfaction increased as they applied mindfulness skills they had learned in the training.

In 2007, Singh and colleagues used the same technologies in a replication study with four mothers of children with developmental disabilities, aggression, and limited social skills (Singh et al., 2007). As in the original study, increased maternal mindfulness was associated with concomitant increases in parenting satisfaction, decreases in problem behaviors in the children, and increases in positive social behaviors among the children. These studies were not designed to analyze the mechanisms by which mindfulness transformed mothers' experiences; however, the authors hypothesized that positive changes "seem to result from a transformation in the way the mindful person relates to events in his or her environment, rather than from learning a set of skills to specifically change behaviors" (Singh et al., 2006, p. 174).

Others have proposed alternative explanations for why positive parenting outcomes may be expected as a result of increased parental mindfulness. Jean Dumas (2005) offered a theoretical foundation for what he termed mindfulness-based parent training (MBPT). According to Dumas, mindfulness in parenting can disrupt ineffective automatized transactional procedures that have been maintained by strong negative emotions. Automatized transactional procedures are not necessarily harmful. In fact, MBPT aims to employ mindful practices to create new automatized transactional procedures in which parents create appropriate distance between themselves and negative emotions, view their own behavior and their child's behavior nonjudgmentally, and develop meaningful action plans. These new automatized transactional procedures may be useful "until they themselves need to be changed in mindful ways" (Dumas, 2005, p. 780).

MBPT has not been explored experimentally and is not without its critics. Proponents of parent-child interaction therapy (Foote, Eyberg, & Schuhmann, 1998) have argued that standard contingency-management interventions presented in this therapy (e.g., positive reinforcement, time-outs, or planned ignoring) combined with key process variables (e.g., the therapist-parent relationship or therapist verbal behavior) may sufficiently decrease the power of these thoughts and feelings without the inclusion of mindfulness strategies (Harwood & Eyberg, 2004).

Parenting gains as a result of mindfulness training may also be explained in terms of undermining experiential avoidance. Parental experiential avoidance may result in parent-child interactions that are topographically positive yet counterproductive. For example, parents may try to reduce the distress of inner experiences (feeling guilty or as though they are bad parents) by providing positive attention, granting privileges that are not deserved, or failing to enforce consequences (Coyne & Wilson, 2004; Greco & Eifert, 2004).

ACT researchers have begun to empirically analyze the relationship between experiential avoidance and parenting risk factors. Early data have indicated that parental experiential avoidance as measured by the AAQ is positively correlated with child depression and anxiety (Shea & Coyne, 2006; Silvia, Conti, Sommerville, & Coyne, 2007), parenting stress (Shea & Coyne, 2006; Silvia et al., 2007), child behavioral problems (Coyne & Thompson, 2009; Shea & Coyne, 2006), and punitive and inconsistent parenting techniques (Shea & Coyne, 2006). Parents who perceived themselves as having less control in their parenting role reported more internalizing problems in their children; this relationship was partially mediated by parental experiential avoidance (Coyne & Thompson, 2009). Similarly, it was found that experiential avoidance significantly predicted inconsistent discipline, poor monitoring, and limited parental involvement, which in turn predicted adolescent behavior problems (Berlin, Sato, Jastrowski, Woods, & Davies, 2005). Therefore, therapeutic approaches that effectively reduce experiential avoidance (e.g., acceptance and mindfulness processes), may be found to enhance outcomes of behavioral parenting therapies.

Blackledge and Hayes (2006) conducted a study using ACT in a group format with twenty parents of children diagnosed with autism, a group with high levels of chronic stress. ACT was presented in workshop format as training, not therapy, with fourteen hours of training in experiential exercises and discussion about the six core ACT processes. Parents' scores on measures of acceptance and mindfulness significantly improved from pretreatment to follow-up, and these improvements were associated with significant reductions in general distress and depression.

Summary of Clinical Work In Acceptance and Mindfulness

In general, acceptance- and mindfulness-based strategies targeting a number of child, adolescent, and parenting problems and challenges have shown promising results. All of the aforementioned studies are outcome studies, and little if anything is currently known about the usefulness of individual treatment components or the effects of particular processes. Additional studies with a greater focus on the mechanisms of action of acceptance- and mindfulness-based interventions are needed to move this work forward. Additionally, many of the studies outlined have a pre- and post-treatment design or are case studies. Randomized controlled trials would further advance our understanding of the effectiveness of acceptance- and mindfulness- based approaches. Finally, it should be noted that the majority of the work outlined has been done with adolescents. Thus, research investigating acceptance and mindfulness with children and associated treatment modifications will be needed prior to drawing any conclusions about the effectiveness of these approaches with children.

CLINICAL CONSIDERATIONS

The primary focus of this chapter has been to describe the state of the scientific literature with regard to assessment and use of acceptance and mindfulness processes among children and adolescents. Efforts to assess the effects of these strategies with children remain in development, as do efforts to identify the most effective methods of intervention. While not the primary focus, there is utility in briefly considering the pragmatics of engaging children in the work of acceptance and mindfulness.

Almost everything on this topic has been published within the past ten years, although elements of this approach, particularly with parents, may be traced back some twenty years to the work of Biglan (1989) with the parents of children with special needs (for a brief history, see Murrell & Scherbarth, 2006). Detailed reviews of this literature can be found elsewhere (Greco & Hayes, 2008; Murrell & Scherbarth, 2006; Murrell, Coyne, & Wilson, 2005; Twohig, Hayes, & Berens, 2007). Here we provide a succinct review of critical issues and key strategies conceptualized as representative of two primary domains of the clinical framework: the structure of the clinical environment and the nature of clinical techniques.

Structure of the Clinical Environment

When working with children, the structure of the clinical environment is likely to have a therapeutic impact and is distinctly different than in acceptance and mindfulness work with adults. Adjustments are both beneficial and necessary when one considers the cognitive and contextual differences that exist for children relative to adults (Semple & Lee, 2008). Caregivers are often encouraged to be involved in acceptance and mindfulness work with children, filling important roles within the therapy session (e.g., participant modeling and development of rapport) and outside of session (e.g., support of home-based practice and promotion of skill generalization and development). As such, establishing an effective working relationship with parents is a key aspect of the clinical environment. In many cases, caregivers are also taught acceptance and mindfulness skills; these skills are inherently useful for caregivers, and learning them also helps caregivers foster use of these skills by the child.

Additional structural changes specifically target parameters of the therapeutic session. Relative to adult acceptance and mindfulness sessions, work with children is often scheduled to be shorter in duration (e.g., 90 rather than 120 minutes), to occur more frequently, and to continue for a longer period of time overall (e.g., twelve rather than eight weeks of treatment). When doing group work with children, fewer children may be included in the group and cotherapists may be added to facilitate interaction and group management. Further, within sessions the amount of time spent on a given activity (e.g., a breathing exercise) may be shortened to increase participation and prevent boredom. Finally, the type of room used for sessions and the physical layout of the therapy room may also be modified to create a child-friendly environment in which there is room for a group to engage in physical activities (Semple, Lee, & Miller, 2006; Murrell et al., 2005; Saltzman & Goldin, 2008).

Nature of Clinical Techniques

Relative to our experience with traditional, evidence-based child and adolescent treatment methods, we have found acceptance- and mindfulness-related techniques to be unique at the level of theory, in their topography, in their function (e.g., fostering willingness to tolerate discomfort rather than managing or controlling anxiety), and at the level of clinical target (e.g., targeting processes rather than behavior). Preliminary evidence has suggested that these techniques may be beneficial in treating a variety of child problems. To date, ACT and other acceptance- and mindfulness-based treatments have been rather independently employed as the primary approach to treatment for various adult concerns. However, in treating children there has been recognition that acceptance- and mindfulness-based techniques and strategies may be most powerful when integrated with other evidence-based practices. A nice example of this has been the initial attempts to integrate elements of ACT with the tradition of behavioral parent training in treating externalizing behavior problems among children (e.g., Blackledge & Hayes, 2006; Coyne & Wilson, 2004; Dumas, 2005). Such strategies may prove to be particularly powerful as they are able to target both child and parent functioning while also allowing parents to model the effective use of acceptance and mindfulness skills that younger children may have difficulty grasping.

The use of age-appropriate metaphors, stories, games, and activities may enhance acceptance and mindfulness processes. Physical activities can be particularly useful in helping children remain engaged in therapy while also helping them conceptualize, in a more concrete way, basic therapeutic concepts. Drawing activities have occasionally been used in just this manner. One such activity involves presenting children with a life-size outline of their body drawn on a large sheet of paper. Children are encouraged to use crayons to connect internal experiences (e.g., emotions and thoughts) with the parts of the body from which they seem to emanate (e.g., the heart or brain). Drawing pictures or writing on the paper may serve the purpose of helping children discriminate between the physical parts of the body and experiential phenomena, which are more elusive and transient. This activity may also lead to discussion about how the child reacts to such experiential phenomena and, ultimately, to a review of ineffective strategies the child may have used to manage or escape such experiences, which is valuable within the acceptance and mindfulness framework (Murrell et al., 2005).

CONCLUSIONS

The adoption of acceptance- and mindfulness-based perspectives and related therapeutic frameworks represents a viable shift in treatment orientation for most childhood problems. Such an orientation goes beyond attending to therapy process issues (e.g., working alliance and therapist facilitation) by prioritizing relevant yet previously neglected individual process issues (e.g., psychological flexibility, willingness, acceptance, and defusion) and targeting these issues using a novel group of practice strategies. To the degree that tools for assessing acceptance and mindfulness among children are developed, and that these strategies are discovered to be effective in addressing childhood problems in psychosocial functioning, further refinement and inclusion in clinical practice will be warranted.

REFERENCES

Altmaier, E., & Maloney, R. (2007). An initial evaluation of a mindful parenting program. *Journal of Clinical Psychology, 63*, 1231-1238.

Arch, J. J., & Craske, M. G. (2006). Mechanisms of mindfulness: Emotion regulation following a focused breathing induction. *Behaviour Research and Therapy, 44*, 1849-1858.

Arch, J. J., & Craske, M. G. (2008). ACT and CBT for anxiety disorders. *Clinical Psychology: Science and Practice, 5*, 263-279.

Berlin, K. S., Sato, A. F., Jastrowski, K. E., Woods, D. W., & Davies, W. H. (2005). *Effects of experiential avoidance on parenting practices and adolescent outcomes.* Unpublished manuscript.

Biglan, A. (1989). A contextual approach to the clinical treatment of parental distress. In G. H. S. Singer & L. K. Irvin (Eds.), *Support for caregiving families: Enabling positive adaptation to disability.* Baltimore: Paul H. Brookes.

Blackledge, J. T., & Hayes, S. C. (2006). Using acceptance and commitment training in the support of parents of children diagnosed with autism. *Child and Family Behavior Therapy, 28*, 1-18.

Bootzin, R. R., & Stevens, S. J. (2005). Adolescents, substance use, and the treatment of insomnia and daytime sleepiness. *Clinical Psychology Review, 25*, 629-644.

Cheron, D. M., Ehrenreich, J. T., & Pincus, D. B. (2009). Assessment of parental experiential avoidance in a clinical sample of children with anxiety disorders. *Child Psychiatry and Human Development, 40*, 383-403.

Coyne, L. W., & Burke, A. M. (2007a). *Observational coding manual, child version: Assessing exposure in the context of a family-based cognitive behavioral treatment for pediatric OCD.* Unpublished manuscript, Suffolk University, Boston, MA.

Coyne, L. W., & Burke, A. M. (2007b). *Observational coding manual, parent version: Assessing exposure in the context of a family-based cognitive behavioral treatment for pediatric OCD.* Unpublished manuscript, Suffolk University, Boston, MA.

Coyne, L. W., & Thompson, A. D. (2009). The effect of parent locus of control on child internalizing problems as mediated by parental experiential avoidance. Poster session presented at the Society for Research in Child Development, Denver, CO.

Coyne, L. W., & Wilson, K. G. (2004). The role of cognitive fusion in impaired parenting: An RFT analysis. *International Journal of Psychology and Psychological Therapy, 4*, 469-487.

Dumas, J. E. (2005). Mindfulness-based parent training: Strategies to lessen the grip of automaticity in families with disruptive children. *Journal of Clinical Child and Adolescent Psychology, 34*, 779-791.

Eifert, G. H., & Heffner, M. (2003). The effects of acceptance versus control contexts on avoidance of panic-related symptoms. *Journal of Behavior Therapy and Experimental Psychiatry, 34*, 293-312.

Foote, R., Eyberg, S., & Schuhmann, E. (1998). Parent-child interaction approaches to the treatment of child conduct problems. In T. Ollendick & R. Prinz (Eds.), *Advances in clinical child psychology.* New York: Plenum.

Greco, L. A., & Baer, R. A. (2006). Child Acceptance and Mindfulness Measure (CAMM). (Available from the first author at the Department of Psychology, University of Missouri, St. Louis.)

Greco, L. A., Blomquist, K., Acra, S., & Mouton, D. (in press). Acceptance and commitment therapy for adolescents with functional abdominal pain: Results of a pilot investigation. *Cognitive and Behavioral Practice.*

Greco, L. A., & Eifert, G. (2004). Treating parent-adolescent conflict: Is acceptance the missing link for an integrative family therapy? *Cognitive and Behavioral Practice, 11*, 305-314.

Greco, L. A., & Hayes, S. C. (2008). *Acceptance and mindfulness treatments for children and adolescents: A practitioner's guide.* Oakland, CA: New Harbinger.

Greco, L. A., Lambert, W., & Baer, R. A. (2008). Psychological inflexibility in childhood and adolescence: Development and evaluation of the Avoidance and Fusion Questionnaire for Youth. *Psychological Assessment,* 20, 93-102.

Harwood, M. D., & Eyberg, S. M. (2004). Therapist verbal behavior early in treatment: Relation to successful completion of parent-child interaction therapy. *Journal of Clinical Child and Adolescent Psychology, 33*, 601-612.

Hayes, S. C. (2004). Acceptance and commitment therapy, relational frame theory, and the third wave of behavioral and cognitive therapies. *Behavior Therapy, 35*, 639-665.

Hayes, S. C. (2008). Climbing our hills: A beginning conversation on the comparison of acceptance and commitment therapy and traditional cognitive behavioral therapy. *Clinical Psychology: Science and Practice, 5*, 286-295.

Hayes, S. C., Barnes-Holmes, D., & Roche, B. (Eds.). (2001). *Relational frame theory: A post-Skinnerian account of human language and cognition.* New York: Kluwer.

Hayes, S. C., Luoma, J. B., Bond, F. W., Masuda, A., & Lillis, J. (2006). Acceptance and commitment therapy: Model, processes and outcomes. *Behaviour Research and Therapy, 44*, 1-25.

Hayes, S. C., Strosahl, K. D., & Wilson, K. G. (1999). *Acceptance and commitment therapy: An experiential approach to behavior change.* New York: Guilford.

Hayes, S. C., Strosahl, K. D., Wilson, K. G., Bissett, R. T., Pistorello, J., Toarmino, D., et al. (2004). Measuring experiential avoidance: A preliminary test of a working model. *Psychological Record, 54*, 553-578.

Hayes, S. C., & Wilson, K. G. (1994). Acceptance and commitment therapy: Altering the verbal support for experiential avoidance. *Behavior Analyst, 17*, 289-303.

Heffner, M., Sperry, J., Eifert, G. H., & Detweiler, M. (2002). Acceptance and commitment therapy in the treatment of an adolescent female with anorexia nervosa: A case example. *Cognitive and Behavioral Practice, 9*, 232-236.

Hofmann, S. G., & Asmundson, G. J. (2008). Acceptance- and mindfulness-based therapy: New wave or old hat? *Clinical Psychology Review, 28*, 1-16.

Kabat-Zinn, J. (1990). *Full catastrophe living: Using the wisdom of your body and mind to face stress, pain, and illness.* New York: Dell Publishing.

Kabat-Zinn, J. (1994). *Wherever you go, there you are: Mindfulness meditation in everyday life.* New York: Hyperion.

Katz, L. Y., Cox, B. J., Gunasekara, S., & Miller, A. L. (2004). Feasibility of applying dialectical behavior therapy to suicidal adolescent inpatients. *Journal of the American Academy of Child and Adolescent Psychiatry, 43*, 276-282.

Lau, M. A., Bishop, S. R., Segal, Z. V., Buis, T., Anderson, N. D., Carlson, L., et al. (2006). The Toronto Mindfulness Scale: Development and validation. *Journal of Clinical Psychology, 62*, 1445-1467.

Lee, J., Semple, R. J., Rosa, D., & Miller, L. (2008). Mindfulness-based cognitive therapy for children: Results of a pilot study. *Journal of Cognitive Psychotherapy, 22*, 15-28.

Linehan, M. (1993). *Skills training manual for treating borderline personality disorder.* New York: Guilford.

Lovibond, S. H., & Lovibond, P. F. (1995). *Manual for the Depression Anxiety Stress Scales.* Sydney: Psychology Foundation.

Lundgren, T., Dahl, J., & Hayes, S. C. (2008). Evaluation of mediators of change in the treatment of epilepsy with acceptance and commitment therapy. *Journal of Behavioral Medicine, 31*, 225-235.

Metzler, C. W., Biglan, A., Noell, J., Ary, D. V., & Ochs, L. (2000). A randomized controlled trial of a behavioral intervention to reduce high-risk sexual behavior among adolescents in STD clinics. *Behavior Therapy, 31*, 27-54.

Miller, A. L., Rathus, J. H., & Linehan, M. M. (2007). *Dialectical behavior therapy with suicidal adolescents.* New York: Guilford.

Miller, A. L., Rathus, J. H., Linehan, M. M., Wetzler, S., & Leigh, E. (1997). Dialectical behavior therapy adapted for suicidal adolescents. *Journal of Practical Psychiatry and Behavioral Health, 3*, 1811-1820.

Miller, A. L., Wyman, W. E., Huppert, J. D., Glassman, S. L., & Rathus, J. H. (2000). Analysis of behavioral skills utilized by suicidal adolescents receiving dialectical behavioral therapy. *Cognitive and Behavioral Practice, 7*, 183-187.

Murrell, A. R., Coyne, L. W., & Wilson, K. G. (2005). ACT with children, adolescents, and their parents. In S. C. Hayes & K. D. Strosahl (Eds.), *A practical guide to acceptance and commitment therapy.* New York: Springer.

Murrell, A. R., & Scherbarth, A. J. (2006). State of the research and literature address: ACT with children, adolescents and parents. *International Journal of Behavioral Consultation and Therapy, 2*, 531-543.

Nelson-Gray, R. O., Keane, S. P., Hurst, R. M., Mitchell, J. T., Warburton, J. B., Chok, J. T., et al. (2006). A modified DBT skills training program for oppositional defiant adolescents: Promising preliminary findings. *Behaviour Research and Therapy, 44*, 1811-1820.

Ott, M. J. (2002). Mindfulness meditation in pediatric clinical practice. *Pediatric Nursing, 28*, 487-490.

Placone-Willey, P. M. (2002). A curriculum for mindful parenting: A model development dissertation. *Dissertations Abstracts International, 63*, 568B.

Rathus, J. H., & Miller, A. L. (2000). DBT for adolescents: Dialectical dilemmas and secondary treatment targets. *Cognitive and Behavioral Practice, 7*, 425-434.

Rathus, J. H., & Miller, A. L. (2002). Dialectical behavior therapy adapted for suicidal adolescents. *Suicidal and Life-Threatening Behavior, 32*, 146-157.

Saltzman, A., & Goldin, P. (2008). Mindfulness-based stress reduction for school-aged children. In L. A. Greco & S. C. Hayes (Eds.), *Acceptance and mindfulness treatment for children and adolescents: A practitioner's guide.* Oakland, CA: New Harbinger.

Segal, Z. V., Williams, J. M. G., & Teasdale, J. D. (2002). *Mindfulness-based cognitive therapy for depression.* New York: Guilford.

Semple, R. J., & Lee, J. (2008). Treating anxiety with mindfulness: Mindfulness-based cognitive therapy for children. In L. A. Greco & S. C. Hayes (Eds.), *Acceptance and mindfulness treatment for children and adolescents: A practitioner's guide.* Oakland, CA: New Harbinger.

Semple, R. J., Lee, J., & Miller, L. F. (2006). Mindfulness-based cognitive therapy for children. In R. A. Baer (Ed.), *Mindfulness-based treatment approaches: Clinician's guide to evidence base and applications.* San Diego, CA: Elsevier.

Semple, R. J., Reid, E. F. G., & Miller, L. F. (2005). Treating anxiety with mindfulness: An open trial of mindfulness training for anxious children. *Journal of Cognitive Psychotherapy: An International Quarterly, 19*, 387-400.

Shea, S. E., & Coyne, L. W. (2006, November). *The implications of emotion regulation and perceived stress on parenting.* Poster session presented at the annual convention of the Association for Behavioral and Cognitive Therapies, Chicago, IL.

Silvia, K. A., Conti, K., Sommerville, S., & Coyne, L. W. (2007, November). *The role of experiential avoidance in perceived parenting stress and child externalizing behavior.* Poster session presented at the annual convention of the Association for Behavioral and Cognitive Therapies, Philadelphia, PA.

Singh, N. N., Lancioni, G. E., Winton, A. S. W., Fisher, B. C., Wahler, R. G., McAleavey, K. M., et al. (2006). Mindful parenting decreases aggression, noncompliance, and self-injury in children with autism. *Journal of Emotional and Behavioral Disorders, 14*, 169-177.

Singh, N. N., Lancioni, G. E., Winton, A. S. W., Singh, J., Curtis, W. J., Wahler, R. G., et al. (2007). Mindful parenting decreases aggression and increases social behavior in children with developmental disabilities. *Behavior Modification, 31*, 749-771.

Sunseri, P. A. (2004). Preliminary outcomes on the use of dialectical behavior therapy to reduce hospitalization among adolescents in residential care. *Residential Treatment for Children and Youth, 21*, 59-76.

Twohig, M. P., Hayes, S. C., & Berens, N. M. (2007). A contemporary behavioral analysis of childhood behavior problems. In D. W. Woods & J. Kantor (Eds.), *A modern behavioral analysis of clinical problems.* Reno, NV: Context Press.

Wahler, R., Rowinski, K., & Williams, K. (2008). Mindful parenting: An inductive search process. In L. A. Greco & S. C. Hayes (Eds.), *Acceptance and mindfulness treatments for children and adolescents: A practitioner's guide.* Oakland, CA: New Harbinger.

Wall, R. B. (2005). Tai chi and mindfulness-based stress reduction in a Boston public middle school. *Journal of Pediatric Health Care, 19*, 230-237.

Wicksell, R. K., Dahl, J., Magnusson, B., & Olsson, G. L. (2005). Using acceptance and commitment therapy in the rehabilitation of an adolescent female with chronic pain: A case example. *Cognitive and Behavioral Practice, 12*, 415-423.

Wicksell, R. K., Melin, L., Lekander, M., & Olsson, G. L. (2009). Evaluating the effectiveness of exposure and acceptance strategies to improve functioning and quality of life in longstanding pediatric pain: A randomized controlled trial. *Pain, 141*, 248-257.

Wicksell, R. K., Melin, L., & Olsson, G. L. (2006). Exposure and acceptance in the rehabilitation of adolescents with idiopathic chronic pain—A pilot study. *European Journal of Pain, 11*, 267-274.

Woodberry, K. A., & Popenoe, E. J. (2008). Implementing dialectical behavior therapy with adolescents and their families in a community outpatient clinic. *Cognitive and Behavioral Practice, 15*, 277-286.

Woodberry, K. A., Roy, R., & Indik, J. (2008). Dialectical behavior therapy for adolescents with borderline features. In L. A. Greco & S. C. Hayes (Eds.), *Acceptance and mindfulness treatment for children and adolescents: A practitioner's guide.* Oakland, CA: New Harbinger.

APPENDIX: AVOIDANCE AND FUSION QUESTIONNAIRE FOR YOUTH (AFQ-Y)

We want to know more about what you think, how you feel, and what you do. Read each sentence. Then choose the number that tells *how true* each sentence is for you.

0	1	2	3	4
Not at all true	A little true	Pretty true	True	Very true

______ 1. My life won't be good until I feel happy.*

______ 2. My thoughts and feelings mess up my life.*

______ 3. If I feel sad or afraid, something must be wrong with me.

______ 4. The bad things I think about myself must be true.*

______ 5. I don't try out new things if I'm afraid of messing up.

______ 6. I must get rid of my worries and fears so I can have a good life.

______ 7. I do all I can to make sure I don't look dumb in front of other people.

______ 8. I try hard to erase hurtful memories from my mind.

______ 9. I wish I could wave a magic wand to make all my sadness go away.

______ 10. If my heart beats fast, there must be something wrong with me.*

______ 11. I push away thoughts and feelings that I don't like.

______ 12. I stop doing things that are important to me whenever I feel bad.*

______ 13. I do worse in school when I have thoughts that make me feel sad.*

_______ 14. I can't be a good friend when I feel upset.*

_______ 15. I can't stand to feel pain or hurt in my body.

_______ 16. I am afraid of my feelings.*

_______ 17. I say things to make me sound cool.

To score the AFQ-Y, sum responses to all items. To score the short form (AFQ-Y8), sum the items with asterisks.

CHAPTER 10

Acceptance and Mindfulness as Processes of Change in Medical Populations

Lance M. McCracken and Kevin E. Vowles, University of Bath, United Kingdom; and Jennifer Gregg and Priscilla Almada, San Jose State University, San Jose, California

It has been argued that all of the most important outcomes in health care are ultimately behavioral (Kaplan, R. M., 1990). This can be taken to imply that if a medical condition has no adverse impact on behavior or if a treatment of such a condition does not improve behavior, it may be of little importance. Of course, this argument takes the term "behavior" to an extreme where death is essentially reinterpreted as the absence of behavior. Be that as it may, this possibly radical view of health places behavior center stage and implies that developments in psychological research and therapy, such as approaches involving processes of acceptance and mindfulness, will necessarily hold great interest for those who wish to understand and improve health.

Among medical conditions, those regarded as chronic have received the most attention from psychologists and those interested in psychological influences on health. These conditions are a major challenge to modern health care systems and are increasing in incidence to the extent that the majority of people will be diagnosed with at least one chronic health condition at some point in life. And as their incidence increases, so do their negative impacts on quality of life, particularly among individuals with multiple chronic conditions (Sprangers et al., 2000). People with chronic medical conditions are significantly more likely to suffer with problems such as depression (9.3 percent versus 3.2 percent for those without chronic health conditions), and the rate of depression more than doubles when more than one chronic condition is present, increasing to 23 percent (Moussavi et al., 2007). These conditions are both directly and indirectly associated with increased mortality in adults, with the indirect effects being conveyed through their impacts on functioning (Andersson, H. I., 2004; Kaplan, M. S., McFarland, Huguet, & Newsom, 2007; Tonelli et al., 2006). All of this is unwelcome news for health care systems that are already overextended (Rothman & Wagner, 2003).

In most cases, chronic conditions are chronic because there are currently no adequate medical solutions for them. Sometimes managing the underlying condition is possible, but even in these cases the effects are often incomplete. In practically all chronic medical conditions another type of management is required—management directed not so much at the underlying condition, but rather at effects of the condition on the patient's emotional, physical, and social functioning.

Developments in acceptance- and mindfulness-based approaches (Baer, 2006; Hayes, Strosahl, & Wilson, 1999) fit well with the treatment needs of those with chronic medical conditions. This stems from the balance of acceptance and control these interventions encourage, their flexibility, and how they foster the capacity to either take action to change one's ongoing experience or learn to sit with it. There are possibly no other approaches within psychology that are quite as good at helping people develop this ability to actively contact unwanted experiences without those experiences leading to behavior patterns of unsuccessfully struggling for control. These approaches also utilize methods that can help clients lighten the effects of immediate, overwhelming, and sometimes seemingly urgent influences on behavior in ways that favor longer-term health and functioning. In doing so, they are able to block responses such as lighting up a cigarette, refusing to exercise, eating excessively, or hiding a problem that has grown out of control for fear of embarrassment.

The present chapter is meant to serve a number of purposes. We will provide a brief review of the major areas where data are available concerning acceptance- and mindfulness-based approaches to chronic medical conditions—chronic pain, diabetes, epilepsy, smoking cessation, tinnitus, and weight loss—addressing both specific chronic conditions and related behavioral problems of primary and secondary prevention. For each condition we will briefly highlight how acceptance- and mindfulness-related processes are pertinent to the particular problem, examine treatment outcome literature where possible, identify relevant process measures, and describe evidence for the role of acceptance- and mindfulness-related processes in treatment outcomes.

CHRONIC PAIN

Several large-scale surveys indicate that approximately one-fifth of adults report chronic pain of some sort (Breivik, Collett, Ventafridda, Cohen, & Gallacher, 2006; Eriksen, Jensen, Sjøgren, Ekholm, & Rasmussen, 2003; Gureje, Von Korff, Simon, & Gater, 1998). Other studies indicate that somewhere around 85 percent of those with chronic pain will continue to report it up to twelve years later (Andersson, H. I., 2004; see also Elliott, Smith, Hannaford, Smith, & Chambers, 2002). The impacts of chronic pain on daily life are many and can be severe, including emotional distress, disturbed sleep, reduced mobility and physical activity, damaged relationships, and restricted work or school performance (see McCracken, 2008, for a review).

Applications of Acceptance and Mindfulness

Essentially all of the experiences of chronic pain are potentially modifiable by psychological influences, and all of the symptom complaints, patterns of altered activity, and usage of health care that arise in its wake are behavior patterns, and as such are as analyzable and treatable as any other behavior patterns of clinical interest. Because pain can be a highly punishing, discouraging, and frightening experience, it can lead rather automatically to patterns of reduced functioning. These behavior patterns enacted by pain sufferers—patterns of not engaging in usual activities, not meeting responsibilities, and essentially not responding normally to the demands of their social contexts—can in turn lead to additional experiences of uncertainty, threat, and loss. This further disrupts healthy functioning and can lead to a downward spiral of withdrawal and avoidance.

For people with chronic pain, daily life can become filled with experiences they have learned to avoid: not just the pain itself, but other physical symptoms, social pressure or presumed scrutiny, guilt or embarrassment about letting others down or performing below former levels, and feelings of fear and anxiety. A fertile mind can easily come to associate feelings of pain with further tissue damage and worsening pain and disability, which can set up a self-perpetuating cycle of increasingly restrictive avoidance. Beyond avoidance, several other processes contribute to the impacts of chronic pain: becoming entangled in catastrophic or other types of misleading thinking (Vowles, McCracken, & Eccleston, 2007), dwelling on aversive past or future events (McCracken & Thompson, 2009), and failing to take action in valued directions (McCracken & Yang, 2006). Each of these processes represents a part of the model of psychological inflexibility underlying acceptance and commitment therapy (Hayes, Luoma, Bond, Masuda, & Lillis, 2006).

Treatments for chronic pain that come from the emerging tradition of acceptance- and mindfulness-based approaches seek to undermine patterns of avoidance; the overwhelming influences of misleading body sensations, emotional experiences, and thoughts; and general psychological inflexibility attendant with chronic pain. These treatments include acceptance, contact with the present moment, committed action, values-directed behavior, self-as-context, and cognitive defusion—each a process proposed in acceptance and commitment therapy (ACT). When mindfulness is the primary organizing process in treatment, it can be regarded as addressing at least four of the ACT processes: acceptance, contact with the present moment, self-as-context, and defusion (Fletcher & Hayes, 2006).

Specific Measures in Chronic Pain

At present, the most frequently used measure of acceptance and mindfulness processes in chronic pain is the Chronic Pain Acceptance Questionnaire (CPAQ, McCracken, 1998). The CPAQ was originally developed by Geiser (1992) in an unpublished doctoral dissertation. Subsequent analyses provided support for a modified version with twenty items and two subscales: activity engagement and pain willingness (McCracken, Vowles, & Eccleston, 2004). Activity engagement reflects the degree to which the respondent participates in activities in the presence of pain, and pain willingness assesses the degree to which the respondent allows pain to be present without attempts to control or avoid it. The CPAQ is included as an appendix to this chapter.

There are many published studies evaluating the psychometric properties and factor structure of the CPAQ (Cheung, Wong, Yap, & Chen, 2008; McCracken et al., 2004; Nicholas & Asghari, 2006; Nilges, Köster, &

Schmidt, 2007; Vowles, McCracken, McLeod, & Eccleston, 2008; Wicksell, Olsson, & Melin, 2009). This instrument has entirely adequate psychometric characteristics. Internal consistency (Cronbach's α) for the total score and subscales has ranged from 0.78 to 0.91. The two-factor structure has been replicated in German-speaking samples (Nilges et al., 2007) and Cantonese-speaking samples (Cheung et al., 2008) and via confirmatory factor analysis in English (Vowles et al., 2008). Both the total and subscale scores have been shown to be strongly related to multiple indices of emotional, physical, and social functioning across no less than thirty-five studies, which have included both cross-sectional and prospective designs in contexts of both assessment and treatment. These studies provide strong support for the construct validity of the CPAQ, as well as for its practical and clinical utility.

Historically, one focus of psychological interventions for chronic pain has been to train patients in coping strategies designed to reduce feelings of pain and the impact of pain on living (e.g., Morley, Eccleston, & Williams, 1999). A measure intended to assess methods of coping as traditionally conceived as well as psychological flexibility based on ACT is the Brief Pain Coping Inventory–2 (BPCI-2; McCracken & Vowles, 2007). Results from the BPCI-2 showed that its two subscales had adequate internal consistency (α = 0.73 for each). Correlation analyses showed that responses reflecting psychological flexibility significantly correlated with measures of emotional and physical functioning and accounted for more variance in these measures than did responses reflecting coping as traditionally conceived.

A cornerstone of ACT work in chronic pain concerns values clarification and values-based action. The Chronic Pain Values Inventory (CPVI; McCracken & Yang, 2006) assesses importance of and success in values-consistent behavior in six domains: family, intimate relations, friends, work, health, and growth or learning. The initial analysis of the CPVI indicated that the importance subscale was somewhat limited by a ceiling effect, as the majority of respondents indicated that most domains were of great importance. The more meaningful measure is probably the success subscale, which has proven utility in prediction of current and future functioning among people with chronic pain (McCracken & Vowles, 2008; McCracken & Yang, 2006). Changes in scores on this subscale have also been related to improvements in functioning during a three-month follow-up period after interdisciplinary intervention (Vowles & McCracken, 2008).

Recently, Wicksell, Renöfält, Olsson, Bond, and Melin (2008) developed the Psychological Inflexibility in Pain Scale (PIPS). This measure of avoidance and fusion for use among people with chronic pain contains sixteen items falling into two subscales derived through factor analysis: avoidance and cognitive fusion—two core processes of the ACT model. Internal consistency of the measure was good (α = 0.75 to 0.90). Multiple regression analyses indicated that scores on both subscales contributed significant variance in the prediction of pain intensity and interference, physical and emotional functioning, and quality of life.

Treatment Outcome and Process

There are currently at least sixteen published studies specifically examining the effect of acceptance- and mindfulness-based treatment methods on functioning in people suffering from chronic pain. Nine of these included multiple components specific to the ACT model (Dahl, Wilson, & Nilsson, 2004; McCracken, MacKichan, & Eccleston, 2007; McCracken, Vowles, & Eccleston, 2005; Vowles et al., 2007; Vowles & McCracken, 2008; Vowles, Wetherell, & Sorrell, 2009; Wicksell, Ahlqvist, Bring, Melin, & Olsson, 2008; Wicksell, Melin, Lekander, & Olsson, 2009; Wicksell, Melin, & Olsson, 2007). The remaining seven studies (Grossman, Tiefenthaler-Gilmer, Raysz, & Kesper, 2007; Kabat-Zinn, 1982; Kabat-Zinn, Lipworth, & Burney, 1985; Kabat-Zinn, Lipworth, Burney, & Sellers, 1986; Morone, Greco, & Weiner, 2008; Sagula & Rice, 2004; Sephton et al., 2007) were more specifically focused on mindfulness training alone, most often in the form of mindfulness-based stress reduction (MBSR; Kabat-Zinn, 1990).

The available evidence suggests that those who participate in acceptance- or mindfulness-based approaches achieve significant reductions in disability, distress, and utilization of health care, as well as significant improvements in physical performance, work or school attendance, and measures of acceptance, mindfulness, and values. Although there is diversity in measures, designs, and sample sizes among these studies, all report improvement in key areas of functioning. In studies that included control conditions, improvements in the acceptance or mindfulness treatment groups were generally superior to the control groups in at least some of these key areas. Further, improvements were essentially sustained at follow-up assessments occurring three to seven months later and three and four years later, particularly in trials of mindfulness (Grossman et al., 2007; Kabat-Zinn et al., 1986).

In addition to evidence supporting the effectiveness of acceptance and mindfulness treatments for chronic pain, several studies have also examined evidence that improvements in the targeted treatment processes, such as acceptance, are meaningfully related to improvements in emotional and physical functioning at follow-up (McCracken et al., 2005; Vowles et al., 2007; Vowles & McCracken, 2008). Only one study (Vowles & McCracken, 2008) examined the relationship between improved success at values-based action and improved functioning; it found a modest correlation at post-treatment that becomes stronger through the follow-up phase. In an earlier study, Dahl and colleagues (2004) found no differences between treatment and control groups on measures of stress, pain, or beliefs that symptoms were caused by work, suggesting that improvement in the treatment group in sick days and medical visits wasn't the product of symptom reduction alone and providing indirect support for the role of the treatment processes that were targeted. Unfortunately, it seems that none of the trials focusing specifically on mindfulness provided data regarding relationships between skill or practice in mindfulness and outcomes. There is, however, at least one cross-sectional study indicating that mindfulness is a significant predictor of functioning above and beyond pain-related acceptance in individuals with chronic pain (McCracken, Gauntlett-Gilbert, & Vowles, 2007).

DIABETES

Diabetes is a major global public health issue. Worldwide, the number of cases was estimated at 171 million in 2000, with a projected increase to 366 million by 2030 (Wild, Roglic, Green, Sicree, & King, 2004). Progression of the disease can involve high rates of severe morbidity and mortality, with complications such as cardiovascular disease, neuropathy, blindness, and end-stage renal disease.

The experience of having diabetes is often distressing. This distress comes from multiple sources and is also related to exacerbation of the disease (Garay-Sevilla, Malacara, Gutiérrez-Roa, & González, 1999). Thus, traditional approaches to psychoeducation have involved attempting to instruct individuals with diabetes to reduce their experience of stress. These approaches often paradoxically create more distress, given that difficult emotions are often unavoidable in diabetes and attempts to not experience distress can be an additional source of stress (Carey et al., 1997; Colditz et al., 1990).

Applications of Acceptance and Mindfulness

As with other chronic diseases, successful management of diabetes is directly related to psychological factors at many levels. At one level, the experience of diabetes includes dealing with a range of thoughts, feelings, and bodily sensations. Key in this level are the normal daily stresses that everyone experiences; thoughts, feelings, and bodily sensations related to having diabetes and urges to eat unhealthful foods and to rest rather than exercise; and worry and anxiety related to testing blood sugar. These private experiences include some content specifically related to diabetes and other content experienced by everyone, whether diabetes is present or not.

A second level includes the person's response to thoughts, feelings, experiences, and urges. Common in diabetes are such responses as denying the presence of the disease, self-soothing by eating when experiencing distress, and eating unhealthful foods in order to make urges to do so go away. Given the often asymptomatic nature of the disease and the fact that people often don't feel different than before they were diagnosed, denial and attempts to eliminate diabetes-related thoughts and feelings are common.

The next level of analysis is also behavioral. When individuals with diabetes deny the presence of the disease or engage in unhealthy behaviors to regulate emotion or eliminate urges, successful management of blood sugar becomes very difficult. When avoidance occurs in response to private events, this may interfere with necessary self-management behaviors, such as adhering to a proper diet and exercise regimen, performing blood sugar tests, adhering to medication regimens, and doing self-checks for foot problems or signs of infection.

Large-scale research conducted with both insulin-dependent and non-insulin-dependent diabetics has demonstrated that potential prevention of complications is related to good blood sugar control and adherence to diabetes self-management recommendations (Diabetes Control and Complications Trial Research Group, 1993; UK Prospective Diabetes Study Group, 1998). Nonadherence, on the other hand, is related to an increase in complications such as heart disease, blindness, neuropathy, and other potentially fatal medical conditions that impair both longevity and quality of life (Glasgow, Ruggierro, Eakin, Dryfoos, & Chobanian, 1997; Gregg, E. W., Gu, Cheng, Narayan, & Cowie, 2007). Further, these complications contribute to more diabetes-related distress, potentially increasing the problem.

To counteract this cycle, acceptance- and mindfulness-based approaches to diabetes generally involve intervening at the level of responses to private events. Other approaches seek to intervene at the level of the private events themselves, but as noted above, the experience of having diabetes is often inherently distressing, and in many respects that is unchangeable. It is difficult if not impossible to eliminate daily stresses, urges, and negative thoughts and feelings about having diabetes. Therefore, helping individuals develop an open awareness of their private events as they occur allows different self-management responses to emerge even when urges, distress, or other private events are present.

Another key feature in acceptance- and mindfulness-based approaches to diabetes is identifying or clarifying the motivating factors that facilitate increased awareness of negatively evaluated thoughts and feelings related to diabetes. These motivating factors, or values, help create an important context in which patients can have a variety of experiences related to their diabetes and also fully adhere to the self-care behaviors required. Again, diabetes is a difficult disease to manage well, so a consistent focus on values and related goals gives those with the disease a meaningful structure in which to experience the difficult private events associated with the disease.

Specific Measures in Diabetes

Development of diabetes-specific measures of acceptance, mindfulness, or related processes is generally lacking, particularly as compared to developments in the area of chronic pain. The Acceptance and Action Diabetes Questionnaire (AADQ; Gregg, J., 2004) was recently developed for the assessment of aspects of psychological flexibility in relation to diabetes. This eleven-item measure assesses awareness, believability, and mindfulness of diabetes-related thoughts and feelings. For example, one item states, "When I have an upsetting feeling or thought about my diabetes, I try to get rid of that feeling or thought." This item seeks to differentiate the respondent's ability to notice upsetting thoughts or feelings about diabetes from the need to either eliminate them or adhere to them. Although not thoroughly studied at this time, the initial psychometrics of the AADQ appear promising, with good internal consistency ($\alpha = 0.88$; Gregg, J., 2004).

Treatment Outcome and Process

Despite the clear applicability of acceptance and mindfulness approaches to diabetes, very few studies have been conducted to evaluate these approaches among diabetics. In one of the few studies to date, Rosenzweig and colleagues (2007) examined the effects of an eight-week MBSR group intervention, looking particularly at the effects of mindfulness above and beyond the effects of changes in medication, diet, exercise, or other self-care behaviors. The researchers observed a downward trend in HbA1c (a measure of average blood sugar over the previous twelve weeks), a significant reduction in blood pressure, and medium to large improvements in depression, anxiety, and general distress.

Although this study demonstrated an effect for those enrolled in the MBSR intervention and researchers measured participants' hours of mindfulness practice, no direct measure of awareness, acceptance, or mindfulness was administered. Researchers hypothesized that outcomes were mediated by a downregulation of stress reactivity and its subsequent effects on physiological processes involved in the production of cortisol, norepinephrine, beta-endorphin, glucagons, and growth hormone. However, the process of mindfulness and its impact on these physiological processes was not examined.

To our knowledge, only one study has examined the impact upon diabetics of an acceptance- and mindfulness-based treatment in relation to a direct measure of acceptance- or mindfulness-related processes during treatment. J. Gregg, Callaghan, Hayes, and Glenn-Lawson (2007) examined the role of a one-day workshop utilizing basic diabetes education combined with ACT compared to a one-day workshop focused only on education about diabetes, both among a group of low-income patients with type 2 diabetes. The ACT component consisted of clarification of values and brief training in noticing one's thoughts, feelings, bodily sensations, and worries related to diabetes. Self-care behavior, acceptance of negative thoughts and feelings related to diabetes, and HbA1c levels were all measured prior to treatment and three months following the workshop. At follow-up, those in the ACT group reported significantly higher rates of self-care behaviors, such as following a diabetes diet, exercising, and testing blood sugar, compared to those receiving only diabetes education. In addition, those in the ACT group reported significantly higher rates of diabetes-related acceptance as measured by the AADQ compared to the group that only received education about diabetes. In addition, individuals in the ACT group were significantly more likely to have HbA1c levels in the target range at follow-up, despite the two groups being equal on this measure at pretreatment (Gregg, J., et al., 2007).

This study also investigated the mediating effect of acceptance on HbA1c levels and found that combined acceptance and self-management had a mediating effect on the relationship between treatment and the blood measure (Gregg, J., et al., 2007). In other words, in this sample, greater increases in these psychological processes led to better blood glucose outcomes, regardless of which treatment was administered. Given that the ACT group demonstrated higher self-care and psychological flexibility in regard to their diabetes, this intervention appeared to impact HbA1c levels through the hypothesized mechanisms.

A key concern that may not yet be adequately addressed is the guilt, shame, and sense of responsibility that many individuals with diabetes hold regarding the development of their disease. This can contribute to difficulties with being fully aware of one's experience and can also create a focus on unfairness that impairs fully managing one's diabetes. Training in mindfulness or psychological flexibility with this population often includes reminders that the disease can progress even with good adherence, and that complications may arise even when blood sugar levels are generally controlled. This can create a new subset of difficult thoughts and feelings related to the futility of self-management, providing additional experiences of which to be mindful.

EPILEPSY

The estimated number of adults with epilepsy in Europe and North America is about 5 per 1,000 (Forsgren, Beghi, Óun, & Sillanpää, 2005; Theodore et al., 2006). People with epilepsy experience significantly reduced quality of life in comparison to people without epilepsy. They are also more likely to have reduced work status and income and to suffer effects of persistent stigma (Theodore et al., 2006). These aspects of epilepsy point to a clear need for psychological approaches, especially when taken together with poor access to treatment, incomplete management of symptoms with medications, and medication side effects.

Applications of Acceptance and Mindfulness

For many years behavioral methods have been applied to the problem of epilepsy with some successful results, particularly in relation to reduced seizure frequency (Goldstein, 1990). Seizures are directly disrupting to daily functioning. They are also stressful, frightening, and stigmatizing. It has been suggested that the emotional experiences associated with these aspects of epilepsy can themselves contribute to seizures (Dahl, 1992). Based on this situation, the ACT model has been applied to seizures as a means of building behavioral qualities of flexibility, acceptance, defusion, contact with the present moment, and values-directed action around the disposition to experience seizures, the fear and other emotions that seizures occasion, and the thoughts and memories associated with these experiences (Lundgren, Dahl, Melin, & Kies, 2006).

Specific Measures for Epilepsy

Two measures of ACT processes have been used in relation to epilepsy. One is the Acceptance and Action Epilepsy Questionnaire (AAEpQ), a modified version of the Acceptance and Action Questionnaire (AAQ), which is used to assess psychological flexibility (Lundgren, Dahl, & Hayes, 2008). The AAEpQ appears to be adequately internally consistent ($\alpha = 0.65$), and evidence for its validity is based on its close derivation from the AAQ and its sensitivity to ACT-based treatment. The other measure, known as the Values Bull's-Eye, assesses behavioral consistency with respect to valued directions and persistence of valuing in the face of barriers. It has good test-retest reliability ($r = 0.86$) and is adequately internally consistent (α ranging from 0.65 to 0.76; Lundgren et al., 2008).

Treatment Outcome and Process

Lundgren and colleagues (2006) reported on a randomized trial of ACT plus behavioral seizure control therapy in twenty-seven adults who were residents of a center for epilepsy in South Africa or who attended the center daily. All participants had EEG-verified epilepsy that was resistant to medication. Both the ACT-based condition and the comparison, which consisted of "supportive therapy," entailed nine hours of treatment distributed in two individual and two group session during a four-week period. The outcome variables in this trial included seizure frequency and seizure index (frequency multiplied by duration), both taken from daily medical charts, and quality of life, all assessed prior to treatment, after treatment, and at six-month and one-year follow-ups. The quality of life measures included the World Health Organization Quality of Life scale (WHOQOL; World Health Organization, 1996) and the Satisfaction with Life Scale (SWLS;

Diener, Emmons, Larsen, & Griffin, 1985). The ACT condition achieved superior results in each outcome variable at all three assessment occasions occurring after treatment. For example, in the ACT condition a mean of 3.8 seizures per month was reduced to 0.71 seizures at post-treatment and 0.62 one year after treatment, with a large effect size (Cohen's d = 0.89), while in the comparison condition seizure frequency remained unchanged. Satisfaction with life was particularly increased in the ACT condition, with a large effect size at post-treatment (d = 1.72), and an even larger effect size at the one-year follow-up (d = 2.47); once again, the comparison condition showed no improvement at all. It is also remarkable that all of the participants in this study were living below the poverty level and many required translations by nurses or social workers during treatment sessions.

A subsequent study of the same trial data examined mediators of change (Lundgren et al., 2008). Again, one finding that is somewhat unique in the epilepsy treatment trial, in relation to results from acceptance- or mindfulness-based treatments for other conditions, is that the target symptoms were nearly completely eliminated by ACT-based treatment. Mediation of this effect was studied using the AAEpQ and the Bull's-Eye. Analyses showed that the processes of psychological flexibility and consistency and persistence in regard to values mediated changes in total seizure time per month from pretreatment to the one-year follow-up. Similarly, consistency and persistence in regard to values mediated change in quality of life as measured by the WHOQOL and a measure called the Personal Wellbeing Index (PWI; Cummins, 1991), but not the SWLS. Overall, these findings suggest that the dramatic reduction in seizures can be attributed to increases in psychological flexibility and persistence in values-consistent behavior.

SMOKING CESSATION

It may go without saying that smoking, particularly in combination with other risk factors, is significantly injurious to good health. Smoking is regarded as the number one cause of preventable death in many countries. Although smoking cessation interventions were once identified as a success story within behavioral therapies in general, some feel that after a "golden age" for these approaches to smoking cessation twenty or thirty years ago, progress in development in this area ceased due to the lack of a unifying theory of behavior change to guide further development (Gifford et al., 2004).

Applications of Acceptance and Mindfulness

The work on epilepsy implies that unwillingness to have the problem of seizures contributes to the problem of seizures in the sense of more frequent seizures and greater impact on quality of life. In a similar fashion, unwillingness is conceptualized as a core process in the continuation of smoking behavior. Specifically, it is hypothesized that for a subset of smokers, smoking entails a process of attempting to control or avoid aversive experiences, including distressing emotions and sensations associated with nicotine withdrawal. The ACT treatment model for smoking cessation emphasizes contacting aversive experiences, accepting them in an active process of healthy living, and taking direction from goals and values (Gifford et al., 2004).

Specific Measures in Smoking Cessation

The Avoidance and Inflexibility Scale (AIS) is designed to reflect smokers' avoidance behavior in relation to smoking cessation and smoking (Gifford et al., 2004). It has high internal consistency (α = 0.93) and is sensitive to the effects of ACT-based treatment.

Treatment Outcome and Process

Gifford and colleagues (2004) conducted a pilot study with seventy-six participants randomized to either ACT or nicotine replacement therapy (NRT). All participants were self-identified nicotine-dependent smokers who smoked at least ten cigarettes per day for at least one year. Both treatment conditions were seven weeks in duration, including clinic visits at least once per week. The ACT protocol entailed seven fifty-minute individual sessions and seven ninety-minute group sessions. Efficacy analyses indicated that quit rates didn't differ at post-treatment or the six-month follow-up. However, the ACT group had significantly greater quit rates at the one-year follow-up: 35 percent versus 15 percent for NRT. When all missing data were coded as "smoking," the ACT group had a quit rate at one year of 21.2 percent, compared to 9.3 percent for NRT, but this difference wasn't statistically significant. Participants in this study also completed the AIS and measures of withdrawal symptoms and negative affect. Secondary analyses showed that neither withdrawal symptoms nor negative affect were related to quit status at one year, while the AIS score was. Further analyses showed that avoidance and inflexibility significantly mediated the effects of treatment.

TINNITUS

Tinnitus involves the experience of sound, typically ringing, buzzing, or hissing, in the absence of a related external sound source. It is experienced by 10 to 15 percent of the general population and, in severe cases, can have a significant impact on quality of daily functioning, with effects including depression, anxiety, sleep disturbance, and difficulties with concentration (Andersson, G., 2002). Tinnitus is a chronic and largely intractable condition, and the source of significant suffering for those who have it.

Applications of Acceptance and Mindfulness

We identified just three studies of acceptance in relation to tinnitus. However, examining tinnitus reinforces our understanding of acceptance and mindfulness in similarly intractable conditions, such as chronic pain. The rationale for applying acceptance to tinnitus is based on the notion that attempting to alter the experience of tinnitus only increases the behavioral influence of the experience and does not yield either control over tinnitus or better functioning in the long run.

Specific Measures for Tinnitus

Westin, Hayes, and Andersson (2008) created a twelve-item Tinnitus Acceptance Questionnaire (TAQ), based on items from the AAQ and CPAQ, and showed that acceptance is potentially important for quality of life and depression in those who suffer from tinnitus. They also showed that acceptance of tinnitus as measured by the TAQ mediated the influence of baseline tinnitus distress on later quality of life and depression. In an interesting prospective study employing performance on a mental imagery task as the dependent variable, this same group found that, in relation to control participants, participants in an acceptance condition remained significantly more focused on the imagery task without interruption (Westin, Ostergren, & Andersson, 2008).

Treatment Outcome and Process

Although we know of no currently published treatment outcome studies involving acceptance or mindfulness for tinnitus, process analyses are available from a recently published treatment trial (Hesser, Westin, Hayes, & Andersson, 2009) in which nineteen patients completed a measure of tinnitus-related distress before and after treatment and at follow-up. Based on videotapes from treatment sessions, raters coded patients' acceptance and defusion statements. Tinnitus-related distress significantly decreased during treatment ($d = 0.91$). Effects of treatment appeared rapidly, occurring within three sessions. The process analyses showed that ratings of defusion and acceptance from the second session significantly predicted outcomes at six-month follow-up, providing support for the mediating role of these variables in relation to treatment outcome.

WEIGHT LOSS

Worldwide, more than 400 million people meet the World Health Organization criteria for obesity and another 1.6 billion are considered overweight (World Health Organization, 2006). Being obese significantly increases a person's risk for developing a number of health problems, including atherosclerosis, hypertension, high blood pressure, diabetes, gallbladder disease, arthritis, cardiovascular disease, kidney disease, heart failure, stroke, some types of cancer, and pregnancy complications (Centers for Disease Control, 2009; Kenchaiah et al., 2002). Due to increased health impairments and susceptibility to chronic disease, obese individuals are also at greater risk of premature death (Adams et al., 2006).

The rapid growth in obesity rates is even more troubling due to the common problem of maintaining weight loss. While some weight loss programs have proven to be successful, most people regain the weight within three to five years after treatment (Perri, 1998; Wadden, Sternberg, Letizia, Stunkard, & Foster, 1989; Wing, 1998). Maintenance data are so discouraging that it is recommended that affected individuals stay in active weight loss treatment throughout their lives (National Institutes of Health, 1998).

Application of Acceptance and Mindfulness

When considering an acceptance- and mindfulness-based approach to sustained weight loss, it is important to first examine the factors that contribute to gaining and regaining weight. For example, rigid control of eating behavior has, paradoxically, been identified as significantly related to regaining weight following weight loss (Westenhoefer, 1991; Westenhoefer, Stunkard, & Pudel, 1999). And sometimes eating is an attempt to control emotions, which has been termed "emotional eating." Using eating as a means to avoid negative thoughts or feelings can lead to a narrowing of behavior patterns. This can impair the ability to cope with discomfort in the future and to engage in successful long-term weight management because those who engage in this behavior can become increasingly reliant on eating as a coping response. Emotional eating reduces aversive private events, so the behavior is maintained by negative reinforcement (Agras & Telch, 1998; Telch & Agras, 1996).

There is increasing interest in using acceptance- and mindfulness-based treatments to target the specific behaviors affecting weight loss and maintenance of weight loss, such as emotional eating and binge eating (Baer, Fischer, & Huss, 2005a, 2005b; Kristeller, Baer, & Quillian-Wolever, 2006; Kristeller & Hallett, 1999). For example, mindfulness can help the individual "attend to relevant aspects of [the eating] experience in a nonjudgmental manner" (Ludwig & Kabat-Zinn, 2008, p. 1350). Processes of acceptance and mindfulness aim to allow people who are trying to lose weight or maintain weight loss to notice their negative thoughts and feelings and experience them at face value and not as necessary determinants of their behavior, and to allow them to contact these thoughts and feelings without attempting to control them.

Specific Measures for Weight Loss

As with most of the medical concerns reviewed above, there are not yet thoroughly developed measures of psychological flexibility in the field of weight loss. Lillis, Hayes, Bunting, and Masuda (2009) designed the Acceptance and Action Questionnaire for Weight-Related Difficulties (AAQW) to assess weight-related acceptance, self-image, willingness to experience private events related to weight loss and maintenance, and other behaviors related to obesity. The AAQW consists of seventeen items rated on a seven-point Likert scale. Scale items consists of statements such as "It's okay to feel fat." The scale has good internal consistency ($\alpha = 0.88$) and is significantly positively correlated with the AAQ.

Treatment Outcome and Process

While there are several studies examining the effects of acceptance- and mindfulness-based treatments on weight loss and weight maintenance, the processes underlying these treatments typically haven't been measured, with a few exceptions. One randomized controlled trial examined the effectiveness of ACT on weight maintenance for obesity (Lillis et al., 2009). Participants in this study were randomly assigned to either the ACT group (forty participants) or a wait list control group (forty-four participants). Both groups participated in at least six months of a nutrition and exercise weight loss program prior to participation in the study. The ACT intervention was designed to impact acceptance and mindfulness of private events related to eating and exercise behaviors and to get participants connected to their health-related values. Participants in the ACT group had significantly better outcomes in weight loss and maintenance, psychological distress, obesity-related stigma, and self-reported health behaviors. These outcomes were mediated by an increase in acceptance and mindfulness. The relationships between treatment group and body mass index, weight change, stigma, psychological distress, quality of life, binge eating, and physical activity were significantly mediated by acceptance as indicated by scores on the AAQW. These results strongly imply that acceptance- and mindfulness-based interventions may be a step forward in the development of more successful long-term weight control programs.

CONCLUSIONS

People with chronic medical concerns present important challenges to behavior change, not least because they present on the surface with medical conditions, but also because their symptoms or the underlying pathology of their disease can be tightly bound to their behavior, with each affecting the other. As scientists or clinicians, our task is to develop and deliver methods of treatment for these conditions that allow people to maintain their health and functioning. These approaches can be directed at stopping behavior patterns that bring a risk of serious illness or at building behavior patterns that entail better management of underlying disease process. Alternatively, they may be aimed at reducing overwhelming influences of pain or other symptoms on behavior, or at helping those with these conditions meet the social and emotional challenges of their condition more skillfully or with greater equanimity when required.

The literature on acceptance- and mindfulness-based approaches to the range of medical conditions reviewed here demonstrates the broad potential of these approaches. Although all of the results discussed here represent early developments, it appears that these approaches can deeply impact the processes by which these conditions lead to suffering and disability. It also appears they can help people live more effectively with painful or potentially intrusive symptoms that are essentially uncontrollable, as in chronic pain and tinnitus. Through their influence on behavior patterns, these approaches may directly alter the underlying pathology of chronic conditions, such as in diabetes, or conditions where smoking, eating, and exercise play a role in the underlying processes of disease. Finally, and quite dramatically, it appears that these approaches can prevent symptoms of some underlying condition from occurring, such as in epilepsy.

There are commonalities in the conditions reviewed here. In each case the experience of having a chronic condition can be a significant source of emotional distress. In turn, this distress can present dilemmas of short-term relief at the expense of long-term health, leading to unhealthy patterns of avoidance and to significant impacts on daily functioning. Each condition can also be experienced as painfully stigmatizing. In the unique ways that acceptance and mindfulness can undermine avoidance, reduce the impact of judgments and interpretations, promote psychological flexibility, increase values-based action, and promote a compassionate quality in action, they seem uniquely suited to help where these conditions generate their most adverse impacts.

Although the findings of the trials presented here have been predominately supportive, there are also key areas where additional work is needed. First, many of the trials, especially some of the larger ones, didn't include active control conditions, and those utilizing randomization to active control conditions generally had small sample sizes. Second, chronic conditions are by definition long-term conditions. It will be important to understand the outcomes of treatment in the longer term to fully understand their impacts and their value. Third, treatment integrity and therapist adherence to the treatment model are key concerns, particularly as these determine internal validity of treatment comparisons. These were not evaluated in the work presented here. Of course, these limitations are not unique to studies of acceptance and mindfulness alone; they characterize many areas of work where psychological methods are applied to medical conditions. As research proceeds, we anticipate that these issues will be addressed.

Given that chronic medical conditions will probably be a normal part of the human experience in the future, we would do well to develop treatment technologies that are adequate to the task of easing the impact of these conditions. We believe that the applications of acceptance and mindfulness described here represent progress in this regard.

REFERENCES

Adams, K. F., Schatzkin, A., Harris, T. B, Kipnis, V., Mouw, T., Ballard-Barbash, R., et al. (2006). Overweight, obesity, and mortality in a large prospective cohort of persons 50 to 71 years old. *New England Journal of Medicine, 355*, 763-778.

Agras, W. S., & Telch, C. F. (1998). The effects of caloric deprivation and negative affect on binge eating in obese binge-eating disordered women. *Behavior Therapy, 29*, 491-503.

Andersson, G. (2002). Psychological aspects of tinnitus and the application of cognitive-behavioral therapy. *Clinical Psychology Review, 22*, 977-990.

Andersson, H. I. (2004). The course of non-malignant chronic pain: A 12-year follow-up of a cohort from the general population. *European Journal of Pain, 8*, 47-53.

Baer, R. A. (2006). *Mindfulness-based treatment approaches: Clinician's guide to evidence base and applications.* London: Academic Press.

Baer, R. A., Fischer, S., & Huss, D. B. (2005a). Mindfulness and acceptance in the treatment of disordered eating. *Journal of Rational-Emotive and Cognitive-Behavior Therapy, 24*, 281-300.

Baer, R. A., Fischer, S., & Huss, D. B. (2005b). Mindfulness-based cognitive therapy applied to binge eating: A case study. *Cognitive and Behavioral Practice, 12*, 351-358.

Breivik, H., Collett, B., Ventafridda, V., Cohen, R., & Gallacher, D. (2006). Survey of chronic pain in Europe: Prevalence, impact on daily life, and treatment. *European Journal of Pain, 10*, 287-333.

Carey, V. J., Walters, E. E., Colditz, G. A., Solomon, C. G., Willett, W. C., Rosner, B. A., et al. (1997). Body fat distribution and risk of non-insulin-dependent diabetes mellitus in women: The Nurses' Health Study. *American Journal of Epidemiology, 145*, 614 -619.

Centers for Disease Control. (2009). Obesity and overweight. www.cdc.gov/obesity/causes/health.html. Accessed October 3, 2009.

Cheung, N. M., Wong, T. C. M., Yap, J. C. M., & Chen, P. P. (2008). Validation of the Chronic Pain Acceptance Questionnaire (CPAQ) in Cantonese-speaking Chinese patients. *Journal of Pain, 9*, 823-832.

Colditz, G. A., Willett, W. C., Stampfer, M. J., Manson, J. E., Hennekens, C. H., Arky, R. A., et al. (1990). Weight as a risk factor for clinical diabetes in women. *American Journal of Epidemiology, 132*, 501-513.

Cummins, R. A. (1991). The comprehensive Quality of Life Scale—Intellectual disability: An instrument under development. *Australia and New Zealand Journal of Developmental Disabilities, 17*, 259-264.

Dahl, J. (1992). *Epilepsy: A behavior medicine approach to assessment and treatment in children*. Göttingen, Germany: Hogref and Huber.

Dahl, J., Wilson, K. G., & Nilsson, A. (2004). Acceptance and commitment therapy and the treatment of persons at risk for long-term disability resulting from stress and pain symptoms: A preliminary randomized trial. *Behavior Therapy, 35*, 785-801.

Diabetes Control and Complications Trial Research Group. (1993). The effect of intensive treatment of diabetes on the development and progression of long-term complications in insulin-dependent diabetes mellitus. *New England Journal of Medicine, 329*, 977-986.

Diener, E., Emmons, R. A., Larsen, R. J., & Griffin, S. (1985). The Satisfaction With Life Scale. *Journal of Personality and Social Psychology, 49*, 71-75.

Elliott, A. M., Smith, B. H., Hannaford, P. C., Smith, W. C., & Chambers, W. A. (2002). The course of chronic pain in the community: Results of a 4-year follow-up study. *Pain, 99*, 299-307.

Eriksen, J., Jensen, M. K., Sjøgren, P., Ekholm, O., & Rasmussen, N. K. (2003). Epidemiology of chronic non-malignant pain in Denmark. *Pain, 106*, 221-228.

Fletcher, L., & Hayes, S. C. (2006). Relational frame theory, acceptance and commitment therapy, and a functional analytic definition of mindfulness. *Journal of Rational-Emotive and Cognitive-Behavior Therapy, 23*, 315-336.

Forsgren L., Beghi, E., Õun, A., & Sillanpää, M. (2005). The epidemiology of epilepsy in Europe—A systematic review. *European Journal of Neurology, 12*, 245-253.

Garay-Sevilla, M. E., Malacara, J. M., Gutiérrez-Roa, A., & González, E. (1999). Denial of disease in type 2 diabetes mellitus: Its influence on metabolic control and associated factors. *Diabetic Medicine, 16*, 238-244.

Geiser, D. S. (1992). *A comparison of acceptance-focused and control-focused psychological treatments in a chronic pain treatment center.* Unpublished doctoral dissertation, University of Nevada, Reno.

Gifford, E. V., Kohlenberg, B. S., Hayes, S. C., Antonuccio, D. O., Piasecki, M. M., Rasmussen-Hall, M. L., et al. (2004). Acceptance-based treatment for smoking cessation. *Behavior Therapy, 35*, 689-705.

Glasgow, R. E., Ruggiero, L., Eakin, E. G., Dryfoos, J., & Chobanian, L. (1997). Quality of life and associated characteristics in a large national sample of adults with diabetes. *Diabetes Care, 20*, 562-567.

Goldstein, L. (1990). Behavioural and cognitive-behavioural treatments for epilepsy: A progress review. *British Journal of Clinical Psychology, 29*, 257-269.

Gregg, E. W., Gu, Q., Cheng, Y. J., Narayan, K. M., & Cowie, C. C. (2007). Mortality trends in men and women with diabetes, 1971 to 2000. *Annals of Internal Medicine, 147*, 149-155.

Gregg, J. (2004). *A randomized controlled effectiveness trial comparing patient education with and without acceptance and commitment therapy for type 2 diabetes self-management.* Unpublished doctoral dissertation, University of Nevada, Reno.

Gregg, J., Callaghan, G., Hayes, S. C., & Glenn-Lawson, J. (2007). Improving diabetes self-management through acceptance, mindfulness, and values: A randomized controlled trial. *Journal of Consulting and Clinical Psychology, 75*, 336-343.

Grossman, P., Tiefenthaler-Gilmer, U., Raysz, A., & Kesper, U. (2007). Mindfulness training as an intervention for fibromyalgia: Evidence of postintervention and 3-year follow-up benefits in well-being. *Psychotherapy and Psychosomatics, 76*, 226-233.

Gureje, O., Von Korff, M., Simon, G. E., & Gater, R. (1998). Persistent pain and well-being: A World Health Organization study in primary care. *JAMA, 280*, 147-151.

Hayes, S. C., Luoma, J. B., Bond, F. W., Masuda A., & Lillis, J. (2006). Acceptance and commitment therapy: Model, processes and outcomes. *Behaviour Research and Therapy, 44*, 1-25.

Hayes, S. C., Strosahl, K., & Wilson, K. G. (1999). *Acceptance and commitment therapy: An experiential approach to behavior change.* New York: Guilford.

Hesser, H., Westin, V., Hayes, S. C., & Andersson, G. (2009). Clients' in-session acceptance and cognitive defusion behaviors in acceptance-based treatment of tinnitus distress. *Behaviour Research and Therapy, 47*, 523-528.

Kabat-Zinn, J. (1982). An outpatient program in behavioral medicine for chronic pain patients based on the practice of mindfulness meditation: Theoretical considerations and preliminary results. *General Hospital Psychiatry, 4*, 33-47.

Kabat-Zinn, J. (1990). *Full catastrophe living: Using the wisdom of your body and mind to face stress, pain, and illness.* New York: Dell Publishing.

Kabat-Zinn, J., Lipworth, L., & Burney, R. (1985). The clinical use of mindfulness meditation for the self-regulation of chronic pain. *Journal of Behavioral Medicine, 8*, 163-190.

Kabat-Zinn, J., Lipworth, L., Burney, R., & Sellers, W. (1986). Four-year follow-up of a meditation-based program for the self-regulation of chronic pain: Treatment outcomes and compliance. *Clinical Journal of Pain, 2*, 159-173.

Kaplan, M. S., McFarland, B. H., Huguet, N., & Newsom J. T. (2007). Physical illness, functional limitations, and suicide risk: A population-based study. *American Journal of Orthopsychiatry, 77*, 56-60.

Kaplan, R. M. (1990). Behavior as the central outcome in health care. *American Psychologist, 45*, 1211-1220.

Kenchaiah, S., Evans, J. C., Levy, D., Wilson, P. W., Benjamin, E. J., Larson, M. G., et al. (2002). Obesity and the risk of heart failure. *New England Journal of Medicine, 347*, 305-313.

Kristeller, J. L., Baer, R. A., & Quillian-Wolever, R. (2006). Mindfulness-based approaches to eating disorders. In R. A. Baer (Ed.), *Mindfulness-based treatment approaches: Clinician's guide to evidence base and applications.* San Diego, CA: Elsevier.

Kristeller, J. L., & Hallett, C. B. (1999). An exploratory study of a meditation-based intervention for binge eating disorder. *Journal of Health Psychology, 4*, 357-363.

Lillis, J., Hayes, S. C., Bunting, K., & Masuda, A. (2009). Teaching acceptance and mindfulness to improve the lives of the obese: A preliminary test of a theoretical model. *Annals of Behavioral Medicine, 37*, 58-69.

Ludwig, D. S., & Kabat-Zinn, J. (2008). Mindfulness in medicine. *JAMA, 300*, 1350-1352.

Lundgren, T., Dahl, J., & Hayes, S. C. (2008). Evaluation of mediators of change in the treatment of epilepsy with acceptance and commitment therapy. *Journal of Behavioral Medicine, 31*, 225-235.

Lundgren, T., Dahl, J., Melin, L., & Kies, B. (2006). Evaluation of acceptance and commitment therapy for drug refractory epilepsy: A randomized controlled trail in South Africa—A pilot study. *Epilepsia, 47*, 2173-2179.

McCracken, L. M. (1998). Learning to live with the pain: Acceptance of pain predicts adjustment in persons with chronic pain. *Pain, 74*, 21-27.

McCracken, L. M. (2008). Psychological effects of chronic pain: An overview. In P. R. Wilson, P. J. Watson, J. A. Haythornthwaite, & T. S. Jensen (Eds.), *Clinical pain management: Chronic pain*. London: Hodder Arnold.

McCracken, L. M., Gauntlett-Gilbert, J., & Vowles, K. E. (2007). The role of mindfulness in a contextual cognitive-behavioral analysis of chronic pain-related suffering and disability. *Pain, 131*, 63-69.

McCracken, L. M., MacKichan, F., & Eccleston, C. (2007). Contextual cognitive-behavioral therapy for severely disabled chronic pain sufferers: Effectiveness and clinically significant change. *European Journal of Pain, 11*, 314-322.

McCracken L. M., & Thompson M. (2009). Components of mindfulness in patients with chronic pain. *Journal of Psychopathology and Behavior Assessment, 31*, 75-82.

McCracken, L. M., & Vowles, K. E. (2007). Psychological flexibility and traditional pain management strategies in relation to patient functioning with chronic pain: An examination of a revised instrument. *Journal of Pain, 8*, 700-707.

McCracken, L. M., & Vowles, K. E. (2008). A prospective analysis of acceptance and values in patients with chronic pain. *Health Psychology, 27*, 215-220.

McCracken, L. M., Vowles, K. E., & Eccleston, C. (2004). Acceptance of chronic pain: Component analysis and a revised assessment method. *Pain, 107*, 159-166.

McCracken, L. M., Vowles, K. E., & Eccleston, C. (2005). Acceptance-based treatment for persons with complex, long standing chronic pain: A preliminary analysis of treatment outcome in comparison to a waiting phase. *Behaviour Research and Therapy, 43*, 1335-1346.

McCracken, L. M., & Yang, S. (2006). The role of values in a contextual cognitive-behavioral approach to chronic pain. *Pain, 123*, 137-145.

Morley, S., Eccleston, C., & Williams, A. (1999). Systematic review and meta-analysis of randomized controlled trials of cognitive behaviour therapy and behaviour therapy for chronic pain in adults, excluding headache. *Pain, 80*, 1-13.

Morone, N. E., Greco, C. M., & Weiner, D. K. (2008). Mindfulness meditation for the treatment of chronic low back pain in older adults: A randomized controlled pilot study. *Pain, 134*, 310-319.

Moussavi, S., Chatterji, S., Verdes, E., Tandon, A., Patel, V., & Uston, B. (2007). Depression, chronic diseases, and decrements in health: Results from the World Health surveys. *Lancet, 370*, 851-858.

National Institutes of Health. (1998). *Clinical guidelines on the identification, evaluation, and treatment of overweight and obesity in adults: The evidence report.* Bethesda, MD: National Heart, Lung, and Blood Institute.

Nicholas, M. K., & Asghari, A. (2006). Investigating acceptance in adjustment to chronic pain: Is acceptance broader than we thought? *Pain, 124*, 269-279.

Nilges, P., Köster, B., & Schmidt, C. O. (2007). Pain acceptance: Concept and validation of a German version of the Chronic Pain Acceptance Questionnaire. *Schmerz, 21*, 60-67.

Perri, M. G. (1998). The maintenance of treatment effects in the long-term management of obesity. *Clinical Psychology: Science and Practice, 5*, 526-543.

Rosenzweig, S., Reibel, D., Greeson, J., Edman, J., Jasser, S., McMearty, K., et al. (2007). Mindfulness-based stress reduction is associated with improved glycemic control in type 2 diabetes mellitus: A pilot study. *Alternative Therapies, 13*, 36-38.

Rothman, A. A., & Wagner, E. H. (2003). Chronic illness management: What is the role of primary care? *Annals of Internal Medicine, 138*, 256-261.

Sagula, D., & Rice, K. G. (2004). The effectiveness of mindfulness training on the grieving process and emotional well-being of chronic pain patients. *Journal of Clinical Psychology in Medical Settings, 11*, 333-342.

Sephton, S. E., Salmon, P., Weissbecker, I., Ulmer, C., Floyd, A., Hoover, K., et al. (2007). Mindfulness meditation alleviates depressive symptoms in women with fibromyalgia: Results of a randomized clinical trial. *Arthritis and Rheumatism, 57*, 77-85.

Sprangers, M. A. G., de Regt, E. B., Andries, F., van Agt, H., Bijl, R. V., de Boer, J. B., et al. (2000). Which chronic conditions are associated with better or poorer quality of life? *Journal of Clinical Epidemiology, 53*, 895-907.

Telch, C. F., & Agras, W. S. (1996). Do emotional states influence binge eating in the obese? *International Journal of Eating Disorders, 20*, 271-279.

Theodore, W. H., Spencer, S. S., Wiebe, S., Langfitt, J. T., Ali, A., Shafer, P. O., et al. (2006). Epilepsy in North America: A report prepared under the auspices of the Global Campaign Against Epilepsy, the International Bureau for Epilepsy, the International League Against Epilepsy, and the World Health Organization. *Epilepsia, 47*, 1700-1722.

Tonelli, M., Wiebe, N., Culleton, B., House, A., Rabbat, C., Fok, M., et al. (2006). Chronic kidney disease and mortality risk: A systematic review. *Journal of the American Society of Nephrology, 17*, 2034-2047.

UK Prospective Diabetes Study Group. (1998). Effect of intensive blood-glucose control with metformin on complications in overweight patients with type 2 diabetes (UKPD 34). *Lancet, 352*, 854-865.

Vowles, K. E., & McCracken, L. M. (2008). Acceptance and values-based action in chronic pain: A study of effectiveness and treatment process. *Journal of Consulting and Clinical Psychology, 76*, 397-407.

Vowles, K. E., McCracken, L. M., & Eccleston, C. (2007). Processes of behavior change in interdisciplinary treatment of chronic pain: Contributions of pain intensity, catastrophizing, and acceptance. *European Journal of Pain, 11*, 779-787.

Vowles, K. E., McCracken, L. M., McLeod, C., & Eccleston, C. (2008). The Chronic Pain Acceptance Questionnaire: Confirmatory factor analysis and identification of patient subgroups. *Pain, 140*, 284-291.

Vowles, K. E., Wetherell, J. L., & Sorrell, J. T. (2009). Targeting acceptance, mindfulness, and values-based action in chronic pain: Findings of two preliminary trials of an outpatient group-based intervention. *Cognitive and Behavioral Practice, 16*, 49-58.

Wadden, T. A., Sternberg, J. A., Letizia, K. A., Stunkard, A. J., & Foster, G. D. (1989). Treatment of obesity by very low calorie diet, behavior therapy, and their combination: A 5-year perspective. *International Journal of Obesity, 13*, 39-46.

Westenhoefer, J. (1991). Dietary restraint and disinhibition: Is restraint a homogeneous construct? *Appetite, 16*, 45-55.

Westenhoefer, J., Stunkard, A. J., & Pudel, V. (1999). Validation of the flexible and rigid control dimensions of dietary restraint. *International Journal of Eating Disorders, 26*, 53-64.

Westin, V., Hayes, S. C., & Andersson, G. (2008). Is it the sound of your relationship to it? The role of acceptance in predicting tinnitus impact. *Behaviour Research and Therapy, 46*, 1259-1265.

Westin, V., Ostergren, R., & Andersson, G. (2008). The effects of acceptance versus thought suppression for dealing with the intrusiveness of tinnitus. *International Journal of Audiology, 47*, S184-S190.

Wicksell, R. K., Ahlqvist, J., Bring, A., Melin, L., & Olsson, G. L. (2008). Can exposure and acceptance strategies improve functioning and life satisfaction in people with chronic pain and whiplash-associated disorders (WAD)? A randomized controlled trial. *Cognitive Behaviour Therapy, 37,* 169-182.

Wicksell, R. K., Melin, L., Lekander, M., & Olsson, G. L. (2009). Evaluating the effectiveness of exposure and acceptance strategies to improve functioning and quality of life in longstanding pediatric pain: A randomized controlled trial. *Pain, 141,* 248-257.

Wicksell, R. K., Melin, L., & Olsson, G. L. (2007). Exposure and acceptance in the rehabilitation of adolescents with idiopathic chronic pain—A pilot study. *European Journal of Pain, 11,* 267-274.

Wicksell, R. K., Olsson, G. L., & Melin, L. (2009). The Chronic Pain Acceptance Questionnaire (CPAQ)—Further validation including a confirmatory factor analysis and a comparison with the Tampa Scale of Kinesiophobia. *European Journal of Pain, 13,* 760-768.

Wicksell, R. K., Renöfält, J., Olsson G. L., Bond, F. W., & Melin, L. (2008). Avoidance and cognitive fusion—Central components in pain related disability? Development and preliminary validation of the Psychological Inflexibility in Pain Scale (PIPS). *European Journal of Pain, 12,* 491-500.

Wild, S., Roglic, G., Green, A., Sicree, R., & King, H. (2004). Global prevalence of diabetes: Estimates for the year 2000 and projections for 2030. *Diabetes Care, 27,* 1047-1053.

Wing, R. R. (1998). Behavioral approaches to the treatment of obesity. In G. A. Bray, C. Bouchard, & W. P. James (Eds.), *Handbook of obesity.* New York: Marcel Dekker.

World Health Organization. (1996). WHOQOL-BREF introduction, administration and generic version of the assessment. Field trial version. Geneva. Available at www.who.int/mental_health/media/en/76.pdf. Accessed September 22, 2009.

World Health Organization. (2006). Obesity and overweight (fact sheet). www.who.int/mediacentre/factsheets/fs311/en/index.html. Accessed January 30, 2009.

APPENDIX: CHRONIC PAIN ACCEPTANCE QUESTIONNAIRE

Below you will find a list of statements. Please rate the truth of each statement as it applies to you. Use the following rating scale to make your choices. For instance, if you believe a statement is always true, you would write the number 6 in the blank next to that statement.

1	2	3	4	5	6
Never true	Very rarely true	Seldom true	Sometimes true	Almost always true	Always true

________ 1. I am getting on with the business of living no matter what my level of pain is.

________ 2. My life is going well, even though I have chronic pain.

________ 3. It's okay to experience pain.

________ 4. I would gladly sacrifice important things in my life to control this pain better.

________ 5. It's not necessary for me to control my pain in order to handle my life well.

________ 6. Although things have changed, I am living a normal life despite my chronic pain.

________ 7. I need to concentrate on getting rid of my pain.

________ 8. There are many activities I do when I feel pain.

________ 9. I lead a full life even though I have chronic pain. 9. I lead a full life even though I have chronic pain.

________ 10. Controlling pain is less important than other goals in my life.

________ 11. My thoughts and feelings about pain must change before I can take important steps in my life.

________ 12. Despite the pain, I am now sticking to a certain course in my life.

________ 13. Keeping my pain level under control takes first priority whenever I am doing something.

________ 14. Before I can make any serious plans, I have to get some control over my pain.

________ 15. When my pain increases, I can still take care of my responsibilities.

________ 16. I will have better control over my life if I can control my negative thoughts about pain.

________ 17. I avoid putting myself in situations where pain might increase.

________ 18. My worries and fears about what pain will do to me are true.

________ 19. It's a relief to realize that I don't have to change my pain to get on with my life.

________ 20. I have to struggle to do things when I have pain.

SCORING

Activities engagement: Sum items 1, 2, 3, 5, 6, 8, 9, 10, 12, 15, and 19.

Pain Willingness: Reverse items 4, 7, 11, 13, 14, 16, 17, 18, and 20, then sum.

CHAPTER 11

Acceptance and Commitment Training: Promoting Psychological Flexibility in the Workplace

Paul E. Flaxman, City University London; and Frank W. Bond, Goldsmiths College, University of London

Psychological distress among working populations is both highly prevalent and costly. For example, recent surveys conducted in the United Kingdom indicate that between 25 percent and 40 percent of workers in various occupations could be diagnosed with a minor psychiatric disorder, such as anxiety or depression (Hardy, Woods, & Wall, 2003; Stride, Wall, & Catley, 2007; Wall et al., 1997). Similarly, epidemiological studies in the United States suggest an average thirty-day workplace prevalence of 18 percent for any DSM psychiatric disorder, with some variation across occupational groups (ranging from 11 percent to 30 percent; Kessler & Frank, 1997). Moreover, research has shown that greater levels of distress are associated with a significant elevation in both sickness absence and work cutback days, when distressed employees are present at work but unable to perform effectively (Hardy et al., 2003; Kessler & Frank, 1997; Kessler, Merikangas, & Wang, 2008). Mental health problems generally are placing a formidable financial burden on many national economies, and a significant proportion of that burden is attributed to lost work productivity (Kessler et al., 2008; Sobocki, Jönsson, Angst, & Rehnberg, 2006; Thomas & Morris, 2003).

Despite these rather startling prevalence statistics, only a very small percentage of distressed employees receive psychological interventions from mental health professionals. This seems to be the case for the vast ranks of workers likely to be experiencing a common minor psychiatric disorder (White, 2000), as well as for those employees with very high levels of emotional distress (Hilton et al., 2008). Indeed, Hilton and colleagues estimated that 78 percent of Australian employees with clinically significant mental health problems were not currently receiving active treatment. While access to psychological treatments is attracting increased attention from national governments (e.g., Layard, 2006), there remains a clear need for effective and efficient interventions that can be delivered directly to employees in the workplace.

With these issues in mind, in this chapter we provide a rationale for implementing workplace training programs based on acceptance and commitment therapy (ACT). We use the term acceptance and commitment *training* (rather than therapy) in the chapter title to reflect the fact that we are applying ACT principles and procedures to groups of employees outside of the therapeutic consulting room. We begin by briefly reviewing workplace stress management interventions more generally, highlighting the paucity of research examining mechanisms of change. We then provide an overview of the ACT intervention model before setting out our argument for the suitability of ACT for enhancing employees' mental health and performance. This rationale is supported by a review of the research that has established links between higher levels of psychological flexibility and various favorable employee and workplace outcomes, and also by a review of empirical evaluations of ACT as a workplace intervention. In line with the principal focus of this volume, we pay particular attention to the mediators of change through which ACT has been found to increase employees' mental health and performance. Toward the end of the chapter, we highlight the experiential nature of ACT interventions and set out some recommendations for future research on ACT in the workplace.

WORKPLACE STRESS MANAGEMENT INTERVENTIONS

Workplace programs that seek to enhance employees' psychological wellbeing have traditionally been referred to as stress management interventions (SMIs). Broadly speaking, organization-focused SMIs aim to modify problematic aspects of the design and management of work, such as excessive work demands, lack of job control, or poor workplace support, that are reliably associated with psychological strain (e.g., Bond & Bunce, 2001; Cox et al., 2000; Giga, Cooper, & Faragher, 2003). Organization-focused SMIs are advocated by occupational health researchers and policy makers alike because of their potential to reduce work-related stressors at their source (Mackay, Cousins, Kelly, Lee, & McCaig, 2004; Sauter, Hurrel, Fox, Tetrick, & Barling, 1999). Individual-focused workplace SMIs, on the other hand, aim to enhance employees' coping skills and resources so that they can more effectively manage the demands and pressures of work and life. While the present chapter focuses on an individually oriented intervention (ACT), we do not intend to underestimate the importance of organizational initiatives that seek to promote employees' health by targeting work-related stressors. Indeed, some of the research that we review in this chapter indicates that the outcomes of organization-focused SMIs could also be enhanced through the implementation of ACT in the workplace (Bond, Flaxman, & Bunce, 2008).

Workplace stress management training (SMT), an individual-focused approach, has been the most widely implemented and empirically evaluated intervention for promoting mental health in the workplace. SMT programs have traditionally been comprised of a combination of cognitive behavioral therapy (CBT) techniques, such as cognitive restructuring and muscular relaxation training. A large body of research conducted over the past twenty-five years suggests that these interventions are effective in reducing various manifestations of employee distress (e.g., Murphy, 1996; Saunders, Driskell, Johnston, & Salas, 1996; van der Klink, Blonk, Schene, & van Dijk, 2001). In a recent meta-analytic review, Richardson and Rothstein (2008) found a small effect size (Cohen's $d = 0.239$) for various multimodal SMT programs, typically involving a mix of cognitive and relaxation skills, and a large effect size ($d = 1.164$) for interventions classified as purely cognitive behavioral, such as stress inoculation training).

Despite these encouraging outcome findings, SMT researchers have generally failed to examine the mechanisms, or mediators, of change that might underpin these interventions (Bunce, 1997). In particular, although the vast majority of workplace SMT programs have utilized CBT approaches, there is a distinct lack of research examining change in core constructs that stem from CBT theory, such as dysfunctional cognitions or metacognitive skills. This neglect of mediating factors may stem from the lack of a unifying theory of change to explain the effectiveness of multifaceted SMT programs.

For example, some authors have noted that the diverse range of models and techniques typically included in SMT (for example, muscular relaxation, cognitive restructuring, time management, and problem solving) makes it difficult to generate theoretically driven hypotheses about why these interventions actually work (Gardner, Rose, Mason, Tyler, & Cushway, 2005; Huebner, 1988; Orsillo, Roemer, Lerner, & Tull, 2004). This is a significant shortcoming in workplace stress management research, which has generally lagged behind the clinical literature in terms of its theoretical and methodological sophistication. As noted by Kazdin (2007), without an understanding of the mechanisms of change, it is difficult to know how to develop or target an intervention in ways that would optimize its effectiveness.

We believe that this shortcoming can be addressed, at least to some extent, by implementing workplace interventions based on ACT principles and procedures. As we discuss below, ACT is underpinned by an intervention model that is hypothesized to apply across a wide range of human problems and settings. Moreover, this model clearly specifies the core processes of change through which all ACT interventions are presumed to operate.

ACCEPTANCE AND COMMITMENT THERAPY

Acceptance and commitment therapy (ACT) has emerged at the forefront of a new generation of cognitive and behavioral therapies. These so-called third-wave approaches (Hayes, 2004) are comprised of an array of therapeutic models and interventions, but they all share an emphasis on the promotion of mindfulness skills as a route to enhanced life functioning (e.g., Baer, 2006; Hayes, Follette, & Linehan, 2004; Hayes, Strosahl, & Wilson, 1999; Segal, Williams, & Teasdale, 2002).

ACT can be distinguished from other mindfulness-based approaches by its core theoretical and philosophical underpinnings, and by the way it utilizes mindfulness in the service of fostering values-based behavioral effectiveness. To elaborate, ACT stems from a behavior-analytic account of human language and cognition: relational frame theory (RFT; Hayes, Barnes-Holmes, & Roche, 2001). This underlying theory, which is itself supported by a significant program of basic research, gave rise to ACT's generic model of psychopathology. The model posits that two contextual features of language and cognition are central to most forms of human psychological distress: cognitive fusion and experiential avoidance. In brief, *cognitive fusion* refers to the tendency to become so entangled with the literal content of thoughts that those thoughts become indistinguishable from the actual events to which they refer. In a context of fusion, people are likely to be unaware of the process of thinking (that one is, in that moment, experiencing a thought) and less in contact with present-moment experience. Moreover, when a person becomes fused with particular verbal content, that content can exert almost complete dominance over the person's behavior (Strosahl, Hayes, Wilson, & Gifford, 2004).

Experiential avoidance refers to an unwillingness to experience difficult psychological content, such as undesirable thoughts, emotions, and somatic sensations, and associated attempts to change or reduce the frequency of that content, even when doing so is counterproductive, as in thought suppression; harmful, as in drug and alcohol misuse or self-harm; or life constricting, as in situational avoidance (e.g., Hayes et al., 1999; Hayes, Wilson, Gifford, Follette, & Strosahl, 1996; Wegner, Schneider, Carter, & White, 1987). Unfortunately, the belief that it is necessary (or even possible) to remove, reduce, or replace undesirable internal states in order to pursue a vital and satisfying life appears to be perpetuated by our social and verbal communities. A glance at the blatant feel-goodism of product marketing provides evidence of this phenomenon, as does common parlance such as "Don't worry" (Hayes et al., 1999; Kashdan & Breen, 2007).

From an ACT perspective, fusion and avoidance invariably lead to psychological and behavioral inflexibility as undesirable thoughts and emotions take on the functions and importance of the actual real-world events they symbolically represent. When a difficult thought about an undesirable event is experienced as indistinguishable from that event, the thought itself is likely to become something to avoid. Hence, a person might become embroiled in a futile and potentially life-damaging internal struggle aimed at avoiding negatively evaluated private experiences.

In order to undermine these two problematic processes, ACT's intervention model, illustrated in the following figure, promotes *psychological flexibility*, which is defined as the ability to contact the present moment and, based on what the situation affords, persisting with or changing one's behavior in accordance with one's chosen values (Hayes, Strosahl, Bunting, Twohig, & Wilson, 2004; Luoma, Hayes, & Walser, 2007). As illustrated in the figure, ACT cultivates psychological flexibility via six interrelated therapeutic processes. Contact with the present moment, acceptance, defusion, and self-as-context together form a higher-order set of mindfulness and acceptance processes, while contact with the present moment, values, committed action, and self-as-context define a broader set of values-based commitment and behavior change processes. ACT is, at its core, a behavior therapy (Hayes et al., 1999). As a result, mindfulness and acceptance skills are cultivated not for their own sake, but to help build life-enhancing patterns of values-based action.

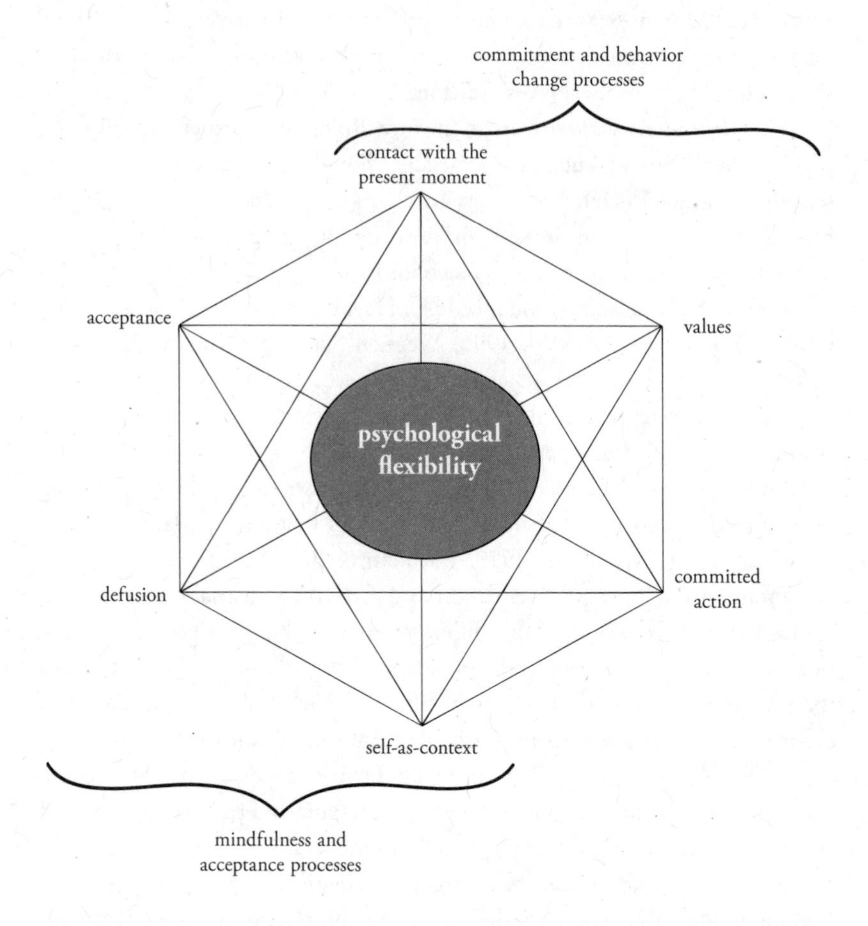

Consistent with the ACT model, the promotion of psychological flexibility appears to have considerable therapeutic utility. Research has found ACT to be effective in the treatment of an unusually wide range of psychological and behavioral problems, including depression, anxiety, eating disorders, burnout, trauma, chronic pain, and psychosis, and ACT has been used successfully in the management of chronic health conditions, such as diabetes and epilepsy. A recent meta-analytic review conducted by Hayes, Luoma, Bond, Masuda, and Lillis (2006) found that ACT interventions resulted in client improvements that were often superior to those observed in a range of other intervention conditions. Moreover, there is mounting empirical evidence to indicate that ACT outcomes are reliably mediated by increases in psychological flexibility or its facets (Hayes et al., 2006).

The principal instrument for measuring psychological flexibility is the Acceptance and Action Questionnaire (AAQ; Hayes, Strosahl, Wilson, et al., 2004). There are nine-item (AAQ-9) and sixteen-item (AAQ-16) versions of the original scale, both of which have been used in occupational health research. Bond and Bunce (2003) conducted a confirmatory factor analysis on the AAQ-16 and found that the scale contains two underlying factors that are consistent with the model of psychological flexibility. (Researchers usually sum across these factors to create an overall psychological flexibility score.) The first factor represents willingness to experience internal events; for example, "I try to suppress thoughts and feelings that I don't like by just not thinking about them" (which is reversed scored). The second factor represents the ability to take action even in the face of unwanted internal events; for example, "When I feel depressed or anxious, I am unable to take care of my responsibilities" (also reversed scored). Responses to these items are rated on a seven-point scale ranging from never true to always true. More recently, the AAQ has been relaunched as a ten-item scale (the AAQ-II). As with the earlier versions of the instrument, the AAQ-II contains both willingness items ("It's okay if I remember something unpleasant") and action items ("My thoughts and feelings do not get in the way of how I want to live my life"). (A paper describing the psychometric properties of the AAQ-II has been submitted for publication; Bond et al., 2009.)

In addition to using the AAQ as an indicator of psychological flexibility, ACT researchers have sought to measure its different facets. In particular, cognitive defusion has been measured with scales that ask respondents how much they believe in the content of particular thoughts. Such an approach is consistent with the idea that ACT helps deliteralize difficult psychological content so as to lessen its impact and the extent to which it functions as a barrier to values-based behavior (Hayes et al., 1999). From an ACT perspective, reducing the believability of negative thoughts (defusion from literal verbal content) is prioritized over trying to change the form or frequency of those thoughts. Both laboratory and clinical studies have indicated that ACT reduces the believability of thoughts, independent of any change in the frequency or content of those thoughts (e.g., Bach & Hayes, 2002; Gaudiano & Herbert, 2006; Masuda, Hayes, Sackett, & Twohig, 2004).

RATIONALE FOR IMPLEMENTING ACT IN THE WORKPLACE

To start at a general level, we propose that the broad applicability of the ACT/RFT model facilitates its use not only in the therapeutic consulting room, but also in nonclinical settings such as the workplace. As we have seen, ACT is based on the assumption that various forms of psychological distress and dysfunctional behavior stem from the same fundamental contextual features of human language and cognition (cognitive fusion and experiential avoidance)—a theoretical assumption supported by empirical demonstrations of ACT's efficacy across a wide range of human difficulties. Indeed, experiential avoidance (a feature of psychological inflexibility) is increasingly viewed as a generalized risk factor with implications for human functioning in general (Biglan, Hayes, & Pistorello, 2008; Hayes et al., 1996; Kashdan, Barrios, Forsyth, & Steger, 2006). Biglan and colleagues (2008), in particular, have set out a convincing argument for conceptualizing experiential avoidance as a core psychological vulnerability factor, with associated implications for prevention. It is notable that their recommendations include delivering ACT in work settings as a promising but currently underutilized preventive intervention strategy.

In addition to the breadth of its underlying model of distress, ACT has a number of technical features that facilitate its delivery in the workplace. First, ACT's mindfulness skills can arguably be developed by most individuals, regardless of their current level of distress. Essentially, mindfulness techniques aim to help people experientially locate a different perspective from which to view all thoughts and emotions. Hence, the tone of the psychological content experienced during mindfulness practice is less important than contacting the healthy "psychological space" that exists between individuals and their thoughts, emotions, and sensations. This aspect of mindfulness training can be particularly useful in the workplace (and other nonclinical settings), where ACT is often delivered to heterogeneous groups of individuals, not all of whom are currently experiencing high levels of distress.

Similarly, the exercises for clarifying values and goals that are central to ACT seem highly suitable for workplace delivery. In our experience, employees are familiar with setting short- and long-term behavioral goals and assessing potential barriers to achieving those goals. Indeed, theories of work motivation and job performance have long emphasized the importance of having employees participate in setting their own work and career goals (e.g., Locke & Latham, 1990). We believe that the values work in ACT can support and extend this practice by promoting personally chosen values as a consistent and powerful guide to work-related goal setting and behavior, and by promoting defusion from psychological barriers to values-consistent action (Bond, Hayes, & Barnes-Holmes, 2006).

Finally, ACT can be delivered effectively in groups, which is the usual format for workplace training programs. In fact, Walser and Pistorello (2004) highlight a number of advantages associated with delivering ACT in groups, including the potential to normalize people's experiences, the opportunity to share insights into ACT's principles and procedures, the creation and sharing of new exercises and metaphors, the opportunity to observe others practicing mindfulness skills and engaging in committed action, and the creation of a context within which people can publicly commit to chosen values. Delivering group-based psychological skills training is, of course, not without its challenges (see Flaxman & Bond; 2006), but our experience suggests that workplace participants generally value discussing and experiencing ACT alongside their coworkers.

In sum, our rationale for advocating ACT in the workplace stems from its generic underlying model of human distress, which supports the conceptualization of experiential avoidance as a generalized diathesis, and ACT's core intervention strategies, which are highly flexible and adaptable to different populations and settings. We believe that our rationale is supported by the growing body of research indicating that ACT principles and interventions generalize to working populations. We provide an overview of this research in the following sections.

The Role of Psychological Flexibility in Occupational Health and Performance

Over the past few years, our own research has sought to examine the relationship between psychological flexibility and various employee and organizational outcomes. For example, Bond and Bunce (2003) conducted a longitudinal study among 412 customer service workers within a financial services organization in the UK to assess the influence of psychological flexibility on mental health, job satisfaction, and performance. Questionnaires (including the AAQ-16) were administrated on two separate occasions, with a one-year time lag between them. Performance was measured by obtaining company records on the average number of computer errors made by each employee. Results indicated that psychological flexibility longitudinally predicted both mental health and performance (but not job satisfaction). These effects were observed even after controlling for three other variables that have received a great deal of attention in occupational health research: job control, negative affectivity, and locus of control (see also Donaldson-Feilder & Bond, 2004).

In addition, this same study tested the hypothesis that psychological flexibility would interact with job control to influence employee well-being and performance. *Job control* is defined as the perceived ability to exert some influence over one's work environment in order to make it more rewarding and less threatening. This widely researched work characteristic occupies a central position in most prominent models of occupational health and performance (e.g., Hackman & Oldham, 1976; Karasek & Theorell, 1990; Terry & Jimmieson, 1999). There is a strong theoretical rationale for examining the interaction between job control and flexibility. Specifically, employees high in psychological flexibility are less likely to waste their limited attentional resources by striving to avoid or control undesirable thoughts and emotions (by engaging in thought suppression or avoidant behavior, for example). With greater attentional resources at their disposal, these workers should be better able to notice when they have job control in any given work situation and can therefore learn how to utilize this control in order to take action that is consistent with their core values and goals. This enhanced capacity for noticing and responding to such opportunities has been described as goal-related context sensitivity (Bond et al., 2008). In support of this hypothesis, Bond and Bunce (2003) found that psychological flexibility moderated the impact of job control on mental health and performance such that the benefits of having greater control were enhanced for those employees with higher levels of psychological flexibility.

Bond and Flaxman (2006) investigated the degree to which psychological flexibility, job control, and their interaction predicted the ability to learn new skills at work. In this study, 448 call center workers in the UK provided data on three separate occasions. At time 1, participants completed questionnaires (including the AAQ-16) and their performance on a new computer software program was assessed. Soon after time 1, all participants attended a five-day training program focused on the new software. After four weeks of using the new software (time 2), the same employees completed a simulated customer service test, yielding scores that provided an objective indicator of work-related learning. Finally, two months after the test (time 3), participants completed a measure of mental health and their average job performance during the three months following the training program was assessed. As predicted, higher psychological flexibility at time 1 was associated with enhanced learning at time 2 and better mental health and performance at time 3. Once again, psychological flexibility was found to enhance the beneficial effects of job control. These findings provide further support for the concept of goal-related context sensitivity, wherein psychological flexibility translates into greater attentional resources, which can be used to enhance learning, task performance, and mental health in the workplace.

Finally, we recently investigated the links between psychological flexibility, job control, and employee well-being within the context of a work reorganization intervention (Bond et al., 2008). Using a quasi-experimental design, we delivered an intervention designed to enhance job control in one unit of a large financial services organization, while a second unit served as the control group. Questionnaire measures were administered prior to the intervention (time 1), and again fourteen months later (time 2), and absence rates for each participant were obtained from organizational records. Results indicated that the work reorganization intervention was effective in improving mental health and reducing absence from work. Further analyses revealed that the beneficial impact of the intervention was enhanced for employees with higher levels of psychological flexibility. That is, workers who had higher levels of psychological flexibility perceived greater levels of job control as a result of the intervention, which led to superior improvements in absence rates and general mental health. These findings are again consistent with the view that psychologically flexible individuals have a greater capacity for noticing and responding to opportunities stemming from increased job control in the work environment.

Of course, the reviewed research is not without its limitations. Most of these investigations have focused on call center employees within the financial services industry (for an exception, see Donaldson-Feilder & Bond, 2004). Nonetheless, this research has allowed us to assess the longitudinal relations between psychological flexibility and objectively measured outcomes, such as performance and absenteeism. Given the increasing interest in psychological flexibility among organizational researchers around the globe (e.g., Stewart, Barnes-Holmes, Barnes-Holmes, Bond, & Hayes, 2006; van Veldhoven & Biron, 2008), we anticipate further studies to help assess the extent to which these findings may be generalized.

One of the great advantages of focusing on psychological flexibility is that it is intimately connected to ACT's clearly specified intervention model and methods. Hence, as well as demonstrating that psychological flexibility is an important characteristic for performance and well-being at work, we can also implement workplace interventions that are specifically designed to help people develop greater flexibility. It is noteworthy that the individual characteristics that have traditionally received attention from occupational health researchers, such as locus of control, coping style, type A behavior patterns, and negative affectivity, do not have such a direct link to intervention. As we describe in the following section, a number of studies have evaluated the extent to which workplace ACT interventions lead to improvements in employees' psychological flexibility, well-being, and work performance.

ACT at Work: Outcomes and Processes of Change

Our review of research on ACT in the workplace is organized into three sections. The first group of studies evaluated ACT as a generic stress management intervention, where ACT-based training was offered to all members of an organization or occupational group with no exclusion criteria imposed. This "preventive" approach is a common feature of workplace SMT practice. Next, we review one study that utilized ACT to improve well-being and sickness absence among a group of workers selected for being at risk for work disability resulting from musculoskeletal pain and stress symptoms. The third group of studies investigated the efficacy of ACT for improving substance abuse counselors' well-being and clinical practice. For each study, we provide information on the research design, duration of the intervention delivered, outcome effects, and results of mediation analyses.

ACT AS WORKPLACE STRESS MANAGEMENT TRAINING

Bond and Bunce (2000) published the first empirical evaluation of ACT as a workplace SMT program. This study compared ACT with a wait list control group and a training program designed to promote innovation and teach workers how to reduce work-related stressors at their source. Both training programs were delivered to small groups of employees using a "2 + 1" format (Barkham & Shapiro, 1990) involving three training sessions: two in consecutive weeks and a third session three months later. Each training session lasted for approximately three hours. The ACT intervention included a number of core strategies already in use in psychotherapy settings. For example, in session 1, participants were encouraged to consider the effectiveness or ineffectiveness of internal control and avoidance strategies for coping with stress symptoms; they also received a summary of the ACT model and practiced a mindfulness exercise. In session 2, the trainer introduced various exercises targeting ACT's cognitive defusion, mindfulness, and self-as-context processes; participants also completed a values assessment exercise and considered how struggling with difficult thoughts and emotions might interfere with achieving valued goals. In the final session, participants practiced and discussed the various techniques introduced in the two earlier sessions; in addition, they were asked to consider psychological barriers to values-consistent goals and to make a public commitment to their most important life values. (The ACT protocol evaluated by Bond & Bunce, 2000, is described in more detail by Bond, 2004, and Bond & Hayes, 2002).

Bond and Bunce examined change on measures of general psychological distress, depression, and propensity to be innovative at work. Measurement points included baseline, three months after the two initial training sessions, and a further three months following the final training session. The findings supported the efficacy of ACT for improving employees' mental health. Specifically, at both post-intervention measurement points ACT participants showed significantly lower levels of distress than those in the innovation training and control groups. ACT also resulted in improvements in innovation potential equivalent to those in the group receiving innovation training. Consistent with ACT's theory of change, mediation analyses revealed that the improvements in mental health and innovation in the ACT condition were either partially or fully mediated by increases in psychological flexibility (as measured by the AAQ-16), but not by changes in dysfunctional cognitive content. In other words, ACT was operating by enhancing acceptance, mindfulness, and values-based behavioral processes, rather than by modifying psychological content.

Flaxman and Bond (Flaxman, 2006; Flaxman & Bond, under review) extended the work of Bond and Bunce (2000) by implementing and evaluating a similar ACT intervention with local government employees in the UK. This research, which also utilized the 2 + 1 delivery method, compared ACT, traditional CBT in the form of stress inoculation training (SIT), and a wait list control group. Measures included psychological distress, thought reappraisal coping strategies, psychological flexibility (as measured by the AAQ-16), and dysfunctional cognitions. Results indicated that ACT and SIT were equally effective in reducing employee distress at three-month and six-month assessment points. Interestingly, there were differences between the two interventions in terms of their impact on thought reappraisal strategies. ACT participants showed a decrease in the use of thought reappraisal, while SIT resulted in a slight increase. This pattern of change is consistent with the contrasting theories underpinning the two interventions. That is, ACT (via mindfulness and cognitive defusion) encourages participants to give up the struggle with difficult cognitive content, while SIT promotes the reappraisal of negatively distorted thoughts via cognitive restructuring.

Mediation tests revealed further theoretically consistent differences between ACT and SIT. Specifically, changes in psychological flexibility and dysfunctional cognitions were tested together as mediators for each intervention. When the competing mediator was controlled, only psychological flexibility mediated the improvements in mental health observed in the ACT group. The pattern of mediation in the SIT condition was less clear, in that neither psychological flexibility nor a change in dysfunctional cognitions functioned as a unique mediator of change. Overall, the results of this research suggest that ACT and traditional CBT (in the form of SIT) can be equally effective for improving employees' mental health, but that they may operate via distinct mechanisms of change.

ACT FOR AT-RISK WORKERS

Whereas the previously mentioned studies employed no participant exclusion criteria, Dahl, Wilson, and Nilsson (2004) delivered ACT to a selected group of Swedish health care workers who were at risk for long-term work disability as a result of stress and musculoskeletal pain. These researchers employed an additive treatment design, in which participants were randomly assigned to one of two groups: medical treatment as usual, which included visits to physicians or other medical specialists and physical therapy interventions; or medical treatment as usual plus ACT. The ACT intervention was delivered via four one-hour individual sessions, conducted weekly at the workplace or in participants' homes. The intervention was designed around four ACT components: clarifying values, promoting cognitive defusion, encouraging values-consistent exposure, and committing to patterns of values-based action. To reiterate, the aim was not to reduce stress and pain symptoms, but to increase participants' ability to pursue valued behavioral goals in the presence of these symptoms.

The two main outcome measures in this study were sick leave utilization (number of sick days), which was objectively measured, and medical utilization (number of visits to a physician or other medical practitioner). At post-treatment, the workers in the ACT group had a mean of 1 sick day over the past month, while those in the group receiving medical treatment took an average of 11.5 sick days. By the six-month follow-up, the difference between the two groups had widened considerably, with the ACT group averaging just 0.5 sick day across the follow-up period, in comparison to an average of 56.1 sick days taken by the group receiving medical treatment only. In view of these differences, it is perhaps not surprising that the ACT participants paid significantly fewer visits to medical practitioners, averaging 1.9 medical visits during the six-month follow-up, compared to 15.1 visits in the comparison group.

Consistent with ACT theory, the superior functioning found among ACT participants in this study could not be attributed to a reduction in the frequency or intensity of difficult thoughts, emotions, or physiological sensations. To elaborate, although ACT reduced sick days and medical utilization to a much greater extent than medical treatment as usual, there were no significant differences between the two groups in terms of impact on stress and pain symptoms. This finding suggests that ACT principally changed the way these at-risk employees were relating to their symptoms of pain and distress (Dahl et al., 2004).

Although this study had a relatively small sample size, the improvement in sick leave attributed to ACT is impressive, especially in view of the fact that workplace stress management researchers rarely evaluate change on such criteria. For example, two recent reviews of the literature found just three studies that had evaluated the impact of traditional CBT interventions on absenteeism, with minimal effects reported (Richardson & Rothstein, 2008; van der Klink et al., 2001). Clearly, additional research is needed to assess whether ACT can reduce sickness absence among other occupational groups.

ACT FOR THE ENHANCEMENT OF ADDICTION COUNSELORS' WELL-BEING AND PERFORMANCE

Other research has focused on evaluating ACT as a method for enhancing the psychological health and performance of substance abuse counselors. Counselors in this field have been targeted for psychological intervention because of their propensity for burnout, and because of the difficulties associated with learning and implementing new treatments designed for clients with substance abuse problems (Luoma, Hayes, Twohig, & Bissett, 2007; Varra, Hayes, Roget, & Fisher, 2008).

Hayes, Bissett, and colleagues (2004) investigated the impact of ACT on stigmatizing attitudes and burnout among counselors in the United States. Counselors were randomly assigned to an ACT intervention, a multicultural awareness program, or an educational control condition that provided instruction on factors linked to the use of methamphetamine and MDMA. All three programs were delivered via one-day workshops. Measures of burnout and stigmatizing attitudes were administered prior to the one-day workshops, immediately after the workshops, and three months later. To measure stigmatization, the counselors responded to items such as "A person would be foolish to marry someone who had a drug or alcohol addiction." As an indicator of cognitive fusion, participants rated the extent to which they believed various negative thoughts about clients with substance abuse problems, such as "My client is not going to change no matter what I do."

Counselors in the ACT group showed no change in stigmatizing attitudes at post-treatment, but by the three-month follow-up, they experienced significantly more favorable attitudes toward their clients compared to the counselors in the educational control condition. The opposite pattern was found for multicultural training, which resulted in a significant improvement in attitudes immediately after treatment, but not at follow-up. Additionally, by the three-month follow-up, ACT participants had significantly lower levels of burnout than participants in the other two groups. Consistent with the ACT model of change, the beneficial impact of ACT on both burnout and stigma was mediated by a reduction in the believability of negative thoughts about clients—an indicator of cognitive defusion.

In a similar study, Varra and colleagues (2008) examined the utility of ACT for enhancing addiction counselors' willingness to use evidence-based pharmacotherapy. The aim was to assess whether a one-day ACT workshop delivered prior to a workshop on treatments for substance abuse problems would enhance adoption of new evidence-based treatment approaches. Sixty counselors were randomly assigned to either the ACT workshop or an educational control condition that involved instruction on addiction prevention and a presentation on leadership styles. Measures included counselors' use of pharmacotherapy, willingness to use pharmacotherapy, perceived barriers to implementing new treatments, and psychological flexibility as measured by the AAQ-16.

At three-month follow-up, counselors who had attended the ACT workshop were more likely to refer their clients for pharmacotherapy, reported a greater willingness to use pharmacotherapy, and had higher levels of psychological flexibility than those in the educational control condition. Interestingly, the counselors in the ACT group perceived more barriers to using new treatments than the controls, but reported a significant decrease in the extent to which they believed that these barriers would interfere with using or learning new treatments, indicating greater cognitive defusion. Reduced believability of barriers and increased psychological flexibility mediated greater use of pharmacotherapy among the counselors who had received the ACT intervention. Thus, helping counselors defuse from psychological barriers to learning and adopting new evidence-based treatments appears to facilitate the integration of those treatments into practice.

Summary of Research on Outcomes and Processes of Change in ACT Workplace Interventions

There is a growing body of evidence that ACT interventions can elicit significant improvements in employees' general mental health. In addition, ACT has shown potential for improving work performance indicators (such as innovation potential) and sickness absence rates. Even among the small group of studies discussed above, we find reliable evidence that ACT effects are mediated by improvements in psychological flexibility or its facets, such as cognitive defusion. The mediation findings are particularly promising, given the lack of attention paid to mechanisms of change in the wider literature on workplace stress management (Bunce, 1997). Moreover, the processes of change observed in these ACT studies mirror those found among clinical populations (see Hayes et al., 2006), providing further support for the breadth of ACT's underlying model of human functioning.

THE EXPERIENTIAL NATURE OF ACT

In an earlier article (Flaxman & Bond, 2006) we outlined a number of practical issues that we have observed when implementing ACT in the workplace. These issues relate to the marketing of ACT to organizations and employees, implementing concurrent work stressor reduction programs, ensuring confidentiality, managing attrition, and dealing with distress that occurs in session. Rather than rehashing those still pertinent observations, here we will highlight the importance of developing an experiential understanding of ACT's core processes. Although we are focusing on ACT in the workplace, this issue applies to all ACT interventions (Luoma, Hayes, & Walser, 2007).

It is crucial for an ACT intervention to provide clients with frequent opportunities for experiential practice. This is designed to ensure that ACT's core processes are not overly intellectualized. To take one example, it is not uncommon for people to seek an intellectual understanding of the self-as-context. During our ACT interventions we have heard numerous views expressed about this core ACT process. For example, people may debate whether this sense of self changes over time, whether it has a spiritual dimension, whether it reflects a sense of nothingness, and so on. Such debates can be encouraging in that they reflect people's fascination with the possibility of an observing self that transcends fluctuating internal content. However, workplace training programs are usually very time limited, and lengthy intellectual discussions (particularly among larger groups) can steal time that could be better used establishing experiential contact with ACT's processes. Generally speaking, groups of employees are probably more familiar, and perhaps more comfortable, with tackling topics at an intellectual level, rather than an experiential level. Hence, we explain at the outset that the training will involve various eyes-closed meditative, or mindfulness, exercises that can provide valuable insight into human functioning, and we frequently reemphasize the importance of this experiential learning. We also tend to introduce an array of such exercises to increase the likelihood that all participants are able to grasp the experiential gist of ACT's mindfulness and acceptance skills.

It is equally important for ACT practitioners to possess an intimate and experiential understanding of ACT's six core processes. Without this level of understanding, the practitioner will be less able to notice when these core processes are being accessed, and when they are not, during an intervention. ACT's technical components need not be delivered in a predetermined order, but the ACT practitioner should always be focused on reinforcing, modeling, and cultivating the processes that interact to produce psychological flexibility. Hence, it is considered essential that ACT trainers and therapists be able to apply ACT principles not only to the psychology of their clients, but also to their own personal and professional experiences (Luoma et al. 2007).

In making these observations on the experiential nature of ACT, we certainly do not wish to discourage therapists and stress management practitioners from learning and applying this approach. Indeed, a recent field effectiveness study found that trainee therapists exposed to both ACT and traditional CBT went on to elicit superior client outcomes with ACT (Lappalainen et al., 2007). Rather, we merely wish to emphasize that learning and delivering ACT requires an experiential grasp of the facets of psychological flexibility, as well as competence in applying its various intervention strategies.

CONCLUSIONS

We have set out a rationale for implementing ACT-based training programs in the workplace. This rationale is based on the breadth of ACT's underlying model, its technical flexibility, and recent empirical work that has demonstrated the benefits of ACT and psychological flexibility for employee well-being and performance.

Although this area of research is still in its infancy, the initial findings are very promising. For example, despite over two decades of stress management research, we still lack an understanding of the mechanisms that underpin change in traditional CBT interventions delivered in work settings (Bunce, 1997; Reynolds, Taylor, & Shapiro, 1993). In contrast, ACT researchers are finding consistent evidence that ACT outcomes are mediated by improvements in psychological flexibility (Hayes et al., 2006). Hence, it would appear that ACT has the potential to advance the theory and practice of workplace stress management. Similarly, we have found evidence that psychological flexibility interacts with an important work characteristic (job control) in the prediction of employee well-being. This suggests that organizational initiatives designed to increase job control would be further enhanced by increasing employees' psychological flexibility. Establishing these links between work characteristics and psychological flexibility is consistent with a recent trend toward greater integration of individual differences into models of occupational health (e.g., Meier, Semmer, Elfering, & Jacobshagen, 2008; Parker, Wall, & Cordery, 2001).

Of course, it will be important to extend these lines of research in order to establish a more prominent role for psychological flexibility in occupational contexts. Our recommendations for future research include evaluating a combination of work redesign and ACT to examine the enhancing effect of psychological flexibility; component analyses to examine whether some ACT processes are more effective than others in the workplace; and further investigation of mediating and moderating variables to enhance understanding of why, and for whom, ACT interventions are effective. We are aware of ongoing efforts to link ACT and RFT principles to various aspects of organizational behavior, including leadership development, organization development, teamwork, organizational culture, and workers' daily well-being (e.g., Bond et al., 2006; Stewart et al., 2006; van Veldhoven & Biron, 2008). In our opinion, this growing interest in ACT and psychological flexibility among organizational researchers holds a great deal of promise for improving the health and performance of employees and their organizations.

REFERENCES

Bach, P. B., & Hayes, S. C. (2002). The use of acceptance and commitment therapy to prevent the rehospitalization of psychotic patients: A randomized controlled trial. *Journal of Consulting and Clinical Psychology, 70*, 1129-1139.

Baer, R. A. (Ed.). (2006). *Mindfulness-based treatment approaches.* San Diego, CA: Elsevier.

Barkham, M., & Shapiro, D. A. (1990). Brief psychotherapeutic interventions for job-related distress: A pilot study of prescriptive and exploratory therapy. *Counselling Psychology Quarterly, 3*, 133-147.

Biglan, A., Hayes, S. C., & Pistorello, J. (2008). Acceptance and commitment: Implications for prevention science. *Prevention Science, 9*, 139-152.

Bond, F. W. (2004). ACT for stress. In S. C. Hayes & K. D. Strosahl (Eds.), *A practical guide to acceptance and commitment therapy.* New York: Springer.

Bond, F. W., & Bunce, D. (2000). Mediators of change in emotion-focused and problem-focused worksite stress management interventions. *Journal of Occupational Health Psychology, 5*, 156-163.

Bond, F. W., & Bunce, D. (2001). Job control mediates change in a work reorganization intervention for stress reduction. *Journal of Occupational Health Psychology, 6*, 290-302.

Bond, F. W., & Bunce, D. (2003). The role of acceptance and job control in mental health, job satisfaction, and work performance. *Journal of Applied Psychology, 88*, 1057-1067.

Bond, F. W., & Flaxman, P. E. (2006). The ability of psychological flexibility and job control to predict learning, job performance, and mental health. *Journal of Organizational Behavior Management, 26*, 113-130.

Bond, F. W., Flaxman, P. E., & Bunce, D. (2008). The influence of psychological flexibility on work redesign: Mediated moderation of a work reorganization intervention. *Journal of Applied Psychology, 93*, 645-654.

Bond, F. W., & Hayes, S. C. (2002). ACT at work. In F. W. Bond & W. Dryden (Eds.), *Handbook of brief cognitive behaviour therapy*. Chichester, UK: Wiley.

Bond, F. W., Hayes, S. C., Baer, R. A., Carpenter, K. M., Orcutt, H. K., Waltz, T., et al. (2009). *Preliminary psychometric properties of the Acceptance and Action Questionnaire–II: A revised measure of psychological flexibility and acceptance.* Unpublished manuscript.

Bond, F. W., Hayes, S. C., & Barnes-Holmes, D. (2006). Psychological flexibility, ACT, and organizational behavior. *Journal of Organizational Behavior Management, 26,* 25-54.

Bunce, D. (1997). What factors are associated with the outcome of individual-focused worksite stress management interventions? *Journal of Occupational and Organizational Psychology, 70*, 1-17.

Cox, T., Griffiths, A., Barlowe, C., Randall, R., Thomson, L., & Rial-Gonzalez, E. (2000). *Organisational interventions for work stress: A risk management approach.* Norwich, UK: Health and Safety Executive/Her Majesty's Stationary Office.

Dahl, J., Wilson, K. G., & Nilsson, A. (2004). Acceptance and commitment therapy and the treatment of persons at risk for long-term disability resulting from stress and pain symptoms: A preliminary randomized trial. *Behavior Therapy, 35*, 785-801.

Donaldson-Feilder, E., & Bond, F. W. (2004). Psychological acceptance and emotional intelligence in relation to workplace well-being. *British Journal of Guidance and Counselling, 34*, 187-203.

Flaxman, P. E. (2006). *Acceptance-based and traditional cognitive-behavioural stress management in the workplace: Investigating the mediators and moderators of change.* Unpublished Ph.D. dissertation, Goldsmiths College, University of London.

Flaxman, P. E., & Bond, F. W. (2006). Acceptance and commitment therapy in the workplace. In R. A. Baer (Ed.), *Mindfulness-based treatment approaches.* San Diego, CA: Elsevier.

Flaxman, P. E., & Bond, F. W. (under review). *A randomised worksite comparison of acceptance and commitment therapy and stress inoculation training.* Manuscript under review.

Gardner, B., Rose, J., Mason, O., Tyler, P., & Cushway, D. (2005). Cognitive therapy and behavioural coping in the management of work-related stress: An intervention study. *Work and Stress, 19*, 137-152.

Gaudiano, B. A., & Herbert, J. D. (2006). Acute treatment of inpatients with psychotic symptoms using acceptance and commitment therapy: Pilot results. *Behaviour Research and Therapy, 44*, 415-437.

Giga, S. I., Cooper, C. L., & Faragher, B. (2003). The development of a framework for a comprehensive approach to stress management interventions at work. *International Journal of Stress Management, 10*, 280-296.

Hackman, J. R., & Oldham, G. R. (1976). Motivation through the design of work: Test of a theory. *Organizational Behavior and Human Performance, 16*, 250-279.

Hardy, G. E., Woods, D., & Wall, T. D. (2003). The impact of psychological distress on absence from work. *Journal of Applied Psychology, 88*, 306-314.

Hayes, S. C. (2004). Acceptance and commitment therapy and the new behavior therapies: Mindfulness, acceptance, and relationship. In S. C. Hayes, V. M. Follette, & M. M. Linehan (Eds.), *Mindfulness and acceptance: Expanding the cognitive-behavioral tradition.* New York: Guilford.

Hayes, S. C., Barnes-Holmes, D., & Roche, B. (2001). *Relational frame theory: A post-Skinnerian account of human language and cognition*. New York: Kluwer.

Hayes, S. C., Bissett, R., Roget, N., Padilla, M., Kohlenberg, B. S., Fisher, G., et al. (2004). The impact of acceptance and commitment training and multicultural training on the stigmatizing attitudes and professional burnout of substance abuse counselors. *Behavior Therapy, 35*, 821-835.

Hayes, S. C., Follette, V. M., & Linehan, M. M. (Eds.). (2004). *Mindfulness and acceptance: Expanding the cognitive-behavioral tradition*. New York: Guilford.

Hayes, S. C., Luoma, J. B., Bond, F. W., Masuda, A., & Lillis, J. (2006). Acceptance and commitment theory: Model, processes and outcomes. *Behaviour Research and Therapy, 44*, 1-25.

Hayes, S. C., Strosahl, K. D., Bunting, K., Twohig, M., & Wilson, K. (2004). What is acceptance and commitment therapy? In S. C. Hayes & K. D. Strosahl (Eds.), *A practical guide to acceptance and commitment therapy*. New York: Springer.

Hayes, S. C., Strosahl, K., & Wilson, K. G. (1999). *Acceptance and commitment therapy: An experiential approach to behavior change*. New York: Guilford.

Hayes, S. C., Strosahl, K. D., Wilson, K. G., Bissett, R. T., Pistorello, J., Toarmino, D., et al. (2004). Measuring experiential avoidance: A preliminary test of a working model. *Psychological Record, 54*, 553-578.

Hayes, S. C., Wilson, K. G., Gifford, E. V., Follette, V. M., & Strosahl, K. (1996). Experiential avoidance and behavioral disorders: A functional dimensional approach to diagnosis and treatment. *Journal of Consulting and Clinical Psychology, 64*, 1152-1168.

Hilton, M. F., Whiteford, H. A., Sheridan, J. S., Cleary, C. M., Chant, D. C., Wang, P. S., et al. (2008). The prevalence of psychological distress in employees and associated occupational risk factors. *Journal of Occupational and Environmental Medicine, 50*, 746-757.

Huebner, L. A. (1988). Some thoughts on the application of cognitive-behavioral therapies. *Counseling Psychologist, 16*, 96-101.

Karasek, R., & Theorell, T. (1990). *Healthy work: Stress, productivity, and the reconstruction of working life*. New York: Basic Books.

Kashdan, T. B., Barrios, V., Forsyth, J. P., & Steger, M. F. (2006). Experiential avoidance as a generalized psychological vulnerability:

Comparisons with coping and emotion regulation strategies. *Behaviour Research and Therapy, 44*, 1301-1320.

Kashdan, T. B., & Breen, W. E. (2007). Materialism and diminished well-being: Experiential avoidance as a mediating mechanism. *Journal of Social and Clinical Psychology, 5*, 521-539.

Kazdin, A. E. (2007). Mediators and mechanisms of change in psychotherapy research. *Annual Review of Clinical Psychology, 3*, 1-27.

Kessler, R. C., & Frank, R. G. (1997). The impact of psychiatric disorders on work loss days. *Psychological Medicine, 27*, 861-873.

Kessler, R. C., Merikangas, K. R., & Wang, P. S. (2008). The prevalence and correlates of workplace depression in the National Comorbidity Survey Replication. *Journal of Occupational and Environmental Medicine, 50*, 381-390.

Lappalainen, R., Lehtonen, T., Skarp, E., Taubert, E., Ojanen, M., & Hayes, S. C. (2007). The impact of CBT and ACT models using psychology trainee therapists: A preliminary controlled effectiveness trial. *Behavior Modification, 31*, 488-511.

Layard, R. (2006). The case for psychological treatment centres. *British Medical Journal, 332*, 1030-1032.

Locke, E. A., & Latham, G. P. (1990). *A theory of goal setting and task performance.* London: Prentice Hall.

Luoma, J. B., Hayes, S. C., Twohig, M. P., & Bissett, R. (2007). Augmenting continuing education with psychologically focused group consultation: Effects on adoption of group counseling. *Psychotherapy: Theory, Research, Practice, Training, 44*, 463-469.

Luoma, J. B., Hayes, S. C., & Walser, R. D. (2007). *Learning ACT: An acceptance and commitment therapy skills-training manual for therapists.* Oakland, CA: New Harbinger; Reno, NV: Context Press.

Mackay, C. J., Cousins, R., Kelly, P. J., Lee, S., & McCaig, R. H. (2004). Management standards and work-related stress in the UK: Policy background and science. *Work and Stress, 18*, 91-112.

Masuda, A., Hayes, S. C., Sackett, C. F., & Twohig, M. P. (2004). Cognitive defusion and self-relevant negative thoughts: Examining the impact of a ninety year old technique. *Behaviour Research and Therapy, 42*, 477-485.

Meier, L. L., Semmer, N. K., Elfering, A., & Jacobshagen, N. (2008). The double meaning of control: Three-way interactions between internal resources, job control, and stressors at work. *Journal of Occupational Health Psychology, 13*, 244-258.

Murphy, L. R. (1996). Stress management in work settings: A critical review. *American Journal of Health Promotion, 11*, 112-135.

Orsillo, S. M., Roemer, L., Lerner, J. B., & Tull, M. T. (2004). Acceptance, mindfulness, and cognitive-behavioral therapy: Comparisons, contrasts, and application to anxiety. In S. C. Hayes, V. M. Follette, & M. M. Linehan (Eds.), *Mindfulness and acceptance: Expanding the cognitive-behavioral tradition*. New York: Guilford.

Parker, S. K., Wall, T. D., & Cordery, J. L. (2001). Future work design research and practice: Towards an elaborated model of work design. *Journal of Occupational and Organizational Psychology, 74*, 413-440.

Reynolds, S., Taylor, E., & Shapiro, D. (1993). Session impact and outcome in stress management training. *Journal of Community and Applied Social Psychology, 3*, 325-337.

Richardson, K. M., & Rothstein, H. R. (2008). Effects of occupational stress management intervention programs: A meta-analysis. *Journal of Occupational Health Psychology, 13*, 69-93.

Saunders, T., Driskell, J. E., Johnston, J. H., & Salas, E. (1996). The effect of stress inoculation training on anxiety and performance. *Journal of Occupational Health Psychology, 1*, 170-186.

Sauter, S. L., Hurrel, J. J., Fox, H. R., Tetrick, L. E., & Barling, J. (1999). Occupational health psychology: An emerging discipline. *Industrial Health, 37*, 199-211.

Segal, Z., Williams, J. M. G., & Teasdale, J. D. (2002). *Mindfulness-based cognitive therapy for depression.* New York: Guilford.

Sobocki, P., Jönsson, B., Angst, J., & Rehnberg, C. (2006). Cost of depression in Europe. *Journal of Mental Health Policy and Economics, 9*, 87-98.

Stewart, I., Barnes-Holmes, D., Barnes-Holmes, Y., Bond, F. W., & Hayes, S. C. (2006). Relational frame theory and industrial/organizational psychology. *Journal of Organizational Behavior Management, 26*, 55-90.

Stride, C., Wall, T. D., & Catley, N. (2007). *Measures of job satisfaction, organisational commitment, mental health and job-related well-being: A benchmarking manual.* Chichester, UK: Wiley.

Strosahl, K. D., Hayes, S. C., Wilson, K. G., & Gifford, E. V. (2004). An ACT primer: Core therapy processes, intervention strategies, and therapist competencies. In S. C. Hayes & K. D. Strosahl (Eds.), *A practical guide to acceptance and commitment therapy.* New York: Springer.

Terry, D. J., & Jimmieson, N. L. (1999). Work control and employee well-being: A decade review. In C. L. Cooper & I. T. Robertson (Eds.), *International review of industrial and organizational psychology.* Chichester, UK: Wiley.

Thomas, C. M., & Morris, S. (2003). Cost of depression among adults in England in 2000. *British Journal of Psychiatry, 183*, 514-519.

Van der Klink, J. J. L., Blonk, R. W. B., Schene, A. H., & van Dijk, F. J. H. (2001). The benefits of interventions for work-related stress. *American Journal of Public Health, 91*, 270-276.

Van Veldhoven, M., & Biron, M. (2008, November). *Psychological workload, employee job strain and psychological flexibility.* Paper presented at the conference of the European Academy of Occupational Health Psychology, Valencia, Spain.

Varra, A. A., Hayes, S. C., Roget, N., & Fisher, G. (2008). A randomized control trial examining the effect of acceptance and commitment training on clinician willingness to use evidence-based pharmacotherapy. *Journal of Consulting and Clinical Psychology, 76*, 449-458.

Wall, T. D., Bolden, R. I., Borrill, C. S., Carter, A. J., Golya, D. A., Hardy, G. E., et al. (1997). Stress in NHS Trust staff: Occupational and gender differences. *British Journal of Psychiatry, 171*, 519-523.

Walser, R. D., & Pistorello, J. (2004). ACT in group format. In S. C. Hayes & K. D. Strosahl (Eds.), *A practical guide to acceptance and commitment therapy.* New York: Springer.

Wegner, D. M., Schneider, D. J., Carter, S. R., & White, T. L. (1987). Paradoxical effects of thought suppression. *Journal of Personality and Social Psychology, 53*, 5-13.

White, J. (2000). *Treating anxiety and stress: A group psycho-educational approach using brief CBT.* Chichester, UK: Wiley.

Index

A

B

C

D

E

F

G

H

Q

R

S

T

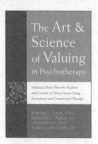

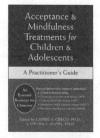